THE NATIONAL TRAILS

1,000 mini adventures on the 17 National Trails of England and Wales

STEPHEN NEALE

C∅NWAY
LONDON · OXFORD · NEW YORK · NEW DELHI · SYDNEY

CONTENTS

PART 1 THE MAGIC PATH 4

THIS IS A PILGRIM'S TALE 6
MAGIC FIX: MOVE, SENSE, OXYTOCIN 9

PART 2 THE TRAILS 18

1. PEDDARS WAY 20
2. YORKSHIRE WOLDS WAY ... 34
3. HADRIAN'S WALL PATH 46
4. THE RIDGEWAY 60
5. THAMES PATH WEST (FRESHWATER) 74
6. THAMES PATH EAST (TIDAL) 90
7. PEMBROKESHIRE COAST PATH SOUTH 102
8. PEMBROKESHIRE COAST PATH NORTH 116
9. PENNINE BRIDLEWAY SOUTH 130
10. PENNINE BRIDLEWAY NORTH 142
11. SOUTH DOWNS WAY 154
12. COTSWOLD WAY 168
13. CLEVELAND WAY 182
14. GLYNDŴR'S WAY 196
15. PENNINE WAY SOUTH 210
16. PENNINE WAY NORTH 226
17. NORTH DOWNS WAY 240
18. OFFA'S DYKE 256
19. COAST TO COAST PATH EAST 270
20. COAST TO COAST PATH WEST 282
21. SOUTH WEST COAST PATH NORTH 296
22. SOUTH WEST COAST PATH SOUTH 308
23. ENGLAND COAST PATH NORTH & EAST 324
24. ENGLAND COAST PATH SOUTH 340

For Dad,
Summer Wind

Marloes

PART 1
THE MAGIC PATH

THIS IS A PILGRIM'S TALE

Something amazing is happening between Cumbria and Yorkshire. More people are walking along a path called the 'Coast to Coast'. This is why.

The trails in England and Wales are thousands of years old. They were trampled by our families, our enemies and our ancestors for a purpose: survival and trade. All-weather foot trails are still with us today (I'll explain why later): The Ridgeway, The Peddars Way, The South West Coast Path, and many more. What's fascinating about the increasing interest in the Coast to Coast is what it teaches us about 21st-century Britain.

Alfred Wainwright stitched together lanes and tracks to form a route for his famous 1973 book, *A Coast to Coast Walk*. Wainwright's trail was no survival or trade path. He crafted a line to

celebrate his love for nature: a totem to beauty. That's a fact worth holding for a moment.

I met a midwife on a trail yesterday. She wore a T-shirt that read, 'I love oxytocin.' Oxytocin is a hormone that's released in the body — notably by human mothers. It is essential to give birth naturally and to produce milk.

But it gets better than that.

Oxytocin is produced by people socialising, listening or telling stories. Or… by couples especially in the first six months of a happy relationship: the honeymoon period.

But it gets better than that.

Oxytocin is produced most when we get intimate with nature: tree hugging, lying on grass, swimming and walking through breeze and birdsong. When all our senses are bombarded by the wild.

If the effect we crave is to feel loved, or to love, its primary cause is intimacy. Without intimacy, we are a shell. A crab carcass. An individual of wants and needs, devoid of the incentive to share and care.

Pilgrimage is the way to get intimate with nature. The easiest way to do that is to walk in the wild, far from houses and fences and roads. The place to immerse yourself in nature is beside water, earth and fire, surrounded by trees. To get truly connected, swim, rest, then fall asleep under those trees, beside a beach. That's why sunbathing or woodland walks are so popular as part of an ancient '*holi day*'. The effect of this intimate connection with nature is an overwhelming release of oxytocin: the love of nature that Wainwright shared. It's also the purpose that medieval and prehistoric 'pilgrims'

Honister Pass

Wood Bay

have described through stories as old as Gilgamesh.

The Coast to Coast is due to be made a National Trail very soon – number 17 in the series. More National Trails will follow.

We are relearning. Humans are moving towards a reconciliation with nature that was unwittingly lost somewhere between the Christianisation of Britain and the post-Enlightenment period, just before 2019. That gap – when magic and alchemy disappeared – was a long psychological sleepwalk we almost woke up from in Covid19. As you read this sentence, 'magic' is being rediscovered by many walkers slowly moving along the Coast to Coast trail from the Irish Sea to the North Sea. A psychological and physical change that is more profound, long-lasting and meaningful than the magic you might have felt at a recent concert, during a night out with friends, or with your last Amazon purchase.

This book is a jumpstart. It's a string of alchemical recipes that will reconnect the bits of ourselves that get separated by the bad decisions we all make daily: the demands of others, work, social media and TV. If a fix of oxytocin is what you or your loved ones are looking for right now, two or three days on the Coast to Coast is a good start. If you live in London, then find the Thames Path; if in Sussex, the North Downs; if in the Midlands the Pennine Way, and so on.

This is not a map to fitness, hormones, wisdom, love or mental health.

But it's a start.

A pilgrim's tale – from the trail.

MAGIC FIX: Move, sense, oxytocin

THIS BOOK HAS THREE OBJECTIVES:

1. To serve as a guide to 1,000 hidden places around the National Trails of England and Wales
2. To reset your senses (see, hear, smell, touch, taste) so you can start to feel better
3. To share some secret path magic

How?

This book was researched, written, edited and put together by more than 100 people between 2023 and 2025.

The National Trails are a collective of paths that cover almost 6,500km (4,000 miles) around England and Wales – equivalent to a pilgrimage from London to Delhi. Walking at 10km (6 miles) a day, it would take two years. In case you haven't got that long, this is a series of 1,000 mini adventures along the way.

Moving slowly, foraging, sleeping, and the ability to carry water in the wild are the 'back to basic' tasks that allow multi- or half-day trips. These adventures will help you connect with nature through your senses. The old ways never became outdated. They just got pushed out when we allowed people with a vested interest to groom our lazy preoccupation with fun cars and fast living.

Carlton Way

Getting started

If any of the adventures in this book inspire you, start with this. Learn how to use a map and compass.

The Thames Path is the perfect introduction, because there's a huge river to follow. Take a real compass – not a digital one. You will never regret it. Get in tune with your sixth 'sense': the sense of direction. Once you're out there navigating, you'll feel like a child who's just been given the gift of sight. Sense of direction is as good a sense as touch and taste, because it will encourage you to start looking up towards the sky, sun and stars, rather than down at a satnav or map.

Next, learn how to carry and filter water without it weighing you down. Then learn which green shoots and tree leaves can be eaten. Bramble tips are a good start. Finally, buy all-weather shoes and clothes.

THE TRAILS

Once you've done some basic preparation, decide which path to explore. The 17 National Trails are like very different children from the same family. Some 'like the Pennine Way' are difficult and rewarding. Others, like the Thames Path, are self-sufficient, and require less attention.

National Trails are defined by three characteristics: fossil, water or trench.

The fossil ridges are carved from chalk or limestone, and they are:

1. North Downs Way
2. South Downs Way
3. Peddars Way
4. Pennine Bridleway
5. Pennine Way
6. The Ridgeway
7. Yorkshire Wolds Way
8. Cotswolds Way
9. Cleveland Way

The waterside paths follow coasts or river, and they are:

1. Pembrokeshire Coast Path
2. Thames Path
3. South West Coast Path
4. England Coast Path
5. Parts of the Cleveland Way, and the Peddars and Norfolk Coast Path (they are also part of the England Coast Path)

The military paths are formed by walls, ditches or escape routes, and they are:

1. Offa's Dyke
2. Glyndŵr's Way
3. Hadrian's Wall Path

Beauty

Travel, trade, defence – these were the platforms that made these trails. Like all rules, they are there to be broken. In fact, it's the link between beauty and nature that is the key part of what makes all the National Trails. The Coast to Coast Path will become the newest National Trail very soon. It was created by author Alfred Wainwright, in honour of its beauty, and his love of getting lost in nature.

Hiding

Being invisible is a skill we inherit before we are born. It's why kids and adults love hide-and-seek. Hiding is the first line of defence when danger threatens. It's why we all duck when something frightens us. Like bird chicks, we're tuned to hide first and, if discovered, fight or flee

Sleeping Bay

Mount Sion

as a last measure These are instincts that got us here as a species after hundreds of thousands of years of success and failure.

You only need to do two things to hide on a National Trail: pitch a bivvy after dark, and set off before sunrise. National Park rangers patrol some areas with heat-seeking cameras to evict wild campers, but usually only where there are particular fire risks, litter problems or areas have become too popular. Just avoid these places whenever possible.

Because hiding is not always possible, wild travel endows us with an even better survival tool: oxytocin.

Oxytocin

Oxytocin is a hormone. It's sometimes called the 'love hormone'. It secretes straight into the bloodstream when we are either in love or in nature, or both. The secrets of oxytocin are bound up in every religion and religious text known, and unknown.

Our prehistoric ancestors understood the benefits of oxytocin. Only they didn't give it a name. They just shared its secret. And, in a sense, that's what this book is. A manifesto on how to boost oxytocin levels while on a National Trail, without needing to know how or why. Oxytocin's greatest secret is that your body produces it while moving overland through the wild on foot. This survival tool is linked, at the simplest level, to our ability as individuals to make a better future for ourselves, without hiding, running or fighting. Oxytocin helps us do this by filling our veins with the hormone that gives us ideas, energised positivity and purpose. We know this is true intuitively and from personal experience. Aristotle held a 'peripatetic' school of philosophy – the word taken from the Greek 'peripatetikos' meaning 'given to walking about.' The co-founder of Apple, Steve Jobs, conducted walking meetings to improve creativity and problem-solving. Beethoven, Nikola Tesla and Darwin are others who walked in nature along so

Carrey Samson

called 'thinking paths' for the same reason. Oxytocin isn't just about purposeful ideas. Because speaking is the natural expression of thought, walking to think, and speak, makes a beneficial outcome more likely when trouble looms. This ancient truth is bound up in almost every story and tale associated with surviving on walk that inevitably involve unexpected danger, from *The Wonderful Wizard of Oz* to the *Epic of Gilgamesh*.

But if in doubt... hide.

Water

The ability to stay hydrated over long distances has less to do with finding water and more to do with carrying. Travellers rarely stock up with enough water because it's heavy. There are three carrying methods that help solve the water problem:

1. Drink and eat properly before leaving, both the night before and on the day. Focus on foods that are a good source of electrolytes, because this will ensure your cells are properly hydrated. A fully hydrated human can last several hours on the trail; carrying an additional three or four litres will cope with most situations.
2. Carry a water filter and the ability to boil water.
3. Use a push-bike as a water carrier along the way. It isn't illegal to push a bike on a footpath, but it can get to be a pain when lifting over gates.

A water strategy can be based around topping up with shop-bought litres at every opportunity. Ideally, I will drink over 60 minutes before setting off on a walk from a town or village, whether I leave at 5am or 9pm. I then carry three more litres. The combination of two litres drunk before setting off and three litres to be drunk for the journey to the next village or town will provide enough water on the hottest of days and climbs.

I carry a filter for emergencies. Or if/when shops close. There are plenty out there, so do some research for the lightest and best.

Food

Foraging food is as easy or complicated as you want to make it. Most people don't forage because they don't think they know how. They will visit the supermarket and buy the same seven fruit and veg each week – tomatoes, lettuce, broccoli, carrots, apples, cucumber and bananas.

Most adults and kids can identify at least seven foods in the wild that are at the top of the food chain when it comes to nutrition and goodness. They're not available all year round like supermarket veg, but here's a seasonal spread: WINTER: dandelion leaves (flowers in spring); blackberry/bramble shoot tips (Feb); SPRING: nettles (March-April), hawthorn blossom (May); SUMMER: dog rose petals (June); AUTUMN: hazelnuts (August-October).

Shelter

The need to find shelter is as important as hiding. Shelter starts with your clothes. Always carry a waterproof stuff bag of dry clothes: 1) a merino wool base layer upper and lower, 2) a micro-thin fleece, 3) a wool hat, 4) cotton trousers, and 5) a combination of hard shell jacket and bottoms, and soft shell coat.

Together with a good sleeping bag and lightweight bivvy, you should enjoy most temperate, low-level hikes.

Venturing out into any wild area without adequate research, with or without the proper equipment, knowledge and training, will inevitably end badly.

HOW MANY MILES?

Go at your own pace.

The paths in this book have been explored at around 10km (6 miles) a day. 10km (6 miles) a day allows you time to notice what's around. A slow walking day passes quicker than time travel, and fills with a thousand thoughts and encounters.

Marloes

To walk the 135km (84 miles) needed to finish Hadrian's Wall, at 10km (6 miles) a day you will need 14 days. If you haven't got a spare 14 days, maybe something in your life needs changing?

Bathe in cold water every morning or night if you get the chance. Even if only for five seconds. It will keep you oiled.

GETTING THERE

Public transport

Almost always efficient, but too fractured to be meaningful as constant travel into and out of the wild. Bus and train journeys are invariably an adventure when they fit with your journey. Look for these places, where train stations and bus stops link with your passage. They are almost as much fun as the paths themselves.

Afternoon teas and parking

Where parking fees have crept up to £12 or £20 per car, it's sometimes better value to make use of investing in restaurants and hotels that combine teas with parking.

A cream tea will rarely cost more than £20 in the poshest tearoom, hotel or riverside restaurant. The upside of investing £20 with a private business is that it makes their day, keeps their business going… best of all, you often get free parking and access to sea views and beach fronts that might otherwise be inaccessible. It may not be in keeping with the spirit of free path access for all, but when it comes to a choice between using a car park app in a National Park or a hotel, I know what I choose.

Directions and parking

Many of the directions to the wild places are linked to public car parks. There's a cost to that — usually from £2 upwards. It may be a price worth paying. I take the view that moving towards public transport wherever possible is more of a luxury than cars.

The best value parking in England is National Trust membership. Membership buys free parking and access to some of the best coast around the South West Coast Path, and the adjoining England Coast Path.

CHURCHES

There are lots of church entries here.
Two reasons:
- Church wardens and parishioners are welcoming most of the time.
- Old churches are built on the places our pagan and non-pagan ancestors considered valuable and sacred – usually where fresh water (springs, waterfalls and rivers) is nearby. Irrespective of your faith, atheism or religion church grounds are precious.

PUBS, B&BS, RESTAURANTS, CAFES AND CAMPSITES

Food and drink are the fuels that power outdoor adventure.

Carrying water and a packed lunch is important; but combining a trail with a treat at a pub, café or sleeping overnight is a magical pleasure.

Something about hotels, pubs and coffee houses. Those featured here are not always the cheapest or best value. While you're out there tramping the trail on lunches of sardines, dandelions and pitta, you will inevitably fall upon places that look perfect, whether that's a £70-a-night bed or a £19 dish of the day.

You'll spot them because they will be packed with customers.

These 17 trails are shaped around survival. They are as much about survival of the hospitality industry as they are about learning the skills of self-sufficient living while on the move: hiding, free food, carrying water, sleep.

THE SENSES – ALL OF THEM

This is a journey through the eight senses – the five you already know about, as well as the senses of direction, balance and feeling. There

The Wainstones

are many more, but eight is enough for now.

Our senses are dulled by the pollution of urban living, domesticity and routine, and then overwhelmed by the fixes we attempt as a pick-me-up. Nature is a respite to all of that. It's a balance. A resetting of the overused senses, and igniting the ones we may have neglected.

For the underused senses, try:

1. **SECRET SWIMS AND HIDDEN BEACHES...**
   TOUCH: Feel the bark of a waterside tree, or the breeze on your face. Go dip your feet and hands in rock pools. Sit on a heather bank and gently stroke the grass with your palm. Or even better, strip off and float on water so the cold runs over your body. If it's winter, buy a £350 wet suit and float in ice. Feel hot sand under your feet. Or rest your toes on a shell bank. Sink feet into warm mud.

2. **WOODLAND**
   SMELL: Enter a wet pine forest and inhale the fumes. Walk through the dense, broadleaf trees of an ancient wood when it's raining. Smell the tree leaf and the wild garlic around the roots. Walk from the wood out onto dunes and fill your nostrils and lungs with the scent of wet air. Waterside woodland in warm weather is the most multisensory environment in the British wild.

For the overused taste buds and noise-weary ears:

1. **WILD CAMPS AND FORAGE**
   TASTE: We've touched on it already, but forage for leaves along the hedgerows. Chew on an oak twig. Learn the difference between wild cherries and feral plums. Walk in late summer when apple trees are heavy with fruit.

St Govan

THE MAGIC PATH

Sandy Haven

Dip your toes and keep it simple. Blackberries, of course, in August and September. Venture out from summer and autumn into spring and winter with bramble tips. The tips can be picked and chewed all day as you walk.

2. **WONDERFUL WILDLIFE**
   HEAR: Listen out for blackbirds singing in the willow tree in June, the crows over the castle ruins, buzzards mewing around the church fields; the trickle of water from the waterfall or brook. The wind in the canopy of the poplars.

3. **ANCIENT, SACRED AND NIGHT SKIES**
   SIGHT: Look down from the top of a grass cliff over a green valley in the Lincolnshire Wolds. Sit on the estuary and watch the tide rise and fall around the creeks and rivers of Essex's England Coast Path. Watch the stars at night along Hadrian's Wall. See a shooting star from the corner of your eye on the Pennine Way. Marvel at your ability to see at night in the wildest, darkest places. Find a fossil on a Dorset beach.
   FEEL: A combination of all the senses... think about what you experienced and enjoyed and what you want to return to. There are more than 1,000 places in this book. They don't begin to scratch the surface of what you can experience.

This is what it is to escape into nature. Like a collection of feelings. And apart from the cost of an occasional afternoon tea, a car park or rail ticket or a night in a B&B... it's still relatively free.

FINAL FIX

You have in your hands a rough guide to sensing your way around England and Wales, along a virtually redundant scaffold of ley lines and opposing forces that collide around the best path network in the world. The coming-together and separation of fresh and salt water, around the fells, valleys and coast of upper, mid and lower earth. An alchemical process that gives birth to more life than you'll see in a thousand episodes of a BBC nature special.

This is a slow journey through the four elements of air, fire, earth and water, via the senses, that will change your life.

For that to happen, you need to make the wild your temporary home; and then you need to make it back home, to tell the stories. Story-telling is the final fix.

If you live to tell the tale, it may change other people's lives too.

KEY TO SYMBOLS

These symbols appear alongside location titles as a guide to the habitat, geology or theme of a place:

 Wild water
 Woodland
 Mother nature
 Good for dark skies
 Accommodation
 Restaurant or café

 Sacred
 Historic
 Trail access
 Top ten

KEY TO ABBREVIATIONS

This is a guide to the directional abbreviations used within the location texts:

N – north
S – south
W – west
E – east
R – right
L – left
FP – footpath

Ln – lane
Rez – reservoir
BW – bridleway
ECP – England Coast Path
FB – footbridge
RB – road bridge

GW – greenway
NT – National Trail
C2C – Coast to Coast Path
SWCP – South West Coast Path
▶ – start
■ – finish

White Horse, Avebury Down

PART 2
THE TRAILS

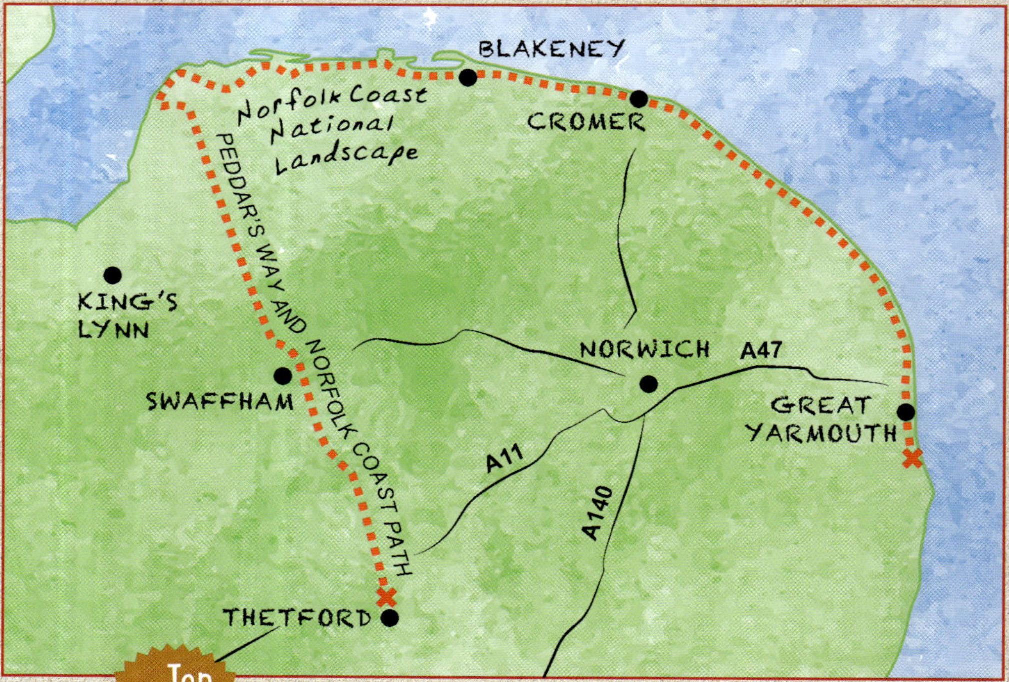

Top TEN

 ▶ **River Nar**, Paddle across a forded Rd. Perfect place for paddling in hot weather or packrafting.
52.698320, 0.685873

Castle and Bailey Gate, Walk around the UK's most impressively preserved Norman castle settlement.
52.703409, 0.690859

 Holme Dunes, Natterjack toads, butterflies and dragonflies congregate here where the Wash meets the N Sea.
52.974048, 0.551176

Seahenge (site of), The original home of Seahenge I and II.
52.977704, 0.548412

 Holkham Gap, Inhale the scent of pine woodland around a vast bay of wet sand.
NR23 1RJ

 High Cape, Explore the lake with views over Wells' marshes.
52.974272, 0.842205

Blakeney Eye, Stand over the (buried) remains of Blakeney Chapel.
NR25 7RP

 Cley Marshes, Listen to the unique water-world of spoonbills, avocets and bearded tits.
NR25 7SB

Water Ln, Fossil-hunt around the location of the famous 'West Runton elephant' find.
52.94173, 1.25137

⊙ **Happisburgh Lighthouse**, Climb the 112 steps when the lighthouse opens on bank holidays.
52.820501, 1.537132

PEDDARS WAY
BEST FOR: CHALK STREAMS

Springs, boreens, pingos

START: KNETTISHALL HEATH COUNTRY PARK
FINISH: HOLME-NEXT-THE-SEA

The Brecks Plantation

The Peddars Way is the place to paddle and explore chalk streams.

These natural wonders rise from springs that are squeezed through chalk bedrock. The chalk filters the water so it is crystal clear and uniquely high in nutrients.

They are favoured by spawning trout and salmon because of their mildly alkaline levels of potassium, nitrate, phosphate and silicate. I've no idea how or why egg-laden salmon know about that.

There are fewer than 250 chalk rivers in the world, and almost all of them are in southern England. Isn't that wonderful?

The Peddars Way crosses several streams after it exits the edge of Thetford Forest, the largest conifer woodland in England.

The combination of chalk river, heath and stream creates a home to some of the rarest habitat and wildlife. The largest stone curlew breeding population is settled here. The best wildflowers grow in the rare heather woodlands.

Chalk rivers, heath and streams form the backdrop to the Brecks' 'pingo' pond system. The 'pingo' is a watery phenomenon found nowhere else in the world but Greenland and Antarctica.

Holme-next-the-Sea

FOREST HOLIDAYS THORPE FOREST
Bungalows for two or more. Wooded holiday short breaks (three nights weekends, or four nights midweek), close to the River Thet. Good deals for two couples, midweek, in winter. Dog-friendly.

Shadwell, Thetford, Norfolk, IP24 2RX

www.forestholidays.co.uk/locations/norfolk/thorpe-forest

03330 110495

COLLEGE FARM B&B, THETFORD
Family-run farmhouse B&B. Three bedrooms or a one-bedroom, self-catered holiday cottage.

College Farm Ln, Thompson, Thetford, Norfolk, IP24 1QG

www.collegefarmnorfolk.co.uk

01953 483318

Knettishall Heath, Thetford
The Peddars Way starts/ends in a wood where wildflowers meet heath, feral ponies, mushrooms and the Icknield Way. It's a good place, under the cover of elm, to think about how the Icknield Way connects this short path by the Little Ouse River, in Norfolk, to Stonehenge – a 30-day walk away 480km (300 miles).
➤ **Find** Knettishall Heath car park, Thetford, IP31 1HL (52.390503, 0.854795). NT is across the Rd.

52.390504, 0.854795

River Thet, Harling/Bridgham parish border, Breckland
Enter water by narrow FB. Explore by packraft. Lots of hiding places in the reeds under willow branches. Listen for jumping fish and voles.
➤ **Find** A11 car park, Roudham, E Harling, NR16 2RF (52.447375, 0.846676) and walk 2.8km (1¾ mile) S.

52.421466, 0.854132

Bridgham Heath to Mill Hill boreen track, Breckland
Unique Breckland heathland. A 11 km (7 miles) rabbit warren of grassy and hard boreen from Bridgham Heath (52.434815, 0.848318) to Shakers Furze Woodland, at Mill Hill (52.528940, 0.811361). Directly N, it starts in the grass and wildflower meadow of the heath and crosses several main roads (52.528980, 0.811554). The stream bridge at Stonebridge is halfway.

52.479987, 0.837079

NATIONAL TRAILS

THE CHEQUERS INN, THETFORD

Thatched pub built in 1600. Classic British dishes and rooms. A 1.6km (1 mile) path detour.

Griston Rd, Thompson, Thetford, Norfolk, IP24 1PX

www.thompsonchequers.co.uk

01953 483360

BROOM HALL COUNTRY HOTEL

Posh 4-star Victorian country house. A 2-acre garden, and 13 acres of parkland. Choice of the Lime Tree Restaurant or more informal Ivy Room, Bar and Terrace.

Richmond Rd, Saham Toney, Watton, Norfolk, IP25 7EX

www.broomhallhotel.co.uk

01953 882125

Madhouse Plantation Tumulus, Wretham
Tomb mound is 50m (165ft) from the FP in a clearing between a potholed track, oak and chestnut trees.
➤ **Find** dead end of Tottington Rd (52.528941, 0.811274) where it meets NT. Facing the metal gate, turn R and walk S, 1km (⅔ mile) along a wooded path.

52.520127, 0.815265

All Saints Church, Threxton
Touch a 13th-century round-tower church. A 2-minute walk N from where the path meets the Threxton Hill Crossways, but worth a visit if the weather turns foul. Interesting stuff inside includes original medieval glass in N window and wood carvings in the pews and stalls. There's a lone yew tree on the E wall for shelter if the church is closed.

52.566488, 0.779866

River Nar, S Acre

LYDNEY HOUSE HOTEL

Renovated Georgian hotel. Reading room, hot tubs, BBQ and dining room.

Lydney House Hotel, Norwich Rd, Swaffham PE37 7QS

www.norfolkholidayrentals.co.uk

07585 210494

THE OSTRICH PUB

Popular walkers' pub for food. Rooms, too. An important service in the village.

Stocks Green, Castle Acre, King's Lynn, Norfolk, PE32 2AE

www.theostrichpub.co.uk

07563 784934

Church, Swaffham

Find rare 11th-century medieval wall paintings, among the oldest in England – as are the amazing stories they feature. Wooded and grass views. Benches and gardens to browse. A 600m (⅓ mile) detour.

52.613667, 0.751398

Houghton Springs, River Wissey, N Pickenham

Somewhere wilder and overgrown to relax for a while after the pace of hard and straight tracks and paths.

▶ **Find** St Mary's Church BW (see above) and follow the NT N for 1km (⅔ mile).

52.620178, 0.749198

Top TEN — River Nar, parish boundary S Acre and Castle Acre

Forded Rd. Perfect place for paddling in hot weather or packrafting. Good views from here up to the Church of St James the Great (see overleaf).

52.698320, 0.685873

Castle Acre Priory, Priory Rd, Castle Acre, King's Lynn

Cluniac monastery dating back to 1090 and Norman church. Recreated herb garden, church full of wood carvings. One of the largest monastic sites, established by the first Cluniac order of monks in England.

52.700893, 0.680801

Castle Acre

PEDDARS WAY 25

THE PIG SHED MOTEL
 Self-check-in with virtual keys enabled on your smartphone. Shares the access Dr to the George & Dragon pub.

Swaffham Rd, King's Lynn, Norfolk, PE32 2BX

www.thepigshedmotel.co.uk

07340 610009

KING WILLIAM IV
 Hotel, courtyard, eatery and coffee house in the countryside.

Heacham Rd, Sedgeford, Hunstanton, Norfolk, PE36 5LU

www.thekingwilliamsedgeford.co.uk

01485 571765

THE DABBLING DUCK PUB
 Local ales, local produce and rooms. Self-catering Duckling Cottage a few doors down.

11 Abbey Rd, Great Massingham, King's Lynn, Norfolk, PE32 2HN

www.thedabblingduck.co.uk

01485 520827

Brancaster

Church of St James the Great, Castle Acre
Medieval paintings, carved pews and other historical wonders.

52.702526, 0.6860667

Top TEN Castle and Bailey Gate, Castle Acre
The UK's most impressively preserved Norman castle settlement is popular with architecture students – 12th century and free to visit. It is rare for an entire castle, village, parish church and monastery to have survived. Together with the priory ruins and church, the castle makes Castle Acre worthy of a half-day visit, minimum.

52.703409, 0.690859

11 Old Stone plinth, Old Smuggling Rd, Little Massingham
A modern stone monument, but interesting. Part of the Norfolk Songline project, the sculpture is inspired by the Peddars Way.
➤ **Find** NT junction with A148 (52.798526, 0.625408) and walk S, 1.6km (1 mile).

52.785404, 0.633696

Harpley Common, Flitcham with Appleton/Harpley
A ½ km (¼ mile) of wooded avenue.
➤ **Find** NT junction with A148 (52.798526, 0.625408) and walk N, 2km (1½ miles).

52.816923, 0.613414

Bunker's Hill boreen, Flitcham with Appleton/Bircham/Harpley border
An 18km (11 miles) boreen track from Roman Rd, Massingham Heath (52.749017, 0.657896) to Fring (52.889939, 0.566277). Directly N, it coincides halfway with the crossroads Anmer Hill/Bunker's Hill burial ground.

52.825657, 0.607559

 ### Ringstead Downs, Ringstead
Hilly detour of wildflowers, chalk and chapel ruins. 500m (¼ mile) from path, S of Ringstead and church below.
➤ **Find** The Gin Trap Inn (52.934096, 0.538752). Facing the pub, turn R and walk S 200m (650ft) to junction. Turn R and follow the Rd S 275m (900ft) to old church track.

52.930072, 0.537446

 ### Peddars Way joins Norfolk Coast Path, Hunstanton/Holme-next-the-Sea/Old Hunstanton parish boundary
Where the Peddars Way joins the Coast Path.
➤ **Find** small car park, Beach Rd, PE36 6LG (52.965142, 0.526329), and walk 1.6km (1 mile) E on ECP.

52.966084, 0.524394

 ### Holme Dunes, Holme-next-the-Sea
Natterjack toads, butterflies and dragonflies congregate here, where The Wash meets the N Sea. In autumn, look for bright orange berries of sea buckthorn. Good for migrating birds in winter.
➤ **Find** small car park, Beach Rd, PE36 6LG (52.965142, 0.526329), and walk 1.6km (1 mile) E on ECP.

52.974048, 0.551176

 ### Seahenge (site of), W Sands, The Wash, Holme-next-the-Sea
The original home of Seahenge I and II. Pine and broadleaf woodland over dunes filled by fresh water. It's also a wonderful place to take a swim. One of the two timber circles is still on Holme beach, the other is at King's Lynn museum. Visibility of Seahenge II comes and goes depending on the tides.
➤ **Find** the end of Beach Rd (52.965142, 0.526329). Walk 2km (1.3 miles) to the R along either the beach or the coast path. Seahenge II can be found about 250m (800ft) offshore. Keep walking E (R) along the sands and slightly inland to explore the trees, Broad Water lake and the Holme Dunes.

52.977704, 0.548412

Gipsy Ln, Brancaster
Tree-lined Ln between marsh (and dunes) and a sacred cross at St Mary's Church.
➤ **Find** the car park in Broad Ln (52.973857, 0.638247), walk 335m (1,000ft) away from the beach and turn R around the marshes and creeks. Follow the path 1km (⅔ mile) to the scrub.

52.966252, 0.626189

Burnham Deepdale
Mow Creek, behind the sand dunes of Brancaster Staithe. Surrounded by FPs and Brancaster village. Church at Deepdale.
➤ **Find** St Mary's Church, Main Rd, PE31 8DD (52.965895, 0.685533). Facing the church, walk L for 100m (330ft) and then turn R onto the FP towards the beach. Continue on another 200m (660ft) to the waterside and turn L along the FP for a 1km (⅔ mile) stroll and creek views all the way to Brancaster Quay.

52.966701, 0.685954

River Burn Estuary, Grey Goose, The Causeway, Burnham Overy Staithe
A swim you'll never forget. Dunes, tidal estuary, surf and solitude.
➤ **Find** the coast path next to the public car park in Burnham Overy Staithe, E Harbour of Way, PE31 8JF (52.964951, 0.745331). Facing the quay, turn R and follow the path 2.4km (1.5 miles) to where the dunes meet the sea. Turn L and walk another 1km (⅔ mile) to rejoin the mouth of the River Burn and wilder parts of the beach. Beware of currents and tides.

52.976800, 0.751820

Scolt Head

Holkham

Top TEN: Holkham Gap, Holkham Beach, Lady Anne's Dr, Holkham

Seals and seabirds on a low-tide island. Kayak or paddleboard to get there, or hike to the pine woodland arc around the bay and wet sands. Hire a boat at high tide.

➤ **Find** Lady Anne's Dr, Holkham, NR23 1RG (52.960859, 0.814705). Parking all the way down to the strip and entrance into the Holkham Estate. Walk through the trees into a natural wonder. (FP from Turnham Deepdale's St Mary's Church to Scolt Head Island dunes via the marshes.)

52.971291, 0.814485

Top TEN: High Cape, Wells-next-the-Sea,

Broadleaf and pine woodland over dunes next to a boating lake and river estuary. Explore the lake and walk inland along Beach Rd and the E Fleet river path to Wells-next-the-Sea. Breathtaking views over Wells' marshes.

➤ **Find** Wells Beach car park (52.972394, 0.849242). Walk to the end of Beach Rd and down the ramp onto the foreshore at low tide. From here, walk L to the pine woodland. If the tide is in, follow the FP L before the beach ramp.

52.974272, 0.842205

PEDDARS WAY   29

🏅 Blakeney Eye, Cley-next-the-Sea

Stand over the (buried) remains of Blakeney Chapel that stood on this islet for 200 years, entirely surrounded by creeks and inlets known collectively as River Glaven. Walk on to Blakeney Point (52.979093, 0.979840). If Holy Island is the focus of human activity, this is nature's equivalent. Claw-shaped spit of sand shaped into a natural harbour by tens of thousands of years of battering by immense energy and power. Visit at low tide on a calm day.

▶ **Find** the end of Beach Rd (52.965289, 1.0476201) and walk E along the sand past Cley Channel, The Hood, Longs Hills and Blakeney Point. It's 6.4km (4 miles) to the furthest point – 12.8km (8 miles) there and back. So take care and watch the tides. An 800m (½ mile) walk is enough to hop over the River Glaven, which runs parallel with the shore onto the islet.

52.966021, 1.037482

🏅 Cley Marshes, Cley-next-the-Sea

A unique water-world of spoonbills, avocets and bearded tits. Gravel-raked coast abandoned by our industry. Like after so many acts of economic vandalism, nature has returned to saline lagoons, reed beds and marsh.

▶ **Find** the car park at the NWT Cley Marshes Visitor Centre, Coast Rd, NR25 7SA (52.954132, 1.055952), and walk N a few metres to marsh and coast path.

52.954035, 1.056236

🚶 Salthouse Marshes, Salthouse

Explore salt tracks and greenways that link up with the coast path from Cley to Gramborough Hill. Most important GW trails out of the front door at Salthouse, cross the A149 and lead down to Little Eye pools and dunes.

▶ **Find** the end of Beach Rd, Holt, NR25 7XW (52.955405, 1.097528). The beach beckons.

52.955649, 1.098044

🏅 Water Ln, W Runton

Fossil-hunt around the location of the famous 'West Runton elephant' find. Mammal and fish petrified remains are common, along with freshwater shells.

▶ **Find** the end of Water Ln, W Runton, Cromer, NR27 9QA (52.941045, 1.250271). There is a car park here. Walk on to the shore and hunt for fossils to the R and L within 100m (330ft).

52.94173, 1.25137

Cromer Lifeboat Station, Cromer
Learn about the savage seas of this coast by exploring a working lifeboat station and meeting its volunteers. Small shop is sometimes open. Look out for fossils in the chalk. Corals and shark remains have been found at this location.

52.933014, 1.301140

Promenade, Overstrand
Chalk is exposed during winter at low tide and is full of fossils. Walk Foulness Beach to Cromer and then back along the clifftops.
➤ **Find** the car park at 50 Pauls Ln, Overstrand, Cromer, NR27 0PF (52.919874, 1.340514). Continue on foot down the ramp to the beach and walk 500m (⅓ mile) R. If the tide is in and high, walk along the promenade.

52.917209, 1.3484994

Sidestrand Cliffs, Overstrand
Look for the colourful cliffs of Sidestrand. Erosion exposes the coloured clays, sands and tills with occasional Jurassic fossils all the way to Overstrand along this secluded beach.

52.909382, 1.362594

Weybourne

PEDDARS WAY   31

 Mundesley Emergency Coast Battery, Mundesley
Look for fossils along the beach. This was once a fossil-rich area because of erosion but thankfully sea defences have protected the coast. Sponges and occasional mammal bones are still found around the N shore of the town.

52.882224,1.431101

 All Saints Parish Church, Mundesley
Church towering over the beach with a rare organ in the corner of the churchyard! The church is also unusual in that it has no spire or tower. Beautiful views.

52.880635, 1.431288

 Happisburgh Lighthouse, Happisburgh
Climb the 112 steps when the lighthouse opens on bank holidays. Happisburgh is most famous for how quickly the coastline is eroding. The upside is the exposure of ancient life. Flint tools and butchered bones have been found on the beach dating back close to a million years. Explore St Mary's Church, 4 Beach Rd, NR12 0PP (52.828471,1.529970)
➤ **Find** what's left of the crumbling Beach Rd (52.821918, 1.537871). There is still a car park over the beach. It's a wonderful place from which to look back at the lighthouse. Walk down the ramp onto the sands for long low-tide walks.

52.820501, 1.537132

 John the Evangelist Church, Waxham
Church on beach Rd at Waxham dating to the 12th century, although some parts predate this to the Saxon period, around AD 850. Bike hire and café next door.

52.778462, 1.617363

 Winterton Dunes, Winterton-on-Sea
Not a part of the Broads. This wooded dune and beach, known as 'The Common', escaped being classified and defined by post-peat industry evacuation. The Common is strangely riddled with FPs: seven run parallel out to the high-tide mark. Visit the Parish Church of the Holy Trinity and All Saints for more on the local area. The tower opens in the summer for views over the wood and dunes.
➤ **Find** Winterton Beach car park, Beach Rd, NR29 4AJ (52.717885, 1.698189). Walk onto the beach and turn L for ½km (⅓ mile) then turn L again on any of the trails into and over the dunes and scrub.

52.719228, 1.689434

Gorleston Splashpad, Great Yarmouth
Swim and kayak. Vast sandy beach, layered in low tide pools. Lots to see on and offshore: boats and people.

52.568707, 1.732488

Beach Rd, Hopton-on-Sea, Great Yarmouth
The Peddars Way starts/ends in Norfolk at the bottom of Beach Rd, Great Yarmouth, to the sound of waves and whining sea birds. It finishes in woodland a long way from sea, but as close to nature as it started. Yin and yang. Fresh water to tidal, across springs, boreens and pingos.
▶ **Find** Potters Resorts, Coast Rd, NR31 9BX (52.534722, 1.731647. Move 200m N to Sea View Rise on the R (E). Follow the Rd for 90m (300ft), take the R turn into Beach Rd and follow the Rd down to the beach, where it joins the point where the ECP meets the Peddars Way/Norfolk Coast Path.

52.536274, 1.737427

Happisburgh

River Nar, S Acre

WILD THINGS TO DO BEFORE YOU DIE

PADDLE barefoot across a forded road

VISIT the UK's best Norman castle settlement

LISTEN to natterjack toads

TOUCH the tide around the original home of Seahenge

INHALE the scent of pine woodland around wet sand

STAND over the (buried) remains of Blakeney Chapel

LISTEN to spoonbills and avocets

FOSSIL HUNT around the location of the famous 'West Runton elephant'

CLIMB the 112 steps of a lighthouse

Top TEN

 ▸ All Saints Church, Walk through snowdrops in a secret church garden. YO43 3LJ

 Thorns Wood, Look for hares between dale views. 53.915023, -0.705615

 St James Church, Find an Anglo-Saxon cross inside the church. YO42 1QU

 Millington, In spring, smell wild garlic in ash woodland. 53.969181, -0.726531

 Nettle Dale, Lie down on a steep bank of tor-grass. 53.977050, -0.700076

 Holme Dale, Move along a grass gorge and chalk valley. 54.006898, -0.652864

 Thixendale, Walk a green canyon on the Chalkland Way. 54.038422, -0.731944

 St Peter's Church, Explore the church, built from the same limestone as York Minster. CYO17 8HU

 Camp Dale, Hunmanby, Touch mounds from the deserted village in a wooded dale. 54.173776, -0.367732

 ▸ Filey Brigg, Cool tired feet at the beach of Filey Bay. 54.217793, -0.272566

YORKSHIRE WOLDS WAY

BEST FOR: LUCID DREAMS

Mad hares, grass ravines, dark night skies

START: HUMBER ESTUARY   FINISH: FILEY BRIGG

Touch the void in lucid dreams. The northernmost chalk streams in Europe are surrounded by no people, no rivers, and almost no towns.

The UK's best-preserved abandoned medieval village epitomises a trail that promotes astral surfing as a virtual art form over social gatherings. The Sufis have been doing it for centuries.

The Yorkshire Wolds landscape is a surreal dreamscape. Peaks and trails are almost as hilly as The Lakes, but mostly absent of water. The Wolds brim and froth with gorges of grass and the occasional magic of the 'dew pond'. Dew ponds have the distinction of being denied by science, while being a phenomenon that exists in the waking world as well as the sleeping one. They are like unicorns that pivot on every plane except the scientific one. Which tells us exactly how science – for all its wonders – can sometimes get it wrong when choosing to gaslight the unexplained.

Touch a dew pond whenever you get a chance. They are known as the 'Water of the Wolds'.

Mad March hares are a common sight along the trail. A comic emblem to the lucid madness and dreamscape sense of it all.

Walk, rather than sleep, under the darkest night skies. It can be unnerving but the eyes soon adapt, and the world suddenly becomes a different place.

Thixendale Grange

THE COUNTRY PARK INN

 Hotel by the riverside.

Cliff Rd, Hessle Foreshore, E Riding of Yorkshire, HU13 0HB

www.thecountrypark.co.uk

01482 640526

Fleet Drain, Hessle, E Riding of Yorkshire

The Yorkshire Wolds Way starts/ends at the end of a small tidal wood. A small brick wall divides the path from the creek that leads out into the Humber a few metres away.

➤ **Find** the car park in Livingstone Rd, Hessle, HU13 0BN. Opposite the Ferry Boat Inn, on the seawall by the old Fleet Drain.

53.717159, -0.435275

Humber Bridge, Hessle

Impressive start to the walk, magnified in part by the scale of the Humber Bridge and the joy of not being on it or in a car. It's a wonderful feeling of calm alongside the brown waters of the Humber.

➤ **Find** Foreshore W car park on Cliff Rd, HU13 0HG (53.714129, -0.448291), under the Humber Bridge.

53.714247, -0.450352

Redcliff Channel, N Ferriby

Look for porpoises in the Humber. A 4.8km (4.8km (3 miles)) riverside FP walk along rocky beach and scrub. Lots of good beachcombing and fossils. Chalk stones on the foreshore.

53.717158, -0.468358

Red Cliff, Welton/N Ferriby

Remarkable prehistoric finds made here. In 1937, three Bronze Age boats made from oak and yew were discovered in the mud.

53.712279, -0.511810

Humber Bridge

YORKSHIRE WOLDS WAY 37

GREEN DRAGON
A 17th-century coaching inn. Pub with 11 en-suite rooms. Good selection of cask ales.

Cowgate, Welton, E Riding of Yorkshire, HU15 1NB

www.marstonsinns.co.uk/inns/green-dragon-hotel-welton

01482 666700

THE TRITON INN
Traditional coaching inn at the foot of the Yorkshire Wolds. Locally sourced foods and ales. Open fire.

Ellerker Rd, Brantingham, Brough, HU15 1QE

https://thetritoninn.com/

01482 667261

THE FOX & CONEY INN
Rooms and food. A 300-year-old Grade II listed inn with rooms. Pub classics in the restaurant, snacks in the bar.

52 Market Pl, S Cave, E Riding of Yorkshire, HU15 2AT

https://thefoxandconeyinn.co.uk/

01430 471050

Holm Dale

Long Plantation, N Ferriby
Oak and beech woodland by beach. Rare example of coastal woodland. Wet in winter but full of good foraging all year.
➤ **Find** Find Ferriby Foreshore Parking, Redcliff Dr, HU14 3DP (53.713889, -0.507025), and walk W then N on the NT 460m.

53.715075, -0.513514

Mill Pond, Welton, E Riding of Yorkshire
Find fungi along the edge of this pine and broadleaf woodland.
➤ **Find** the end of Dale Rd, HU15 1PE (53.735385, -0.545914). Follow the path 275m (900ft) to a pond and springs.

53.737890, -0.543233

S Wold Plantation, Elloughton-cum-Brough
Listen to blackbirds singing in relays along the length of the trail. Tangled broadleaf for birds.
➤ **Find** where the NT meets the Rd beside a small lay-by at Elloughton Dale, Brough (53.748097, -0.556334). Walk N into the woodland.

53.749858, -0.558083

All Saints Church, Brantingham
Picture-postcard church view set against sloping woodland and Brantingham Dales.

53.758616, -0.570291

MANOR FARM CAMPSITE

 (Wolds Way walkers only). Showers and water. Super clean and friendly.

Goodmanham, Market Weighton, E Riding of Yorkshire, YO43 3JA

THE FIDDLE DRILL

 Village café for treats and teas. Special place for walkers and locals.

Main St, Goodmanham, Market Weighton, E Riding of Yorkshire, YO43 3JA

www.facebook.com/fiddledrill?locale=en_GB

07598 512478

Dismantled railway line, S Cave

A 800m (½ mile) walk along the old railway beside Weedley Springs and Drewton Springs. Always something special about treading the rails of history. The grassy Swin Dale is a typical dry Wolds valley.

▶ **Find** lay-by at Comberdale Hill, Brough, HU15 2BE (53.781996, -0.568357). Follow the path/old Rd W 500m (⅓ mile) until it meets the NT. Turn R and N onto Comber Dale and follow the NT 800m (½ mile) until it reaches the dismantled railway.

53.785916, -0.575230

Hunsley Dale, Rowley/S Cave

Look for shelter along this lightly wooded track. A 1.6km (1 mile) trek through broadleaf woodland.

▶ **Find** junction where Whin Ln, High Hunsley, YO43 4TW meets the NT. Walk S 1.6km (1 mile) to woodland.

53.793861, -0.569724

Hessleskew Ln, Sancton/Market Weighton

A 3.2km (2 miles) BW and boreen through fields of crops. Directly N from Flower Hill, Newbald to Arras Cottages, just past the A1079.

53.848662, -0.590737

Thixen Dale

THE GOODMANHAM ARMS

 Considered one of the best pubs in Yorkshire. Great food, ales and its own microbrewery. The combination of this pub's remarkable reputation and nearby campsite and Fiddle Drill make Goodmanham village a highlight of the walk.

Main St, Goodmanham, E Riding of Yorkshire, YO43 3JA

01430 873849

 ### Rifle Butts Quarry, Mill Beck, Goodmanham
Wildflower oasis fed by springs (including Mill Beck), off Spring Rd, YO43 3JA. There's a lot of geological interest in this place and many fossils have been found. The reserve is the crossing of two great trails: the Wolds Way and the Hudson Way rail trail.

53.871960, -0.635015

 ### St Helen's Well
Sacred well that survived an outlived railway track, under ash trees. Ancient site still loved by locals.

53.870476, -0.645905

 ### All Saints Church, Main St, Goodmanham
Church famous for its stained glass windows and the early introduction of Christianity into Yorkshire.

53.876928, -0.648103

 ### The Lake, Pond Wood, Londesborough
Watch red kites circling the woods inbetween dales of Londesborough Park. Gets very boggy in winter.
➤Find A614 parking, Londesborough (53.884260, -0.665309) and walk 1.6km (1 mile) N.

53.894031, -0.671516

 ### All Saints Church, Low St, Londesborough
Snowdrop walk and secret garden to rear of church. Backs onto deer park and wild wood area known as 'The Wilderness'. Church guidebook has history of the village.

53.897332, -0.679680

 ### Church Ln, Londesborough
A 1.6km (1 mile) boreen between All Saints Church and Partridge Hall. Passes scrub woodland on SW, halfway along the hill.
➤Find All Saints Church (see above) and walk NW on the NT 1km (⅔ mile).

53.903546, -0.692970

 Top TEN ### Thorns Wood, Nunburnholme
Look for hares and dale views from the N tip of Thorns Wood.
➤Find driveway to Stonehouse E & Son, YO42 1RD (53.907853, -0.700929). From the main Rd, walk along the Dr (part of the NT) and follow for 800m (½ mile) into the wood

53.915023, -0.705615

THE WOLDS RETREAT

 A 4-star B&B. Part of a meditation centre at the foot of the Wolds. The World Peace Café is worth a visit, as are the 50 acres of park and woodland area.

Kilnwick Percy Hall, Pocklington, York, E Riding of Yorkshire, YO42 1UF

www.madhyamakaorgbed-and-breakfastpocklington-york-2

01759 304832

THE RAMBLERS' REST

 B&B and tearoom in a former farm cottage, said to be one of the oldest cottages in the village. Homemade food for walkers, cyclists and visitors.

Main St, Millington, York, E Riding of Yorkshire, YO42 1TX

www.ramblersrestmillington.co.uk

01759 305220 (tearoom), 01759 303292 (B&B)

 ### Nunburnholme Beck, Nunburnholme

Rest and hide from weather at FB over wooded beck. The beck once fed fishponds that the church monks used for food.
➤**Find** St James Church (see below) and walk NE and then SE 275m (900ft) along the NT to beck.

53.920139, -0.707771

 ### Top TEN St James Church, Nunburnholme

➤**Find** Anglo-Saxon cross inside the church. Small, but interesting churchyard. Bench outside for travellers and walkers.

53.919221, -0.710529

 ### Bratt Wood boreen, Bratt Ln, Nunburnholme

A 3.2km (2 miles) boreen from Bratt Wood, Lowfield Ln, to Chalkland Way, Warren Dale (53.945239, -0.738925) via Wold Farm and Low Warrendale Farm. Most of the Ln seems to have been downgraded from a GW, but thankfully retained by both landowners and LA as an important BW for the area. It is also a pretty walk through rural and brownfield landscapes. The best of it is Bratt Wood in the S and the twisting, slopes and S-bends of the boreen right at the end in the N before Millington Ln, Jenny Firkin Wood (see overleaf).

53.923487, -0.714271

St Nicholas' Church, Ganton

YORKSHIRE WOLDS WAY

THE GAIT INN

Village pub for cooked food and hand-pull beers. Dog-friendly.

Millington, E Riding of Yorkshire, YO42 1TX

www.thegaitinn.co.uk
01759 302045

SEAWAYS

Glamping, camping and holiday lets. Seaways Café next door. The Manor Inn pub also has rooms in the village.

Fimber Rd, Fridaythorpe, Driffield, E Riding of Yorkshire, YO25 9RX

www.seawayscafe.co.uk
07789 263728

 ## Jenny Firkin Wood and Pond, Nunburnholme
Oasis of woodland and watery ponds that once served the ancient church. A worthwhile detour to explore for a few hours. The church alone is special (53.937805, -0.741825).
▶ **Find** Millington Ln, Jenny Firkin Wood crossroads, YO42 1UE (53.945269, -0.738863) and walk S 275m (900ft) to wooded track on the R.

53.941122, -0.740614

 ## Whinny Hill, Warter/Nunburnholme
Look for chalk-grass 'herbs' salad burnet and wild thyme around this prehistoric burial site. Good views W and NW. Salad burnet has a rosette at the bottom of the flower stem and its flowers are speckled red.

53.951299, -0.725054

 ## Millington Wood, Warter
Top TEN
Bluebells in April in ash woodland. Wild garlic in spring. Rare baneberries grow between hazel and maple. The berries are not for eating as they are poisonous – the clue is in the name.
▶ **Find** Lily Dale car park, YO42 1TZ (53.966128, -0.723688).

53.969181, -0.726531

 ## Cow Moor, Warter, Millington
On W side of the path is a linear earthwork dating back to the Iron Age. The double dyke is thought to have been created by La Tène tribes to contain and protect cattle.
▶ **Find** Lily Dale car park, YO42 1TZ (53.966128, -0.723688). Walk away from the wood and E 275m (900ft) on the Rd until lakeside track on the R. Walk over FB and 180m (590ft) SE-E to NT. Turn L and walk N on the NT 275m (900ft).

53.970898, -0.711518

Nettle Dale, Huggate
Top TEN
As isolated as it gets within 300m (985ft) of a Rd. In a sense, the best of all Wolds. A steep bank of tor-grass and hedging that looks a bit like a vast 'crescent' man-made mound over the chalk valley.
▶ **Find** Cow Moor (above) and keep walking N 800m (½ mile) then take BW R into plantation.

53.977050, -0.700076

Wharram Percy

RACHEL'S WALNUT COTTAGE TEA ROOM

 Tea and coffee served in bone china. Homemade cakes. Rachel's speciality is freshly baked fruit scones with jam and cream.

Pocklington Ln, Huggate, E Riding of Yorkshire, YO42 1YJ

www.rachelswalnutcotta getearoom.co.uk

01377 288378

🌙 Holme Dale, Huggate

Move along a grass gorge that epitomises this landscape – a corridor banked by two great hills that look like nature has set a trap. Scattered remnants of a chalk valley area and two dales that have been inhabited for thousands of years... and a village, until the Black Death wiped out the inhabitants.

▶**Find** St Mary's Church, Church Ln, YO25 9RT (54.021827, -0.666450), and follow NT S for 1.6km (1 mile).

54.006898, -0.652864

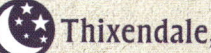 St Mary's Church, Fridaythorpe

Stand under the giant ash tree and admire the ornate Edwardian clock, dated 1903. It's quite a scene. Carvings inside.

54.021827, -0.666450

🔟 Thixen Dale, Thixendale

A 800m (½ mile) long boreen into and out of the village. The Ln is lined with wildflowers in spring.

▶**Find** The Cross Keys Inn (see overleaf) and walk the NT S 1.6km (1 mile).

54.034566, -0.713668

🌙 Thixendale, Ryedale

A 800m (½ mile) detour to see another of the Wolds' greatest landmarks, the green canyon on the Chalkland Way. BW leads all the way to Millham Dale, which is worth the trouble.

▶**Find** The Cross Keys Inn (see overleaf) and walk 275m (900ft) NW on the NT. Ignore the NT turning and keep walking on the Rd, another 180m (590ft) to join the Chalkland Way on the L as it leaves the Rd. Follow the BW 800m (½ mile).

54.038422, -0.731944

YORKSHIRE WOLDS WAY 43

WOLDS INN

Restaurant and rooms in the highest pub on the Yorkshire Wolds. Chef's blackboards specials are... special.

Driffield Rd, Huggate, E Riding of Yorkshire, YO42 1YH

www.woldsinn.com/
01377 288217

THE CROSS KEYS INN

Popular B&B and food for walkers on the way. Wood-burning stove and old stable yard converted to bedrooms.

Thixendale, Malton, N Yorkshire, YO17 9TG

www.crosskeysthixendale.co.uk
01377 288316

WOLDS WAY CARAVAN AND CAMPING

Toilets, showers, shop and laundry for tents and caravans. Also a Finnish Log House that sleeps four people.

W Wold Farm, W Knapton, Malton, N
Yorkshire, YO17 8JE

woldsway caravan andcamping.co.uk

St Mary's Church, Thixendale
Grade II listed church. Full of interesting artefacts and history.

54.039199, -0.715377

The Warrens, Birdsall
Isolated, views N on the E-tracking BW.
▶Find dead-end dirt Rd, Birdsall, Malton (54.054797, -0.730992) and walk 275m (900ft) E.

54.054938, -0.719757

Vessey Hill BW, Wharram
A 6.4km (4 miles) boreen and BW E and then N from Vessey Hill (54.049181, -0.728577) to Wharram-le-Street (54.082077, -0.679845). Take the detour to Wharram Percy Medieval Village (54.056749, -0.690518).

54.054555, -0.698128

Wharram Percy Medieval Village, Malton
Church ruins, fishpond and springs, surrounded in thin air and wildflowers. Highlight is the point: Wharram Percy is a deserted medieval village.

54.066437, -0.689348

St Mary's Church, Malton
Grade I listed, Anglo-Saxon nave and doorway, Norman tower.

54.081952, -0.681011

Beacon Wold wooded FP, Thorpe Bassett
Pine woodland with views through the trees at intervals (54.129387, -0.667200).
▶Find where the NT meets the High St, Settrington, YO17 8BQ (54.123671, -0.675602). Walk 365m (1,200ft) N.

54.127371, -0.671697

Rowgate Dew Pond, Thorpe Bassett
The famous water of the Wolds at Ryedale.

54.133133, -0.670717

Milburn Fields FP, Keld Ln, Thorpe Bassett
A 1.6km (1 mile) boreen N from Rowgate (54.133775, -0.670224) to Wintringham Beck BW (54.148131, -0.664931).
▶Find Beacon Wold FP (see above) and walk 2km (1¼ miles) N.

54.140534, -0.667583

THE DAWNAY ARMS

 Lunches, dinners, drinks and room, a an 800m (½-mile) detour from the trail.

Church St, W Heslerton, Malton, N Yorkshire, YO17 8RQ

www.facebook.com/profile.php?id=61554769905698

01944 319171

THE GANTON GREYHOUND

 Food and 15 rooms next door to Ganton Golf Club.

Ganton, Nr Scarborough, N Yorkshire, YO12 4NX

www.thegantongreyhound.co.uk

01944 710116

St Peter's Church, Wintringham

This church was built from the same limestone as York Minster. Rare stained glass windows featuring 14th-century saints. Jacobean wood carvings inside.

54.146969, -0.642902

Deepdale Plantation, Wintringham

Pine and broadleaf woodland to rest and escape bad weather.
▶**Find** Wolds Way Caravan and Camping (see p43) and follow the BW W out of the camp for 800m (½ mile) until it meets the NT. Turn L at the NT and walk S 550m (1,800ft).

54.152950, -0.637711

Enclosure Rites, Wintringham

Look for this installation that is part of the E Yorkshire hidden art trail.

54.156715, -0.637347

St Nicholas' Church, Ganton

Touch the church building set back in woodland and gardens. Impressive 14th-century spire.

54.184407, -0.484152

Fairy Dale

YORKSHIRE WOLDS WAY   45

THE SHIP INN
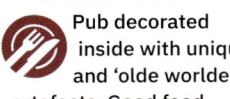
Pub decorated inside with unique and 'olde worlde' artefacts. Good food.

W St, Filey, N Yorkshire, YO14 0ER

www.facebook.com/profile.php?id=100063194710362

01723 514639

WHITE LODGE HOTEL

Hotel where the train meets the sea and the ECP. It's a lovely place to rest after the walk. Sea view at the end of Filey's famous Victorian Crescent. Great base for rock-pooling. There are 20 en-suite rooms, restaurant, bar and a large outside terrace.

The Crescent, Filey, N Yorkshire, YO14 9JX

www.whitelodgehotelfiley.co.uk

01723 514771

Camp Dale, Hunmanby
Excellent diversion from the earthworks down towards the Camp Dale loop. This wooded dale was last inhabited by villagers in the Middle Ages. Now deserted, the area is littered with mounds from previous inhabitants.
▶ **Find** The Ship Inn (see left) and walk W on the Rd and NT 4.8km (3 miles).

54.173776, -0.367732

Filey Brigg Cliffs, Filey
Views and brews. Where the Wolds Way meets Cleveland Way.
▶ **Find** Filey station, Filey, YO14 9PE (54.210013, -0.293647). Walk N 90m (300ft) to Station Avenue to join the NT. Turn R and walk E 800m (½ mile) to Filey Sands, and then 2.4km (1½ miles) N to Filey Brigg.

54.217793, -0.272566

Filey Brigg Cliffs, Scarborough
The Yorkshire Wolds Way starts/ends by cooling tired feet at the beach of Filey Bay, to the sounds of people and water. The path finishes on a clifftop, a long way from the Humber, and in a very different landscape. Sea to river, across grass ravines, steep climbs, gorges and chalk streams. You will have slept under some of the darkest skies in England.
▶ **Find** Country Park car park, Country Park Caravan Site, YO14 9ET (54.215036, -0.285031), and walk N 800m (½ mile) to path start.

54.217793, -0.272566

WILD THINGS TO DO BEFORE YOU DIE

TOUCH a dew pond

MOVE barefoot along a grassy chalk valley gorge

WALK through snowdrops in a secret garden

LOOK for hares over grass gorges

FIND an Anglo-Saxon church cross

SMELL wild garlic in ash woodland

LIE DOWN down on a steep bank of tor-grass

EXPLORE a church built from the same limestone as York Minster

FEEL the mounds of a deserted village

COOL tired feet at the beach of Filey Bay

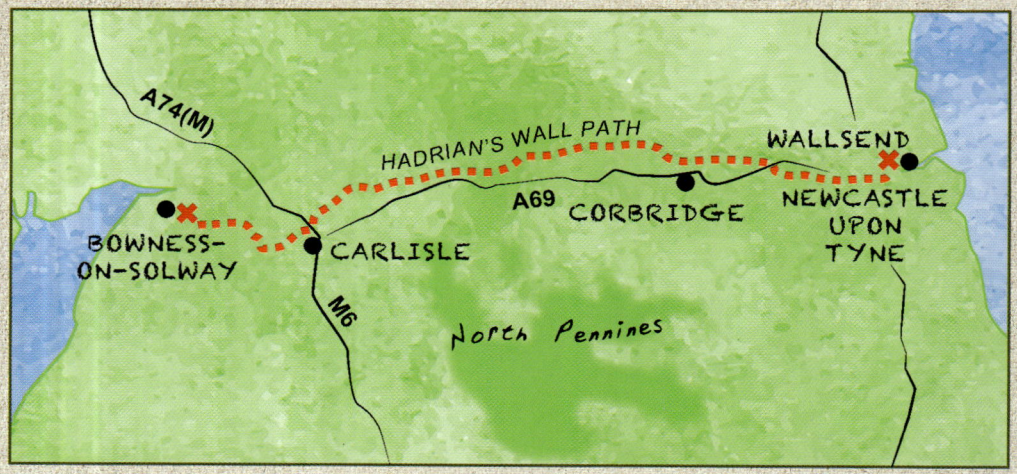

Top TEN

 ▶ Tyne Bridge, Look for kittiwakes nesting under the Tyne Bridge.
54.968466, -1.606688

 Sewingshields Crags, Feel the energy around where Arthur and his Knights are supposed to be sleeping before their return.
55.024544, -2.314234

Broomlee Lough, Watch carnivorous plants catch flies.
55.020463, -2.324134

 Crag Lough, Look for cranberries around peat wetlands.
55.005727, -2.359877

 Cawfield Quarry, Rest under the UK's darkest night sky, and watch northern lights.
54.993706, -2.447881

 Hare Hill, Touch the tallest remaining stretch of Hadrian's Wall.
54.974283, -2.682518

 River Eden, Explore, hide, and look for otters on the riverside walk between willows and water.
54.924678, -2.870866

 Burgh Marsh, Listen to the entire world population of Svalbard-breeding barnacle geese.
54.922561, -3.083610

 Coast Rd walk, Move along the Solway Path when it floods on spring tides.
54.924288, -3.107477

 ◉ Old Harbour Wall, Watch fishermen catch sea trout and salmon using ancient nets.
54.948669, -3.185628

Thorny Doors

HADRIAN'S WALL PATH

BEST FOR: STAR-WATCHING

Northern lights, carnivorous lakes, apocalyptic spring tides

START: THE TYNE FINISH: THE SOLWAY

Hadrian's Wall is one of the best places in the UK for touching stars — and one of the few places to regularly see the northern lights.

A volcanic ridge across N England, Hadrian's Wall Path is threaded by ruined watchtowers, forts and temples that form part of the old wall.

Wait for a clear night to visit the clifftops. Then get down and around the eutrophic apocalyptic lakes, and the carnivorous sundew beneath the whin sill clefts.

Take a torch, but keep it switched off. If you have the time, arrive before sunset and allow your eyes to adjust to the changing phases. The skies, light and water can combine to create unique reflections of unimaginable beauty. Auras, green flashes, rainbows and unique cloud formations are common.

Once your eyes have adjusted enough and the moon lights up the way, look skyward for the North Star, the anchor around which it's possible to start exploring the celestial map.

Consider combining star-watching with night-time rambles looking for bats or listening to owls.

LIOSI'S SICILIAN CAFE BAR

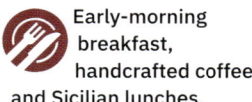 **Early-morning breakfast, handcrafted coffee and Sicilian lunches.**

4 Swordfish House, Amethyst Rd, Newcastle upon Tyne, Tyne and Wear, NE4 7YL

www.liosiscafe.com

01912 733303

HEDLEY'S RIVERSIDE COFFEE SHOP

 **Family-run coffee shop in the beautiful Tyne Riverside Country Park.**

Grange Rd, Newburn, Newcastle upon Tyne, Tyne and Wear, NE15 8ND

www.facebook.com/p/Hedleys-riverside-coffee-shop-100037636432647

THE SWAN

 **Seasonal dishes and cask ales in what was once a cottage beside a blacksmith's shop. The Swan began life as an ale house in 1842.**

Heddon-on-the-Wall, Newcastle upon Tyne, Tyne and Wear, NE15 0DR

www.vintageinn.co.uk/restaurants/north-east/swan-at-heddon#/

01661 853161

Chester's Fort

🅝 Station Rd, Walker Riverside Industrial Park, Wallsend

Hadrian's Wall Path starts/ends in an urban setting, beside a Gothic clock. The trail is sometimes followed by an annoying highway, but it all ends well in the isolation of the Solway, where the tide occasionally floods the Rd like some sort of vengeful punishment for lining much of the eastern end in fast traffic. An interesting separation of opposites on a path that is, for some, the best in the entire NT collective.

▶**Find** Wallsend station, Station Rd, Wallsend, N Tyneside, NE28 6RJ. Walk S on Station Rd towards the river, for 90m (300ft).

54.988644, -1.530991

Walker Riverside Park, Newcastle upon Tyne, Tyne and Wear

Feel the history. Look for the skeletal hulls of Victorian coal 'wherries' that stick up from the mud at low tide. Find fishing-line graveyards on the Tyne's sandy shore and rock pools. Wooded walk and river views are best at midday. A feral wilderness, not for late-night walks past the park.

▶**Find** Walker Riverside Park E, NE6 3TP (54.960981, -1.550614). Walk to the River Tyne 27m (88ft) S and then, facing the river, turn R and walk 90m (300ft) into the park.

54.960602, -1.552406

HADRIAN'S WALL PATH 49

ROBIN HOOD INN

Large, comfortable rooms; wines and whiskies at a gin bar.

Military Rd, E Wallhouses, Corbridge, Northumberland, NE18 0LL

robinhoodinnhadrianswall.co.uk

01434 672549

PINE DINING, VALLUM FARM

Classy restaurant in an old cow barn to admire Hadrian's Wall and the sloping Northumberland landscape.

Military Rd, E Wallhouses, Corbridge, Northumberland, NE18 0LL

www.restaurantpine.co.uk

01434 671202

THE RIVERSIDE KITCHEN

Home-cooked food using local ingredients on the wall path, close to the Chesters Roman Fort.

www.theriversidekitchen.co.uk

Chollerford, Hexham, Northumberland, NE46 4EW

01434 689850

Tyne Bridge, Newcastle upon Tyne
Top TEN

Look for kittiwakes nesting under the Tyne Bridge. The Gateshead Millennium Bridge gets most attention, but the Tyne Bridge is the most impressive of the seven bridges between Newcastle and Gateshead – not least for the kittiwakes. Opened by King George V in 1928. Best seen from the neighbouring Swing Bridge for perfect views of the city.

54.968466, -1.606688

Ryton Island, Gateshead
Wilder than the neighbouring country park. Tree-lined path, perfect for hiding.

▶ **Find** the car park at Blayney Row, NE15 8ND (54.934094, -1.755303). Walk S 45m (147ft) to riverside. Facing the water, turn R and walk W 500m (⅓ mile) along the NT.

54.981392, -1.763630

Vindobala, Roman Cistern, Heddon-on-the-Wall
Look for ditches and ridges either side of the Rd. There's not much wall to see along this stretch, so a minor detour to this Roman site is an idea. There are information boards.

55.001728, -1.826426

Whittle Dene Reservoirs, Stamfordham
Listen to jumping trout feeding on the surface in summer. Herons fish here, as do humans.

55.009134, -1.896241

Fozy Moss

GEORGE HOTEL

 Single, twin and double rooms. Swimming pool and gym.

B6320, Chollerford, Hexham, Northumberland, NE46 4EW

www.bespokehotels.com/the-george-hotel

01434 681611

GREENCARTS CAMPSITE AND BUNK HOUSE

 Camping fields, barn and bunkhouse. Campers get access to washroom, showers, washer and dryer. Log baskets for lighting fires at night.

Greencarts Farm, Humshaugh, Northumberland, NE46 4BW

wwwgreencarts.co.uk

01434 681320

YHA THE SILL AT HADRIAN'S WALL, BARDON MILL

 The hostel is next to The Sill: National Landscape Discovery Centre, which, together with Northumberland National Park Authority, investigates the unique landscape.

Close to the Roman Army Museum and the Roman fort at Vindolanda.

Military Rd, Bardon Mill, Hexham, Northumberland, NE47 7AN

www.yha.org.uk/hostel/yha-the-sill-at-hadrians-wall

Housesteads Fort

 ### St Oswald's in Lee Church, Hexham

Unique part of British history marked by a wooden cross and church. This is where Christianity was brought to northern England before it landed at Lindisfarne. More character than a Tolkien novel, as is the history. Read up before arriving, but there are lots of info boards.

55.020560, -2.100242

 ### Planetrees Roman Wall, Chollerford

Good for photos of human-made wall against the contrast of wild hillside.

▶**Find** lay-by B6318, NE46 4EX (55.021032, -2.111185), and walk 27m (88ft) N.

55.020969, -2.112577

 ### Brunton Turret, Chollerford

A significant part of the wall and a turret. Important part of the transition between 'broad wall' and 'narrow wall', so this detour is worthwhile. Information boards explain more; there's also an artist's impression of how it would have looked. Access from the A6079.

▶**Find** car park Front Street, A6079, NE46 4EF (55.019029, -2.130337) and walk 800m (½ mile) N on the NT, which runs along the Rd.

55.023602, -2.124386

Chesters Roman Fort and Museum, Chollerford

Ruins, fort, bathhouse and River Tyne. One of the most impressive legacies of the wall, making it a must-see. The bathhouse is good.

55.026718, -2.139112

THE TWICE BREWED INN

 Home-brewed ales served up at a B&B with a Dark Skies Observatory. Fires, beer garden, and on-site Brew House. The inn has its own astronomer team and large aperture telescopes. Planets, galaxies, nebulae and nuts. Dedicated dog-friendly rooms.

Bardon Mill, Hexham, Northumberland, NE47 7AN

www.twicebrewedinn.co.uk

01434 344534

WINSHIELDS CAMPSITE

 Campsite with bunkhouse in a converted stone barn a short walk from Hadrian's Wall and the Pennine Way. Campervans on hardstanding, but pitches cannot take large tents.

Winshields Inn, Hexham, Northumberland, NE47 7AN

www.winshieldscampsite.co.uk

07968 102780

Black Carts Turret, Walwick
Touch a large section of preserved wall. Beautiful place to rest, especially at sunset.

55.035755, -2.182279

Temple of Mithras and Brocolitia Fort, Newbrough
The path dissects temple and fort. Sit in the temple, look back at the fort, and let your imagination ride.
▶ **Find** Brocolitia car park, B6318, NE46 4DB (55.035641, -2.220262), and exit by the W gate into the fort.

55.033821, -2.222661

Sewingshields Crags, Hexham
Top Ten
Some of the best views on the wall from 30m (100ft) cliff. Isolated, so some care needed. Where Arthur and his Knights are supposed to be sleeping before their return. Explore this place.

55.024544, -2.314234

Broomlee Lough, Hexham
Top Ten
Look for carnivorous plants. Sundew on bog mosses of fresh water. Purple, and occasionally white, funnel flowers. Pennine Way runs along this section of wall.

55.020463, -2.324134

Housesteads Roman Fort, Haydon Bridge, Hexham
Vast fort and breathtaking wall views.
▶ **Find** Housesteads Visitor Centre, B6318, NE47 6NN (55.009880, -2.323455) and walk N on FP 457m (1,500ft) to fort. From the fort, walk 730m (2,400ft) W to where the Pennine Way and Hadrian's Wall NT part.

55.013783, -2.330338

Sewingshields

HADRIAN'S WALL CAMPSITE

 Award-winning campsite, less than 2km from the wall. Motorhomes, caravans, tents or glamping.

The Tilery, Melkridge, Haltwhistle, Northumberland, NE49 9PG

www.hadrianswallcampsite.co.uk

01434 320495

GREENHEAD HOTEL AND HOSTEL

 A 48-bed hostel, seven en-suite bedrooms and restaurant. Dog-friendly.

Main Rd, Greenhead, Brampton, Cumbria, CA8 7HB

www.greenheadbrampton.co.uk

01697 747411

HADRIAN'S HOLIDAY LODGES AND TOURS

 B&B and self-catering lodges near the wall. Organic breakfasts.

Four Wynds, Longbyre, Greenhead, Northumberland, CA8 7HN

www.hadriansholidays.com

01697 747972

Top TEN ## Crag Lough, Bardon Mill/Henshaw

Look for cranberries around the lough's raised peat wetlands. The heather mires between here and Scotland are the best in England. The wall meets the Pennine Way as it tracks N. Elevated views over the lough.

55.005727, -2.359877

 ## Sycamore Gap, Henshaw

The most famous section of the path.

55.003349, -2.374314

 ## Steel Rigg, Henshaw

Rugged, steep climb, but worth it. Go find out.

➤ **Find** Steel Rigg car park, Henshaw, NE47 7AN (55.003608, -2.390767), and walk to the NT a few metres away for views along the trail path and cliff.

55.002232, -2.388954

Winshield Crags, Henshaw

Touch the highest point on the wall. Winshield Crags tower to 1,131ft (345m). The Whin Sill at its most spectacular.

55.001928, -2.404557

Winshield Crags

HADRIAN'S WALL PATH   53

CHAPEL HOUSE FARM WALKERS CAMPSITE

 Budget-priced campsite that takes walk-ins. Farmyard toilet/handwash facilities.

Chapel House Farm, Gilsland, Northumberland/Cumbria border, CA8 7EL

www.chapelhousefarmgilsland.com

07717 700049

BROOKSIDE VILLA B&B, HADRIAN'S WALL

 Award-winning B&B by the wall. Bike storage, guest lounge, terrace and packed lunches.

Gilsland, Northumberland/Cumbria border, CA8 7DA

www.brooksidevilla.com/

01697 747300

Cawfields

Top TEN — Cawfield Quarry, Melkridge
The UK's darkest night sky comes with occasional northern lights. This is the best view on the wall... water and skyline waves against rock.
▶ **Find** Cawfield Quarry car park Pennine Way, NE49 9PJ (54.992938, -2.450183). Walk E on path 45m to the waterside.

54.993706, -2.447881

King Arthur's Well, Greenhead
Touch medieval story-telling. Wells and wall ruins, too.

54.993584, -2.499511

Walltown Crags, Greenhead
Feel the power of this place. Roughly halfway along the trail is where Scotland and the N Pennines merge.
▶ **Find** Walltown Visitor Centre car park, Walltown Quarry, CA8 7HZ (54.986939, -2.519806). Exit the car park by the quarry gate E and walk along the NT E 1.6km (1 mile).

54.992513, -2.507376

Remains of Thirlwall Castle, Thirlwall
Lots of information boards on the castle and fortified tower house. Dates back 700 years. Built from stone dismantled from the wall at the nearby Roman fort.
▶ **Find** Thirlwall View car park, B6318, CA8 7HL (54.986258, -2.536550), and walk over the railway line on the NT, then 365m (1,200ft) N along the river to the castle. Alternatively, cross the Rd and follow the Pennine Way S towards the Roman Camp (54.982599, -2.545822).

54.988558, -2.534201

Hole Gap

COOMBE CRAG CAMPING
A working dairy and sheep farm on the wall. Basic site for cyclists, walkers and wall visitors.

Coombe Crag Farm, The Banks, Lanercost, Cumbria, CA8 2BU
www.coombecragcamping.co.uk
07969 834808

FLORRIE'S ON THE WALL
Bunkhouse and café.

Kingbank, Walton, Cumbria, CA8 2DH
www.florriesonthewall.co.uk
01697 741704

River Irthing Falls, Waterhead/Upper Denton
Lie down on a warm day and feel the water spray. A steep path has a river view and place to rest. The Willowford FB is made from the same rust-like steel used for the Angel of the North.
▶**Find** Birdoswald car park, Brampton, CA8 7DD (54.991607, -2.600738). Exit the car park by the roadside gate and walk S onto the NT. Turn R and walk E 800m (½ mile) to riverside.

54.990306, -2.593274

Denton Scar, Waterhead/Upper Denton, Carlisle, Cumbria
Get lost among the trees and on Irthing riverbank E. It's quite a place to explore.
▶**Find** Banks E Turret from Hadrian's Wall car park, Brampton, CA8 2JH (54.975181, -2.665221) and walk 1.6km (1 mile) E along the NT into Combcrag Wood. Ignore the L turn on the NT and instead follow the FP S down through the wood to the riverside.

54.977071, -2.640604

NATIONAL TRAILS

OLD VICARAGE BREWERY, WALTON

 The Old Vicarage hosts a microbrewery, bar and B&B. Dog-friendly. Evening meals and packed lunches on request.

3 Irthing View, Walton, Brampton CA8 2DP

www.oldvicaragebrewery.co.uk

01697 543002

WALTON TEAROOM

 All-day breakfasts, soups and cream teas. Dog-friendly.

Walton, Brampton, Cumbria, CA8 2DJ

07954 704734

Hare Hill, Waterhead/Upper Denton

Touch the tallest remaining stretch of Hadrian's Wall: 3m (10ft) high. Hare Hill is the last piece of upstanding wall when walking W, or the first piece if walking E.

▶**Find** Banks E Turret from Hadrian's Wall car park, Brampton, CA8 2JH (54.975181, -2.665221) and walk 1km (⅔ mile) W along the NT to Hare Hill.

54.974283, -2.682518

St Mary's Church, Walton

Church by a village green. Vast cemetery to explore. Keep looking for raised areas of ground that are the tell-tale signs of buried wall after Hare Hill.

54.972673, -2.748091

Cambeckhill Weir, Irthington

Place to get lost in trees. Ferns, twisted woodland, water and shingle riverbanks to explore.

▶**Find** Walton tearoom (see left) and walk S through village down to NT. Where NT leaves the Rd (54.970766, -2.749125), walk W 1.6km (1 mile) to weir.

54.967339, -2.765719

Thorny Doors

Milecastle 76 on Solway

BLEATARN FARM CAMPSITE

Hot showers and hook-up on the path. Toilets, showers and dishwashing.

Irthington, Carlisle, Cumbria, CA6 4ND

07795 490579

 ### River Eden, Stanwix Rural/Wetheral
Explore, hide, and look for otters on the riverside walk between willows and water.

54.924678, -2.870866

 ### Memorial Bridge Beach, River Eden, Stanwix
A natural navel of sand beach in the shadow of Memorial Bridge. Lovely place to hide or rest. Good view from the bridge and lots of wildflowers around the riverbank.
▶**Find** Rickerby Park car park, Carlisle, CA3 9AA (54.904024, -2.927572), set back in a quiet picnic space. Walk down 20m (65ft) to the riverside and, facing the water, turn L, following the FP, 800m (½ mile) to the bridge.

54.899073, -2.922440

 ### Stanwix Riverbank, Edentown
Wooded walk around meander of River Eden where sparrowhawks catch small birds. Visit in summer, when the young fledglings start to hunt.

54.905571, -2.947000

 ### St Kentigern's Church, Grinsdale
Riverside church on FP is a detour. Good for packrafting.

54.912916, -2.980518

NATIONAL TRAILS

HADRIAN'S WALL PATH   57

THE DROVER'S REST

Family-run inn on the wall. Try the homemade and hot-smoked Cumberland sausages, served in a homemade bun.

Monkhill, Burgh by Sands, Carlisle CA5 6DB
www.droversrestinn.com
01228 576141

GREYHOUND INN

Real ales, food and campervan stopover. Steak pie top dish.

Burgh by Sands, Carlisle, Cumbria, CA5 6AN
01228 576888

HILLSIDE FARM

B&B and bunk barn with views over the Solway Firth marshes.

Boustead Hill, Burgh by Sands, Cumbria, CA5 6AA
www.hadrianswalkbnb.co.uk
01228 576398

St Anne's Island, River Eden, Kingmoor/Beaumont
One of the only islands on the path. This sandy eyelet sits on the River Eden. Packraft or paddle when water levels are low.
▶ **Find** St Mary Church, Beaumont, CA5 6EA (54.924121, -3.018845), and walk NE 275m (900ft) to the riverside. Facing the water, turn R and walk SE 800m (½ mile) to FP.

54.919540, -3.010439

St Michael's Church, Burgh by Sands
Church built from stones taken from the wall. The church gives back with a walkers' drinking tap.

54.922173, -3.048815

Top TEN
Burgh Marsh E, Eden Estuary, Rockcliffe/Burgh by Sands
Listen to the entire world population of Svalbard-breeding barnacle geese. All 28,000 birds migrate from the Arctic to Solway in autumn. The most isolated part of the wall is here...
▶ **Find** the 1.6km (1 mile) FP (54.922506, -3.083367) from the cattle grid out onto the marsh. The Solway co-joins with Eden Estuary salt marsh. If kayaking further upstream, look out for Atlantic salmon and even otters.

54.922561, -3.083610

Burgh Marsh W, Eden Estuary, Rockcliffe/Burgh by Sands
Feel the estuary breeze carrying the croak calls of rare natterjack toads. They feed and mate around the edges of Solway's dunes, heath, marshes and shellfish beds.
▶ **Find** the shorter FP, 1.2km (¾ mile) W along the path (54.924013, -3.102671) from the Burgh Marsh E entry above.

54.928134, -3.104603

Top TEN
Coast Rd walk, Burgh by Sands
Move along the Solway Path. This place feels like the edge of a precipice, only rescued by the realisation that buses sometimes run here. Other than that, a lucid dreamscape of apocalyptic magic. A wonderful place to walk. The path floods occasionally on spring tides, which makes it more special. An alchemical trap for many reasons. Check tide times.
▶ **Find** Drumburgh Castle (see p58) and walk 2.8km (1¾ miles) E on the coast Rd until the FP N onto marsh, opposite Bousted Hill.

54.924288, -3.107477

CROFT HOUSE B&B

 Good start or end to the path.

Boustead Hill, Carlisle, Cumbria, CA5 6AA

01228 576929

THE KINGS ARMS INN

 Inn on the Solway Firth at the start/end of Hadrian's Wall. B&B and bar.

Bowness-on-Solway, Wigton CA7 5AF

www.kingsarmsbowness.co.uk

01697 351426

SHORE GATE HOUSE B&B

 A 17th-century mill house with wide watery views over to the Scottish coast.

Bowness-on-Solway, Wigton CA7 5BH

www.shoregatehouse.co.uk

01697 744622

Drumburgh Castle, Bowness

Heraldic birds carved into entrance, altar stone from Roman temple in garden. A pele tower was originally built here by Robert le Brun in 1307, on what was once a tower of Hadrian's Wall.

54.960602, -1.552406

Old Harbour Wall, Bowness

TOP TEN

Look for fishermen who catch sea trout and salmon on their run up the Solway from June until late summer. Known as 'Haaf Netters', the fishermen stand chest-deep in the sea and push framed nets to scoop up fish that swim towards them. The method was introduced by Vikings more than 1,500 years ago and has been used in the Solway Firth ever since.

▶**Find** The Kings Arms Inn (see left) and walk 2.4km (1½ miles) E along the coastal Rd to the Old Harbour Rd.

54.948669, -3.185628

Bowness, Allerdale

Hadrian's Wall Path starts/ends on the Solway. Perhaps one of the most inspiring ends in the entire trail series. No pavement. Just hard, quiet Rd. Grass verges, wall flowers, beach, estuary mud, sea and blue sky. The end of a volcanic ridge of ruin, sprinkled in northern lights, giant toads and carnivorous lakes.

▶**Find** Bowness-on-Solway parking, Bowness-on-Solway, Wigton, CA7 5AF (54.952690, -3.220385) and walk 500m (⅓ mile) through the town to NT start.

54.953911, -3.211616

Sewingshields

WILD THINGS TO DO BEFORE YOU DIE

WATCH fishermen catch sea trout and salmon in traditional nets

LISTEN to kittiwakes nesting under the Tyne Bridge

FEEL the energy around sleeping Arthur and his Knights

TASTE wild cranberries around the lough's raised peat wetlands

REST under the northern lights

TOUCH the tallest part of Hadrian's Wall

LOOK for otters on the riverside

LISTEN to the entire world population of Svalbard-breeding barnacle geese

PADDLE along the Solway Path when it floods

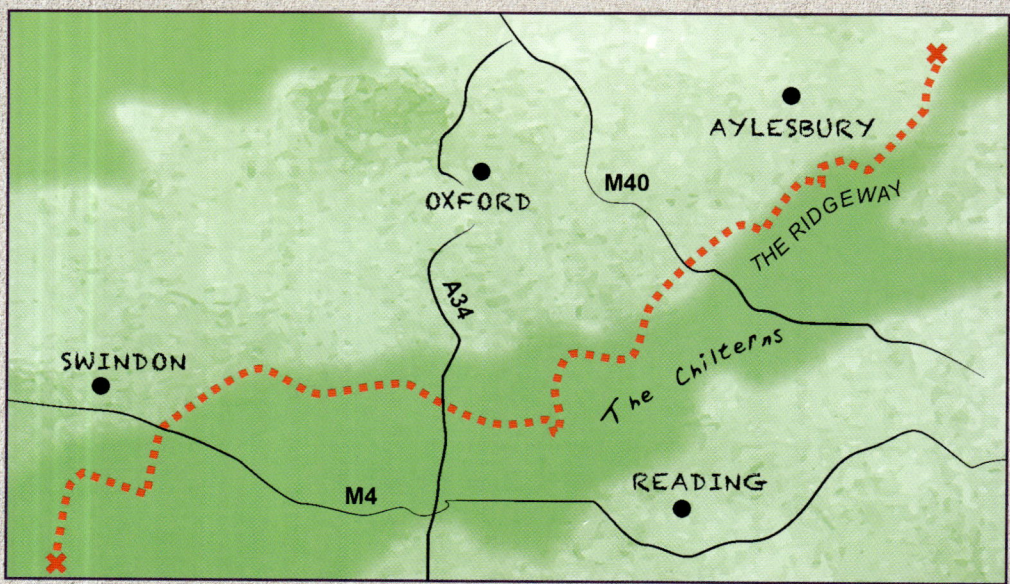

Top TEN

- **Overton Hill,** Feel the thin air around 5,000-year-old stone circles.
  51.412484, -1.830608
- **Valley of Stones,** Walk the space that is home to the largest collection of sarsen stones in Britain.
  51.438191, -1.803457
- **The Polisher Stone,** Touch a power source of immeasurable energy.
  51.442322, -1.816496
- **Wayland's Smithy,** Enter a Neolithic long barrow that is as impressive as any tomb you'll find in Britain.
  51.566677, -1.596092
- **Dragon Hill,** Stand on the Ln or FP over a chalk hill that has had the top artificially removed.
  51.577679, -1.569155

- **Goring and Streatley Bridge,** Watch the world go by from a bridge over the Thames.
  51.522966, -1.142716
- **Pulpit Hill Hillfort,** Explore an Iron Age hillfort at the top of one of the largest deciduous woodlands on the trail.
  51.737529, -0.797297
- **Ellesborough Warren,** Walk around the largest box woodland in the UK.
  51.747193, -0.791995
- **Bacombe Hill,** Photograph giant fungi.
  51.754521, -0.761992
- **Grand Union Canal,** An encounter with Britain's most important canal. This meeting links the Icknield Way with the Thames Path and Peddars Way.
  51.799507, -0.626604

THE RIDGEWAY

BEST FOR: MAGIC

Druids, dragons, valley of stones

START: WESSEX DOWNS   FINISH: CHILTERN HILLS

The Ridgeway is more connected to magic, wizards and wise women than any other National Trail in England and Wales. It has seen everything from dragons and knights to stone circles and barrows.

Fire, chalk and stream are the secrets druids associated with purpose: long life and good health. The wise knew where to find the purest source, and then how to both protect and defend it while making use of the plants, minerals and life-healing properties of fresh water. These are the origins of our sacred places, temples and churches.

Secularism thrives in places where old priorities are, thankfully, easy to come by. Water today is fresh and prolific from the tap. But that statement of fact it as profound in its sense of what we have lost as it is in what we have gained. Tap water has freed us from the burden of chalk stream portage and protection but enslaved us to the profit and whim of utility and sewage companies whose purpose is shareholder. Polluting the chalk streams we once held sacred is of no importance to anyone other than frustrated, toothless campaigners.

Two of our most sacred establishments – Stonehenge and Canterbury Cathedral – sit at the head of chalk streams. Our pollution of the water – and we are all to blame – is tantamount to pissing on pews of wisdom.

The contempt that we as individuals, and the water companies, have for our purest rivers is lazy, and there's a reason for that. Distance from nature is how we interpret what's good about life, and what it is to be safe. But it's a pendulum that has swung too far on the back of our arrogance. Our belief that past ideas were no more than folklore and old wives tales. The net result is that magic eludes us. And we need some of it back. The Ridgeway is the place to rethink.

Amesbury

Silbury Hill

The Ridgeway, W Overton
The Ridgeway starts/ends in what feels like a transit camp for time travellers. It's at the pivot of a prehistoric wilderness. An energy-filled air of excitement and anticipation that is something like the sensation of entering a cinema or theatre before a rare performance. Five Round Barrows are a few metres to the E. This place is significantly better than Stonehenge, for no other reason than it is connected to an entire column of sensations, symbols and tombs that reveal themselves over the next 140km (87 miles).
➤**Find** the Ridgeway and Sanctuary car park, A4, SN8 1QG (51.411541, -1.830554).

51.411552, -1.830604

Overton Hill, W Overton
Feel the thin air around a path surrounded by stone circles and mounds. The timber and stone circus is believed to be at least 5,000 years old. The Sanctuary was once connected to Avebury circle (a must-visit) by an avenue of stones, known as 'West Kennet Avenue'.

51.412484, -1.830608

THE RIDGEWAY 63

THE CROWN INN

Overnight stopovers for motorhomes and food. Steak pie is good. A 2.4km (1½ mile) detour from the path.

Broad Hinton, Swindon, Wiltshire, SN4 9PA

www.crownatbroadhinton.co.uk

01793 731302

THE WELL GUEST HOUSE

B&B. Single, doubles, twins and triples. Popular with walkers – just 5 minutes from Junction 15 of the M4. Packed lunches for Ridgeway walkers. Supper served at 7pm and must be pre-arranged. Secure cycle storage. Luggage transfer.

Marlborough Rd, Ogbourne St George, Wiltshire, SN8 1SQ

www.thewellguesthouse.co.uk

01672 841445

Small Barrows, W Overton
Touch a beech tree, part of the grove of trees around a barrow mound. Good views. An important place to relax and feel close to prehistoric Britain.

51.418159, -1.833260

Six Round Barrows, W Kennett
Move around the old beech trees that mark each barrow in this peaceful tomb. The burials are part of the huge, ancient cemetery W of the Ridgeway around Overton Hill.

51.416334, -1.835801

The Toad Stone, Fyfield Down, Herepath
Feel this ancient marker. It was either a guide, a sacred stone or both. The Toad Stone is at the centre of the valley of sarsens. Also known as 'frog rock'.

51.435116, -1.807894

Green Street, Overton Down
Sense the space around the crossroads where The Ridgeway meets another prehistoric path, the Green Street Trail. This was once part of the Rd from Bath to London.

51.436437, -1.821585

Top TEN — Valley of Stones, Fyfield Down
Walk the space that is home to the largest collection of sarsen stones in Britain. These rocks were used at both Avebury stone circle and Stonehenge. A shrine in every sense.

51.438191, -1.803457

Avebury Down

THE VILLAGE INN

Locally sourced, home-cooked pub food.

Bell Ln, Liddington, Swindon, Wiltshire, SN4 0HE

www.villageinn-liddington.co.uk

01793 790314

Top TEN The Polisher Stone, Marlborough Down
A rare opportunity to touch a power source of immeasurable energy. A polissoir: a sarsen stone used by prehistoric ancestors to sharpen tools and axes.

51.442322, -1.816496

Barbury Castle, Wroughton
Touch the ruins of a vast Iron Age fort. Grass covers the ruin and ramparts. The castle spreads over the entire plateau. Ancient chariots have been found here. Uffcott chalk stream is a 1km (⅔ mile) detour N (51.488068, -1.817329). Walk 1.6km (1 mile) E to Smeathe's Ridge for the best views.
▶**Find** Barbury Castle car park, Swindon, SN4 0QH (51.484327, -1.777391). Car park is on NT. Walk 800m (½ mile) NW to the site.

51.485158, -1.787008

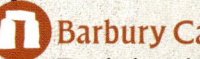 Chantry Meadow Chalk Stream, Southend
Listen to poetry: the flow of a chalk stream. Look for brown trout and pea mussels.

51.466184, -1.719149

Chiseldon and Marlborough Railway Path, Southend
Feel echoes of the past on this disused railway line. Southend is a hamlet of timber-framed houses, some made from local chalk blocks known as 'clunch'.

51.458404, -1.712547

White Horse, Avebury Down

THE RIDGEWAY

Wayland's Smithy

HELEN BROWNING'S ROYAL OAK

 Pig farm, farm shop, hotel and restaurant, set in 1,500 acres of organic farmland. Woodland and water, high ground and low ground, and a 14.5km (9 miles) boundary. 'You hardly need to leave the place,' say the owners. Close enough to the trail to ensure you do.

Cues Ln, Bishopstone, Swindon, Wiltshire, SN6 8PP

www.helenbrownings organic.co.uk

01793 790481

 ### Hall Wood, Bytham Rd, Southend
Look for chanterelles and boletes in autumn between giant beech trees. Sunken tree-lined trail of flint and chalk is good for shelter and shade.

51.459842, -1.704590

 ### Liddington Castle, Badbury
The hillfort marks the highest point on the trail (275m), with views over the M4.

51.515852, -1.699928

 ### Wayland's Smithy, Ashbury
Top TEN
A Neolithic long barrow that is as impressive as any tomb you'll find in Britain. Built more than 7,000 years ago.
▶**Find** B4000 car park, Swindon, SN6 8LN (51.557265, -1.607144). Facing the car park, turn L and walk NE, 1.6km (1 mile) to the site.

51.566677, -1.596092

 ### Uffington Castle, Uffington
Explore the ramparts. Coins found here have been dated to the Dobunni tribe.

51.574848, -1.569157

THE WHITE HORSE, FARINGDON

 One of Britain's oldest inns comes with thatched roof, oak beams and log fires. Almost 500 years old, Thomas Hughes of *Tom Brown's School Days* fame is said to have written his books here. The White Horse is mentioned in JK Rowling's *Lethal White*.

Marsh Way, Woolstone, Faringdon, Oxfordshire, SN7 7QL

www.whitehorsewoolstone.co.uk

01367 820726

COURT HILL CENTRE

 Bunkhouse, camping and tearooms. Former Youth Hostel Association (YHA), now managed by the Court Hill Trust.

Court Hill Rd, Letcombe Regis, Wantage, Oxfordshire, OX12 9NE

www.courthill.org.uk

01235 760253

THE HARROW PUB

 A country pub with cricket green views, 1.6km (1 mile) S of the trail.

Main St, W Ilsley, Newbury, Berkshire, RG20 7AR

www.theharrowwestilsley.co.uk

01635 261993

 ## White Horse, White Horse Hill, Uffington

White horse views provide these hills with something beyond sensations. Dated to 1600 BC, and the Bronze Age. Best appreciated from the valley below (51.583446, -1.576800).

▶**Find** White Horse Hill car park, Faringdon, SN7 7QJ (51.577230, -1.578408). Exit the car park and turn L, walk S 500m (⅓ mile) onto NT. Turn L and walk E 1.6km (1 mile) to site.

51.577508, -1.564846

 ## The Manger, Woolstone, Vale of White Horse

Look for brown hares around the largest and best areas of chalk grassland on the trail.

51.576857, -1.571576

 ## Dragon Hill, Vale of White Horse

Stand on a chalk hill that has had the top artificially removed. The bare plateau of chalk has never grown grass since its cap was removed in prehistory. Like all mysteries, there's a good story to go with it. Kate Bush used the hill for the video to her song 'Cloudbusting'.

51.579195, -1.568543

 ## Devil's Punchbowl, Childrey

Best on a cloudy day. Watch sunlight break across the bowl like a glistening cut-glass grail.

51.561618, -1.499792

 ## Letcombe Castle (Segsbury Camp), Wantage

Feel the wide space of time. This Iron Age hillfort is so large it can be difficult to appreciate the atmosphere. The southern rampart runs parallel to The Ridgeway for 400m (¼ mile), evidence the track predates the fort.

51.555781, -1.447989

 ## Yew Down, Lockinge, Vale of White Horse

Listen to barking deer. Look for them seen in large groups around the wooded edges.

▶**Find** Ridgeway car park, Wantage, OX12 8QX (51.562233, -1.340928) and walk 4km (2½ miles) W to the site.

51.555347, -1.394570

Whitehorse Hill

THE SWAN AT COMPTON

 A travellers' hub. Six bedrooms. Popular for the Ridgeway, the Thames and cycling King Alfred's Way.

High St, Compton, Newbury, Berkshire, RG20 6NJ

www.swanatcompton.co.uk

01635 885700

Monument and Barrow, Betterton Down, Vale of White Horse

Touch the monument. It's a bit unloved, but all the better for that, surrounded by nettles on all sides. The cross is on a marble column and dedicated to a soldier lost in the Crimea. It is mounted on a barrow that is more than 4,000 years old – a tribute, no doubt, to another or person someone cared about.

➤**Find** Yew Down (see left) and walk 275m (900ft) E to the site.

51.556887, -1.389781

Gore Hill Underpass, Chilton

Touch the murals of modernity: a concrete underpass decorated in art history. Shows how art, memory and purpose can be used to tame ugliness as much as wild nature.

51.547716, -1.294221

Fox Barrow, Several Down

Look NE for bulbous mounds of barrows. Fox Barrow is the only barrow given a name.

51.539334, -1.276023

Lowbury Hill, Streatley

Celtic temple on hill. An 800m (½ mile) detour can be turned into a circular navigation of the hill, rejoining the Ridgeway W, along the GW The Fair Mile. The hill trig point is the highest point on the Berkshire Downs (189m).

➤**Find** Wheel Orchard car park, RG8 9QE (51.521951, -1.137169), and walk 2.4km (1½ miles) W until FP to the R. Take detour 800m (½ mile) and N, to the site.

51.536492, -1.219124

THE BELL INN

A place of history, stories and charm – has been in same family for 250 years. Old-school time travel. Homemade rolls, real ale and a beer garden.

Bell Ln, Aldworth, Reading, Berkshire, RG8 9TL

www.facebook.com/profile.php?id=100057442510552

01635 578272

KING WILLIAM IV

Old brick-and-flint pub with three dining areas and large inglenook fireplace. Brakspear beer straight from the barrel. Gardens with views.

Hailey, Ipsden, Wallingford, Oxfordshire, OX10 6AD

www.kingwilliamhailey.co.uk

01491 681845

YHA STREATLEY-ON-THAMES

Victorian house at the crossroads of the Thames Path and Ridgeway NTs.

Reading Rd, Streatley, Reading, Berkshire, RG8 9JJ

www.yha.org.uk/hostel/yha-streatley-on-thames

03453 719044

Devil's Bowl

Top TEN Goring and Streatley Bridge, Goring-on-Thames
Bridge over the Thames. The Ridgeway and Thames Path meet briefly in a climax of water, weirs and trade.

51.522966, -1.142716

St Andrew's Church, S Stoke
Touch the flint wall in the church. Church is close to banks of the Thames, set in woodland. Cool place for rest or shelter.

51.548020, -1.137630

Boat Launch, Ferry Ln, N Stoke, Oxfordshire
Boat launch across the Thames. Southern access has been blocked and declassified to FP. N side remains as GW. The church connects to the River Thames.

51.564270, -1.133480

St Mary the Virgin Church, Wallingford
Look for medieval wall paintings in the church dating back to the 14th century.

51.571500, -1.122698

Grim's Ditch, Crowmarsh
Inhale the subtle scent of bluebells and wood anemones in spring along this second section of Grim's Ditch. The earthworks are thought to date to at least 1000 BC.

51.582401, -1.076704

St Botolph's Church, Swyncombe
Masses of snowdrops from January or February – some say the best showing in the UK.

51.606600, -1.015977

68 NATIONAL TRAILS

THE RIDGEWAY 69

PERCH & PIKE

 Rooms, drink and food. A 17th-century flint-built inn and converted barn with log fires. Eat in the restaurant or garden terrace. Dogs in the bar, but not in restaurant or letting rooms.

The Street, S Stoke, Reading, Berkshire, RG8 0JS

www.perchandpike.co.uk

01491 520647

RIDGEWAY VIEW CAMPSITE

 Family-friendly, campervan and dog-friendly site. Campfires are allowed. A back-to-basics site. Cold-water showers and Portaloo toilets.

Sheepcote Farm Bungalow, Mongewell, Wallingford, Oxfordshire, OX10 8BP

www.ridgewayadventures.co.uk/camping

07552 533381

THE MAKER SPACE AT THE CROWN

The future of eats and drinks? A remarkable place to make, shop and eat… if you have the time. Part workshop, part café. This rather neglected 300-year-old pub in the Chilterns has been turned into workrooms, store and café.

Gangsdown Hill, Nuffield, Henley-on-Thames, Oxfordshire, RG9 5SJ

www.themakerspace.co.uk/maker-hq

Aston Rowant Park, Watlington

Look for twayblade; its flowers look like a green man. There is a chalk stream near Lewknor church (51.674718, -0.970380), but it's a 1.6km (1 mile) detour.

▶ **Find** Cowleaze Woods car park, OX49 5HX (51.654967, -0.952021) and exit car park onto BW track NE. After 230m (755ft), turn L and take FP into park.

51.661967, -0.951601

Chinnor Hill Nature Reserve, Chinnor

Move between huge beech trees. The rare Chiltern gentian grows here on the hills.

▶ **Find** Chinnor Hill Nature Reserve car park, OX39 4BH (51.695692, -0.892444) and walk on BW NE, 800m (½ mile) to site.

51.700288, -0.893020

Whiteleaf Cross, Brush Hill Local Nature Reserve, Princes Risborough

Find the cross on the dome. Whiteleaf Cross is a chalk hill figure at least 400 years old and is the best place to get close to red kites as they glide between and beneath the beech trees.

▶ **Find** Whiteleaf Cross car park, Peters Ln, HP27 0RP (51.725575, -0.809233), and walk 365m (1,200ft) N to site.

51.724217, -0.810647

Lord Wantage Memorial

WHITE MARK FARM

Small Camping & Caravanning Club Certificated Site, with room for 30 tents at the foot of the Chiltern Hills. Pubs in Wallington a 800m (½ mile) walk away.

82 Hill Rd, Watlington, Oxfordshire, OX49 5AF

www.whitemarkfarm.co.uk

01491 612295

THE PLOUGH AT CADSDEN

Perhaps the most famous pub in England. Close to Chequers, the country seat of British prime ministers. The pub claims to be popular with visitors from all over the world. Quality food and decent rooms.

Longdown Hill, Cadsden, Princes Risborough, Buckinghamshire, HP27 0NB

https://ploughatcadsden.co.uk

01844 343302

Top TEN — Pulpit Hill Hillfort, Pulpit Hill Nature Reserve, Great and Little Kimble cum Marsh

An Iron Age hillfort at the top of one of the largest deciduous woodlands – a 6.4km (4 miles) stretch of broadleaf and pine trees from Little Kimble in the N to Speed in the S.

▶ **Find** Pulpit Hill car park, HP27 0NB (51.737529, -0.797297) and walk to the site.

51.737529, -0.797297

Top TEN — Ellesborough Warren, Aylesbury

The largest box woodland in the UK. Look for one of the rarest flowers in England: the pasqueflower; a large, purple, hairy and bell-shaped flower on the steep chalk slopes of grass.

51.747193, -0.791995

Coombe Hill, Ellesboroug

The only place in Britain to find the fringed gentian flower. There is a monument here to the men killed in the Boer War.

▶ **Find** National Trust – Chilterns Countryside, Lodge Hill, HP17 0UR (51.748466, -0.767784), and walk 800m (½ mile) N on FP to site.

51.753241, -0.771897

Tadpole Bridge, River Thames, Goring

THE RIDGEWAY   71

> **THE GREYHOUND PUB**
>
> Check out the Greyhound grill menu. Also a gluten-free menu. Room available for overnight.
>
> Chesham Rd, Wigginton, Tring, Hertfordshire, HP23 6EH
>
> www.greyhoundtring.co.uk
>
> 01442 824631

Top TEN Bacombe Hill, Wendover
Photograph giant fungi. The largest mushrooms you will ever find grow in this ancient oak wood, underneath bramble, birch, hawthorn and gorse.

51.754521, -0.761992

St Mary's Church, Wendover
Touch a flint tower surrounded in yew trees. There are two huge trees at the entrance, a female on the R and the male on the L. A large pond sits on the other side of the way.

51.757944, -0.739141

Barn Wood, Great Missenden
Bathe in autumn sunshine coming through the trees. They look best when in red, yellow and browns. The most wooded section of the entire trail has the most variety: beech, oak and pine.

51.748412, -0.714681

Bull's Wood, Tring
Smell lime flowers in spring. This avenue of trees through Tring Park was planted by the Rothschild family. Look for small tree rodents known as 'glis-glis'. They are like grey squirrels, but with larger black eyes. Another Rothschild introduction into the area.

51.785224, -0.649525

Top TEN Grand Union Canal, Tring
Have an encounter with Britain's most important canal. This meeting links the Icknield Way, Thames Path, Coast Path and Peddars Way.
▶**Find** Tring Station car park, HP23 5QR (51.801250, -0.621818), and walk 275m (900ft) W to FB.

51.799507, -0.626604

Aldbury Nowers Wood, Tring
A place to hide. Find woodland via the tree-lined track. The path follows Grim's Ditch. The wood is riddled with tumuli (mostly on the E side) and disused pits.
▶**Find** Pitstone Hill car park, HP23 5RX (51.825337, -0.6157189), and walk 1.6km (1 mile) SW to site.

51.811855, -0.621180

Incombe Hole, Ivinghoe
The spectacular cliff of Incombe Hole towers over bulbous hills.
▶**Find** Beacon Rd car park (51.833706, -0.602249) and walk N, 550m (1,800ft) to NT. Turn L, and walk 640m (2,100ft) S to site.

51.830522, -0.607035

Goodmerhill Wood

TOWN FARM CAMPSITE

Family-run campsite in Chiltern hills. Pitch up, park up or rent a tent. Cottages also available.

Town Farm, Ivinghoe, Leighton Buzzard, Bedfordshire, LU7 9EL

www.townfarmcamping.co.uk

01296 668455

Ivinghoe Hills, Leighton Buzzard, Ivinghoe Aston

Watch birds fly purposefully N and S against changing skies. This is a transit hub for raptors.

51.837379, -0.607414

Beacon Hill, Leighton Buzzard, Ivinghoe Beacon

The Ridgeway starts/ends at the Icknield Way, at Beacon Hill. A cool or cold place, depending on when you arrive, with tail and headlights from the B489 beaming back. The sights and sound of owls hooting, rabbits, sunsets, and chalk. Hawks frequently fly over the valley below Beacon Hill. The views are incredible, not least at dawn. To watch the headlights and tail-lights of traffic commuting to work while sucking in the wild cold air makes this one of the top ends of any trail. The druids, dragons and sarsen stones in between mark this as the best trail in the collection.

➤**Find** Beacon Rd car park (51.833706, -0.602249) and walk N, 1km (⅔ mile) to NT start/end.

51.842303, -0.607306

WILD THINGS TO DO BEFORE YOU DIE

WALK the largest collection of sarsen stones in Britain

TOUCH a power source of immeasurable energy

ENTER a Neolithic long barrow

STAND over a chalk hill

FEEL the air around 5,000-year-old stone circles

EXPLORE an Iron Age hillfort

PHOTOGRAPH giant fungi

FORAGE around the largest box woodland in the UK

KAYAK along Britain's most important canal

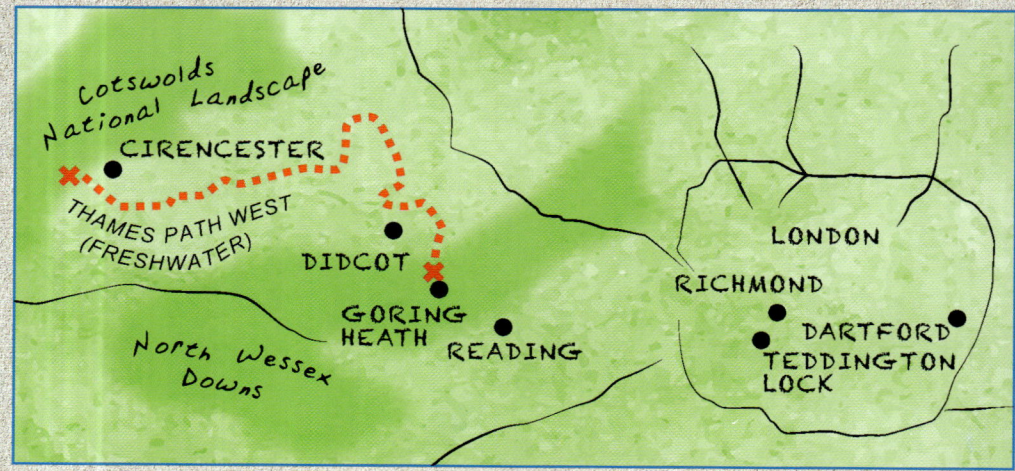

 Neigh Bridge Lakes, Listen to the cackle and whistles of breeding snipe and curlew around the UK's largest water park.
51.651994, -1.976247

Maidenhead Railway Bridge, Touch the genius of Isambard Kingdom Brunel architecture: a brick-built bridge across the Thames.
51.521129, -0.700905

St John's Lock, Move around and explore the first lock on the Thames.
51.689868, -1.680833

 Godstow Abbey, Watch bats at dusk around the abbey ruin.
51.777985, -1.299095

 Thames Lido, Swim in this fabulous lido.
51.460167, -0.965334

 River Wye Chalk Stream, One of two chalk streams that feed into the Thames.
51.570183, -0.711078

 Boveney Lock and Weir, Kayak or canoe the busy Thames.
51.490950, -0.640952

 Ankerwycke Yew, Feel the presence of a tree that lived 500 years before Christ.
51.445448, -0.561526

Cock Marsh, Touch burial mounds with easy river access for packrafts.
51.575351, -0.722144

 **Teddington Lock FB,** Explore the tidal pivot of the Thames.
Find Teddington Lock, Teddington Lock, Teddington TW11 9NG

THAMES PATH WEST (FRESHWATER)

BEST FOR: BIRDSONG

Nightingales, salmon, secret islands

START: COTSWOLDS   FINISH: GORING HEATH

The freshwater Thames is many things, but its hosting of birdsong is beyond the pleasure of listening to a rippling stream or a laughing child. Blackbirds are star performers.

From the water source in Gloucestershire to the tidal Teddington Lock, birds will take turns to sing almost the entire length, one bird handing to the next in a series of relays that span 177km (110 miles). For every three or four blackbirds, there is one robin, filling the melodic spaces in this birdsong relay.

The Thames unifies urban, agricultural, rich and poor, historic parks and old commons, woodland, reservoirs and quarries. But it is separated and divided by birds' song.

Warblers throw up rifts around the marl lakes of the Cotswold Water Park, and then later in the reediest sections of the river. Skylarks wrestle with wind while wheeling above their nest sites. Nationally important wildfowl rasp around the gravel pits. Nightingales shine over riverside scrub. But only the blackbirds sing for the pure joy of it all... all day long, whether from an alder over a Bronze Age tomb or a churchyard willow.

Other than the campsite owners that provide free pitches to Pennine walkers, blackbirds are the most generous givers on the path circuit.

Kelmscott to Tadpole Bridge

Thames Source, Kemble

Source of the River Thames, Coates
The Thames Path E starts/ends at the shallow pile of stones that marks the official source of the river. Touch the stones. The sunken ground spans a 50ft radius. The bowl is surrounded by a grove of trees. A giant ash rises to the E, and then a circle of oak, maple, blackthorn, elder, horse chestnut and willow. A meadow of grasses, nettles, buttercups and occasional thistles. The Thames head stone monument will likely outlive the ash and the oak that tower above it. A memorial to what our ancestors most celebrated. Poetry: water on the move.
➤**Find** The Thames Head Inn, Tetbury Rd, GL7 6NZ (51.687094, -2.029209). Facing the pub (with the car park to your L), turn R and continue about 460m (1,500ft) along the A433. The FP straddles either side of the Rd. Turn L into the field and walk about 640m (2,100ft) to the stone monument.

51.694605, -2.030545

Old Covert, Kemble and Ewen
Taste nettles in a spring-laden oak woodland. The riverside is a narrow path lined with birch, and occasional bracket fungi. There are plenty of plants to eat in spring.
➤**Find** the source of the Thames (see above) and walk 4km (2½ miles) E to the woodland. Kemble Railway station, 460m (1,500ft) SW of the trail, is about halfway.

51.674935, -1.991235

THAMES PATH WEST (FRESHWATER) 77

THE VALE HOTEL

A 16th-century hotel with a restaurant and a bar. Single and double rooms.

The Vale Hotel, 32 High St, Cricklade, Wiltshire, SN6 6AY

www.valehotel.uk

07733 110731

TROUT INN, LECHLADE
Pub by the weir pool to St. John's Lock. Riverside garden. Family-run inn with real ales, ciders, wines and spirits. Daily blackboard specials.

St John's Bridge, Faringdon Rd, Lechlade, Gloucestershire, GL7 3HA

www.thetroutinn.com

01367 252313

THE PLOUGH INN

Pub classics or snacks for sharing. Bedrooms upstairs in the 17th century stone building. A 5-minute walk across the fields from the Thames Path.

Kelmscott, Lechlade, GL7 3HG

www.theploughinnkelmscott.com

01367 253543

 ## Neigh Bridge Lake, Somerford Keynes
Top TEN

Listen to the cackle and whistles of breeding snipes, curlews and golden plovers around the UK's largest water park. Carved by humans from more than 140 gravel pits, taken over by nature as a resettlement. More than 20,000 waterfowl, of at least 40 different species. This is the most extensive marl lake system in Britain. This is a very special place.

▶ **Find** the Neigh Bridge Country Park car park, GL7 5DX (51.650861, -1.975694), which sits beside the FP. Walk 45m (150ft) N or S to the edge of the lake.

51.651994, -1.976247

 ## Minety Ln Lakes, Somerford Keynes

Look for Daubenton's bats over the lake. Best just before dusk. Pochard and smew also feed here.

▶ **Find** the Neigh Bridge Country Park car park (see above) and follow the trail 800m (½ mile) SE to the lake.

51.647146, -1.964748

 ## N Meadow, Cricklade

Try to smell a natural wonder. More than 500,000 snake's-head fritillary flowers bloom here on good years.

51.650047, -1.866907

St John the Baptist Church, Inglesham

Inhale the air of purpose. William Morris, the 19th-century land campaigner and craftsman, renovated this church while he lived a few km away at Kelmscott. Lots of fading wall art that celebrates nature.

51.684269, -1.704410

Chimney Meadows

THE TROUT AT TADPOLE BRIDGE, FARINGDON

 Riverside pub with bedrooms in the heart of Oxfordshire. The food focus is fish and seafood, but there are also steaks and Sunday roasts. There is a bar and riverside garden. Each bedroom is named after a fishing fly. Explore the remote bridge.

Buckland Rd, Buckland Marsh, Faringdon SN7 8RF

www.butcombe.com/the-trout-at-tadpole-bridge-oxfordshire

01367 870382

THE MAYBUSH NEWBRIDGE, NEWBRIDGE

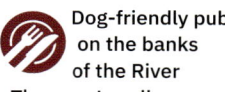 Dog-friendly pub on the banks of the River Thames. Locally sourced, homemade food.

Abingdon Rd, Newbridge, Oxfordshire, OX29 7QD

www.themaybushnewbridge.co.uk/

01865 300101

Top TEN St John's Lock, Lechlade on Thames

Move around and explore the first lock on the river. Six of the 45 non-tidal locks on the river are between Lechlade and Newbridge. These locks are the most remote and beautiful in England, so well worth a stopover. Layered in a sense of timeless charm that can be uniquely felt.

51.689868, -1.680833

Church of St Mary the Virgin, Faringdon

Touch a 13th-century church. The building is next to Buscot Old Parsonage, a few metres from the River Thames. The visit requires a 500m (⅓ mile) detour via Buscot lock, as the church is on the other side of the bank from the NT. The lock is beautiful and remote.

51.681574, -1.673346

Radcot Bridge, Grafton and Radcot

The oldest bridge on the Thames has three Gothic arches that span the river like a cathedral roof. This old bridge was saved from demolition because boat traffic was diverted along the Thames' other channel.

51.693645, -1.588662

Radcot Lock, Old Man's Bridge, Great Faringdon, Vale of White Horse

Listen to the sound of passing river traffic in summer. A place to stop and rest.

51.69974169548363, -1.5724784317702007

Shifford Cut FB, Chimney

Listen to jumping fish while sitting next to the wooden bridge.
▶ **Find** The Trout at Tadpole Bridge (see above) and walk 3.2km (2 miles) E.

51.704926, -1.470698

Newbridge, Northmoor

Watch swans swim over the steely waters around the 12-arch bridge. This was originally a 51-arch structure, built by the monks of Deerhurst Priory, in the 13th century.

51.710049, -1.416944

Bablock Hythe, Appleton-with-Eaton, Vale of White Horse

Packraft onto E bank to walk the riverside FP rather than following the Thames Path inland. This is a famous Thames crossing, used by the Romans. A ferry service worked here for more than 1,000 years. Ferries do still run occasionally.

51.735081, -1.371640

St John's Lock

 ### Farmoor Rez, Vale of White Horse
Tread the Rez path for 800m (½ mile). This is a detour and rejoins the Thames at an island of trees (51.755180, -1.364823).
➤**Find** Farmoor Rez parking space, OX2 9NS (51.752496, -1.347507), and walk 460m (1,500ft) S to the Rez FP. Walk 2.4km (1½ miles) clockwise around the water. The NT is 275m (900ft) further on at the FB.

51.751420, -1.363781

 ### Swinford Toll Bridge, Swinford
Watch for the sheer madness of it all... a 5p charge to queue in a car. Swinford Bridge is one of only two remaining Thames toll bridges. Free to pedestrians.

51.774540, -1.359333

 ### Wytham Great Wood, Cumnor
Smell the scent of mushrooms, hazel, oak, pine and birch. Bluebells in spring. There is a YouTube channel on Wytham Woods. Apply for your permit beforehand.

51.777749, -1.345969

 ### Hagley Pool Peninsula, Gosford and Water Eaton
A raft of woodland. A beautiful place to shelter from rain or shine, heat or cold.

51.786037, -1.304199

 ### Godstow Abbey, Godstow
Bats at dusk around the abbey ruin. The shell of a small chapel remains, with a large abbey wall. Good for wildflowers. The abbey featured in Thomas Hardy's *Jude the Obscure*.

51.777985, -1.299095

THE TROUT INN, WOLVERCOTE

Pub, bar and restaurant overlooking the river, with its own garden.

195 Godstow Rd, Wolvercote, Oxford, Oxfordshire, OX2 8PN

www.thetroutoxford.co.uk

01865 510930

Fiddlers Island, Bailey Bridge, Medley

No need to packraft – Fiddlers Island spans the N end of the ancient Port Meadow to Oxford station.

51.760755, -1.277761

Iffley Lock Boat Rollers, Iffley

Feel the slow movement of a lock around the edge of a busy city.

51.729413, -1.240715

Sandford Lock, Sandford-on-Thames

Balance along the edge of this island walk. This lock, public house and FB is a place to river-watch. The Thames shifts back to rural as fast as it was urbanised by Oxford. Feel how quickly the city merges back to wild. Sanford lock and weir is the greatest fall of water on the Thames.

51.708163, -1.232710

Orchard Lake Woods, Culham

Smell pine along more than 3.2km (2 miles) of woodland. There is a large lake (51.669022, -1.249861) through the trees where orchids grow in spring and summer. There are also many oaks in this planted wood.

51.667484, -1.246031

Culham Lock

THAMES PATH WEST (FRESHWATER)

 Abingdon Abbey, Northcourt
Abbey remains between the Thames and abbey stream.
51.671762, -1.274624

 Abingdon Lock and Weir, Abingdon-on-Thame
Relax on the 'island' by the weir. There are free moorings. Explore Barton Fields wildflower meadows on N side. There is good cycling here.
▶**Find** Rye Farm car park, Culham Rd, OX14 3NN (51 667635, -1.277469). Walk N to the Thames and NT. Turn R, facing the water, and walk E 550m (1,800ft) to the lock.
51.670377, -1.26944

 St Ethelwold's House, Abingdon
A retreat and meditation centre by the river. Rooms can be hired at affordable rates.
www.ethelwoldhouse.com
51.668598, -1.282177

 Sutton Pools, Sutton Courtenay, Vale of White Horse
Lots of islands make this a magical place. Best explored by packraft. The pools are a 300m (985ft) detour from the Thames at Culham Cut, but worth it.
51.646626, -1.272749

 St Michael's and All Angels Church, Abingdon
Look down from the hillside church over the Thames. The site pre-dates the Christian church and is said to be on the St Michael's ley line. The church's stained glass gives more than a nod to its pagan past. Scenes include St Michael slaying a blue dragon. The graveyard has many gravestones worth exploring. William Dyke, said to have fired the first shot at the Battle of Waterloo, is here.
51.655335, -1.210390

 Castle Hill, Little Wittenham
Look down the Thames Valley from an Iron Age fort. Views via Little Wittenham church and Wittenham Clumps are best at sunset or sunrise. It's a steep 3.2km (2 miles) detour, but worth it.
51.627577, -1.178826

 Wallingford Castle, Winterbrook
Built by the Normans and demolished by Cromwell.
51.602966, -1.123451

THE MILLER OF MANSFIELD INN, GORING

 An 18th-century grade II listed coaching inn.

High St, Goring, Reading RG8 9AW

www.themillerofmansfield.com

01491 913990

 ### Bow Bridge, Cholsey
Look for lamprey and bullhead fish swimming in the shallows near Wallingford. This wooded riverside path is an important moment in the NT canon: where the Thames Path meets the Ridgeway on the opposite bank.

51.576805, -1.126552

 ### St Mary the Virgin Church, N Stoke
The meeting of the two NTs across the river via packraft. N Stoke church is on the other side of the river (the Ridgeway runs through the churchyard). The two trails meet fully at Goring.

51.571488, -1.122860

 ### Goring and Streatley Bridge
Two villages, two counties, two NTs, river, roads, houses and station squeezed in the narrowest part of the Thames Valley. The Chiltern Hills to the E. Berkshire Downs to the W.

51.523156, -1.141952

 ### St Margaret's Church, Mapledurham
Filming location for Michael Caine movie The Eagle has Landed. The Mapledurham Watermill is beautiful, and featured in Black Sabbath's 1970 debut album.

51.485029, -1.036439

 ### Rivermead Park, Caversham Heights
Listen to honking geese. Sit on benches beside big daisies along Reading's rural N fringe.
▶**Find** Tilehurst station, Reading, RG31 6TH (51.471739, -1.029638), and walk 460m (1,500ft) NW to the railway FB over to the Thames. Facing the water, turn R and walk SE 3.2km (2 miles) to the park.

51.466662, -0.994712

 ### Thames Lido, Reading
This fabulous lido was formerly an Edwardian outdoor swimming pool. There is also a bar, restaurant and hot baths.
www.thameslido.com

51.460167, -0.965334

 ### River Kennet, Horseshoe Bridge, Reading
Find where the River Kennet enters the River Thames underneath the old Horseshoe Bridge. This is an important access point, as the Kennet river flows into the Kennet and Avon Canal, to Bath, and onwto the Cotswold Way. It's an important link for anyone planning to walk all the NTs.

51.458660, -0.949707

The Beetle and Wedge, Moulsford

Caversham Lakes, Reading
Open swimming, walking and people-watching. Explore this entire complex for a whole day... ideally by packraft.
51.462852, -0.946099

Sonning Lock, Sonning
Flower- and plant-filled lock at the end of a wooded path.
51.473341, -0.917234

St Andrew's Church, Sonning
One of the Thames' most beautiful churches, inside and out. This place gets overlooked because it is surrounded by so many lakes. The graveyard is huge and interesting, surrounded by a red-brick wall, sometimes sunshine, and calm.
51.474168, -0.913463

Poplar Eyot, Shiplake, Wokingham
Travel to the island. The bank is littered in large fallen branches for mooring and hiding places.
51.518158, -0.878988

Marsh Meadows, Henley-on-Thame
Listen to wintering populations of tufted duck, pochard, goosander. A quiet meadow in summertime.
➤ **Find** car park in Mill Ln, RG9 4HD (51.528926, -0.890746). Exit the car park, turn L and walk 137m (450ft) E to the riverbank. Turn L onto the NT and walk 180m (590ft).
51.530853, -0.892018

Wallingford

Hambleden Lock, Remenham
Balance over a beautiful lock, with a weir that connects both sides of the river. Hambleden Mill, Mill End, on the other side is worth crossing the river for. There is access to one of two chalk streams feeding into the Thames (51.562016, -0.868066).

51.559349, -0.873238

Magpie Island, Remenham
Touch the water while sliding down from the sloping bank. Navigate by packraft between two offshore islands.

51.547933, -0.856545

Hurley Weir, Hurley
Move over the river in a packraft. Care is needed around the weir, but afloat is a good way to see one of the Thames' best beauty spots. Gets busy in summer.

51.551571, -0.811364

Temple Lock, Hurley, Buckinghamshire
A man-made bridge onto one of the Thames' most vegetated islands. A working weir and lock make this a special place for both humans and wildlife.

51.551945, -0.793873

THAMES PATH WEST (FRESHWATER)   85

THE BOUNTY

Café and snack bar on the riverside, with garden and decking.

Cockmarsh, Bourne End, Berkshire, SL8 5RG

01628 520056

 ### All Saints Church, Bisham
An Anglo-Saxon church that sits on the opposite side of the path, next to Bisham Abbey.

51.561299, -0.777971

 ### Riverwoods, Marlow
Wooded beauty spot for shelter and shade.
▶ **Find** Spade Oak car park, Coldmoorholme Ln, SL8 5PS (51.580092, -0.725863) and walk 137m (450ft) S to the riverbank. Facing the river, turn R and walk W 2.4km (1½ miles) to the tree-lined riverbank.

51.567622, -0.752667

 ### Cock Marsh, Cookham
Touch burial mounds. Easy access to the river for packrafts, or cross the river via the railway FB.
▶ **Find** Spade Oak car park, Coldmoorholme Ln, SL8 5PS (51.580092, -0.725863) and walk 137m (450ft) S to the riverbank. Facing the river, turn L and walk E 1km (⅔ mile) to the railway bridge across the river.

51.575351, -0.722144

 ### Sashes Island, Hedsor Water
Listen along one of the quietest parts of the Thames. This is a good place to see shoveler and overwintering smew ducks.

51.565558, -0.699143

 ### River Wye Chalk Stream, Bourne End
One of two chalk streams that feed into the Thames. The Wye is on the E bank, opposite the path. Packraft across for access.

51.570183, -0.711078

 ### Whitebrook Wood, Battlemead Common (summer only)
Enjoy the smell of rain on leaves along some of the best woodland on both sides of the river.

51.543122, -0.693934

 ### Ray Mill Island, Boat Ramp
Wooded, open area to picnic or hire boats. Beside Taplow Bridge, the island gets busy in summer.

51.534664, -0.698565

THE LENSBURY, TEDDINGTON

Rooms, food and drink along 25 acres of riverside grounds. The Lensbury Club was first formed in 1920 as the sports and social club for employees of the Dutch petroleum giant Shell, close to Teddington Lock. Then acquired by London & Regional Hotels in 2019.

The Lensbury, Broom Rd, Teddington, TW11 9NU
www.lensbury.com
020 8614 6400
01628 520056

Maidenhead Railway Bridge
Top TEN

Touch the genius of Isambard Kingdom Brunel architecture: a brick-built bridge across the Thames. Completed in 1838, the unique arches were controversial before the bridge opened the following year. Some engineers thought it would collapse under the weight of trains.

51.521129, -0.700905

St Mary Magdalene Church, Boveney

Touch the old oak doors and medieval tiles in this riverside church. Built in the 12th century. Look for bats at dusk.

51.490950, -0.640952

Boveney Lock and Weir
Top TEN

A kayak/canoe portage. Always fun to sit and watch. Best in school holidays when river traffic is busiest.

51.490950, -0.640952

The Brocas, Eton

Two cathedrals of power: views of Windsor Castle from Eton.

51.485808, -0.611701

Goring

Beale Wildlife Park

 ### Lime Avenue, Windsor
Travel the N path or paddle the Thames. The S side is closed for security reasons.

51.483875, -0.586677

 ### Magna Carta Memorial, Nr Old Windsor
Monument surrounded by woods, where the Magna Carta is supposed to have been signed by King John in June 1215.
▶ **Find** the riverbank opposite Magna Carta Island and then leave the river by crossing the Rd into the park.

51.444439, -0.566043

 ### Ankerwycke Yew, Runnymede
Not on the path, but one of the most impressive detours. Touch what is believed to be a 2,500-year-old tree; it has an 8m (26ft) girth. Ruins of a Benedictine nunnery are nearby. The meadows of Runnymede are opposite.

51.445448, -0.561526

 ### Staines Wood, Staines Bridge
Taste chestnuts in autumn. This chestnut and maple woodland is beside the M25.

51.433273, -0.516867

 ### Staines Bridge, Runnymede
Move across onto the N bank via one of the river's most impressive bridges. This was once the upper limit of the tidal reach.

51.433273, -0.516867

Sonning

The London Stone, Birch Green
A stone marker at the spot on the Thames where Richard I granted the Corporation of London control and rights.

51.432474, -0.513976

Dumsey Meadow, Chertsey
Famous swim spot for locals. Trees, meadows and parakeets.

51.389686, -0.479472

Shepperton Lock and Weir, Laleham
Lock and islands. There is a pedestrian ferry to Weybridge 100m E. Cross the river by packraft when ferry not running. The S bank has fewer roads, so better than N.

51.414795, -0.500372

Canbury Gardens, Norbiton
Kingston riverside laden in avenues of riverside trees that are best seen in autumn.
▶**Find** Kingston Station, Wood St, KT1 1UJ (51.412618, -0.301068) and walk 460m (1,500ft) W to the riverside. Turn R along the river and walk 365m (1,200ft).

51.415005, -0.307479

THAMES PATH WEST (FRESHWATER)

 The Half Mile Tree, Kingston upon Thames
Touch a famous horse chestnut. This one is a timeless marker post between Teddington Lock and Richmond. Although the tree is old, it replaced the original marker tree that was also here for hundreds of years.
▶ **Find** Canbury Gardens (see left) and continue N for 1km (⅔ mile).

51.424160, -0.306875

 Teddington Lock, Richmond-upon-Thames
The Thames Path's fresh water starts/ends here not by force of nature, but by force of human intervention. For all that, it is an impressive pivot of change. You'll feel the energy around the steel FB. Between the FB and the Thames you will need to navigate numerous gates, tired limbs, the sound of nightingales, secret islands and jumping trout. But you're in good company. Salmon turn from the sea to the freshwater Thames each year to spawn. To reach their breeding grounds, those incredible fish bypass 20 Thames weirs and 17 more on the Kennet.
▶ **Find** Teddington Lock, Teddington, TW11 9NG

51.431057, -0.321477

WILD THINGS TO DO BEFORE YOU DIE

LISTEN to the cackle and whistles of birds around the UK's largest water park

TOUCH the genius of Isambard Kingdom Brunel

MOVE around the first lock on the Thames

WATCH bats at dusk around abbey ruins

SWIM at a fabulous Lido

EXPLORE a chalk stream

CANOE the busy Thames

FEEL a tree that lived 500 years before Christ

TOUCH burial mounds

EXPLORE the tidal pivot of the River Thames

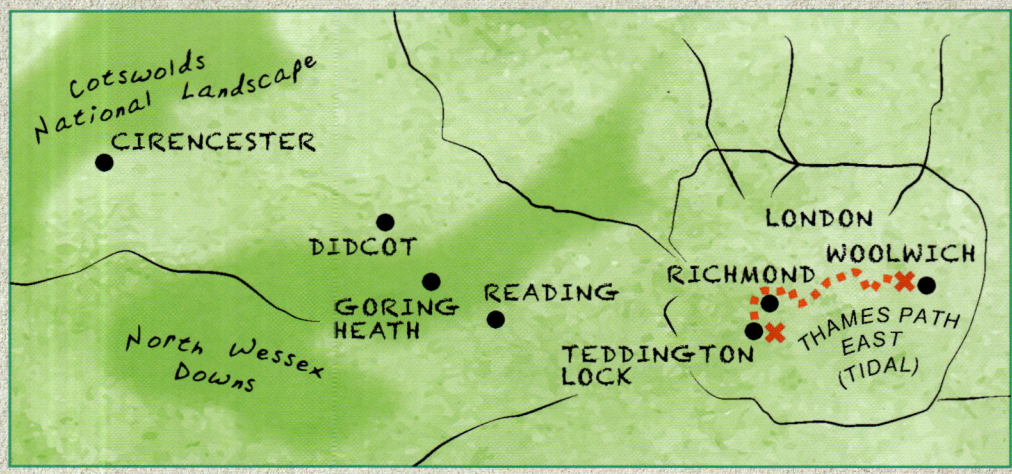

Top TEN

 Old Ship, Eat and drink Thames views from fireside or terrace.
51.490275, -0.239940

 The Wharf, Savour an afternoon tea by the river.
51.430912, -0.325127

 Chelsea Embankment Gardens, Stroll along tree-lined avenues beside Albert Bridge.
51.483470, -0.165756

 Houses of Parliament, Look for peregrines from Westminster Bridge.
51.500963, -0.123543

 Boudiccan Rebellion, Touch the statue to Boudicca – 27 years in the making.
51.500803, -0.121852

The Oyster Shed, Fresh food and wines with panoramic Thames views.
www.oystershed.co.uk

Tower Of London, England's most iconic building, epitomised by the phrase 'sent to the Tower'.
51.506904, -0.075556

 Barnes Towpath, Stand under one of more than 40 native black poplars that line what is arguably the most beautiful wooded section of the tidal Thames. These trees are thought to be the last remnants of an extremely rare wild species.
51.477943, -0.226857

The London Peace Pagoda, Touch the peace pagoda presented to Londoners in 1980 by the founder of a Japanese Buddhist movement.
51.481980, -0.159067

 The Mayflower Pub, The oldest pub on the River Thames has one of the greatest stories.
www.mayflowerpub.co.uk

THAMES PATH EAST (TIDAL)

BEST FOR: SLOW FOOD

Palaces, ancient trees, tidal cuisine

START: TEDDINGTON LOCK   FINISH: WOOLWICH

The tidal Thames is home to the world's best cuisine.

From Rick Stein to the River Café, the greatest city in the world serves a platter that embodies its unique waterway: wild, local, and (multi) cultural.

The Thames trail is the merging and pulling apart of opposites. Just as the fake gothic art of Pugin's Parliament architecture showcases the chaos of natural curves and ornate pagan gods to temper the order of elite governance, so the pull of Epping Forest fungi, line-caught Thames bass and Richmond's wood-pasture mushrooms blend with park-reared venison.

Wet woodland and the oldest yew trees in England line the Thames riverbank.

Tidal Thames is not really about nature. Nor is it about the worst of human nurture. From the flood barrier to the London Olympic Park, everything in London is a contradiction: peregrine falcons roost in Parliament, sand martins burrow in the banks of human-made reservoirs.

Nature is constantly chipping away at and eroding the seat of human utility. Woodpeckers wrestle with invasive parakeets for air and tree space, while blackbirds outsing migratory nightingales in the riverside scrub scrum.

London has the largest urban peregrine falcon population in the world... after New York. The Houses of Parliament are their favourite nesting platforms. Our seat of power over the chaos of nature is usurped by both pigeon and wild predator.

London chefs get that alchemical delivery better than any other class of cook in the world.

If you can find a table view that looks out onto the wild Thames in a storm, while picking away at Harwich lobster, with a plate of Thames strawberries, there's nothing better.

Teddington Lock to Kew Bridge

THE WHARF, TEDDINGTON

'Afternoon Tea by the River' at The Wharf. Choose from a range of teas served with finger sandwiches, and Homemade scones with clotted cream and jam. Also coffee, cocktails, pre-lunch aperitifs or bar snacks.

The Wharf, 22 Manor Rd, Teddington, Richmond-upon-Thames, TW11 8BG,

www.wharfteddington.com

020 8977 6333

THE WHITE SWAN, TWICKENHAM

A pub of two rooms: a terrace balcony and a garden on the riverbank. Visit at high tide, when the garden may end up in the river, but never for long. Staff sometimes wade through the water with a few plates or glasses in hand.

The White Swan, Riverside, Twickenham, TW1 3DN

www.whiteswantwickenham.co.uk

020 8744 2951

THE BELL & CROWN

Riverside pub, licensed as the Bell & Crown in 1787. Peaceful benches right by the water.

11-13 Thames Rd, Strand on the Green, London, W4 3PL

www.bell-and-crown.co.uk

020 8994 4164

Teddington Lock, Ham

The Tidal Thames Path starts/ends at the gateway to the greatest city in the world. London is a forager's paradise. Nuts, greens, berries and unlimited fresh water between the ancient trees. A complex of three locks in the London Borough of Richmond marks the coming together of fresh and tidal Thames...

▶ **Find** where the river path meets Riverside Dr, Richmond, TW10 7RP (51.432993, -0.318604). Just before the parked cars, follow the hard path 365m (1,200ft) down to the Thames. The Teddington Lock FB can be crossed to the other side of the river.

51.430090, -0.322110

Marble Hill, Twickenham

Walk through 500m (⅓ mile) of tree-lined path.

▶ **Find** Orleans Gardens beside public toilets (51.447381, -0.3160300). Walk down to the marina and, facing the water, turn L along the path then walk 500m (⅓ mile) to the wooded foreshore.

51.449232, -0.308374

Syon Park and All Saints Church, Isleworth

Wonderful church with parking access direct into the tidal Thames beside a stunning park with public access. Take in the view from both sides of the Thames. Sacred.

51.471347, -0.319738

Teddington Lock Footbridge

NATIONAL TRAILS

Ham Lands

BULLS HEAD, MORTLAKE

 Great value food with views from the river path over Kew Railway Bridge.

373 Lonsdale Rd, Mortlake, Richmond, London SW13 9PY

www.chefandbrewer.com/pubs/greater-london/bulls-head

020 8994 1204

OLD SHIP

 Cask-conditioned beers and a seasonal dining menu. Lovely views all year, from cosy cold days in front of the fires to summer days on the terrace. Short walk from Ravenscourt Park, Stanford Brook and Hammersmith Underground stations.

25 Upper Mall, Hammersmith, W6 9TD

www.oldshiphammersmith.co.uk

020 8748 2593

THE BLUE BOAT, FULHAM REACH

Open-plan kitchen for some real theatre of food on the riverside.

Fulham Reach, Distillery Wharf, Parr's Way, Fulham W6 9GD,

www.theblueboat.co.uk

02030 922090

Chiswick Eyot, Hounslow

One of the numerous small islands or eyots on the River Thames. Accessible from the N bank (Chiswick) during low tides. Not much to see apart from willow (it's the last remaining continuously cultivated withy bed on the Thames). Riverside parking and access to the river.

➤**Find** riverside at the junction of Chiswick Ln S and Chiswick Mall. Weekend street parking is easier than midweek. Nearest Underground station is Stamford Brook, 800m (½ mile) N of the river.

51.487288, -0.247706

Hurlingham Park, Lower Hurlingham

Boat launch or walk at low tide under the canopy of trees on E side of the park. Find the wooded area next to the river and the boat ramp.

➤**Find** Putney Bridge Underground station, SW6 3UH (51.468424, -0.208752). Exit the E side of the station and walk 640m (0.4 miles) to Hurlingham Park. Pass through the public car park and cross the park to the exit in Broomhouse Ln. Walk 180m (590ft) to the bottom of the Ln to the wooded area next to the river and the boat ramp.

51.464975, -0.197786

Chelsea Embankment Gardens, Kensington

Top TEN

Tree-lined avenues. Good views across Albert Bridge and the River Thames.

➤**Find** S Kensington Underground station, Pelham St, SW7 2NB. Walk just under 1.6km (1 mile) to the river.

51.483470, -0.165756

Westminster Boating Base, Pimlico

Youth club in a beautiful small riverside park. Courses from beginner to advanced in canoeing and kayaking. Riverfront balconies are available to hire.

www.westminsterboatingbase.co.uk/activities/kayak-canoe

51.485460, -0.134782

River Lane, Petersham

PREMIER INN
 Budget accommodation 140m (460ft) from Putney Bridge Underground station and 70m from the river path.

3 Putney Bridge Approach, Hurlingham, Fulham, SW6 3JD

www.premierinn.com
03333 211273

TATTERSHALL CASTLE
 Old steam ferry converted to a pub. Fish and chips on the deck. Opposite the London Eye and between Westminster and Embankment Underground stations.

Victoria Embankment, SW1A 2H

www.thetattershallcastle.co.uk
020 7839 6548

THE OYSTER SHED
 Panoramic sun-drenched views across the River Thames. Freshest food, finest wines, quality cask ales with views of the Tower of London and The Shard.

The Oyster Shed, 1 Angel Ln, London EC4R 3AB

www.oystershed.co.uk
020 7256 3240

THE DICKENS INN
 Pub with restaurant housed in a beautiful 18th-century warehouse in the heart of St Katharine Docks.

The Dickens Inn, Wapping, E1W 1UH

www.dickensinn.co.uk
020 7488 2208

Houses of Parliament, Westminster Bridge
Look and listen for peregrines from Westminster Bridge. More than 30 breeding pairs live in London and their favourite hunting grounds is Parliament (Tate Modern also good).

51.500963, -0.123543

Boudiccan Rebellion, Westminster Bridge
Statue on Westminster Bridge, with views of Westminster Palace, London Eye, Big Ben and the Thames. Boudicca was a legendary queen of the Iceni tribe who led an uprising against the Roman armies in AD 60. English sculptor Thomas Thornycroft spent 27 years working on the statue, until just before he died in 1885. It was erected at Westminster in 1902.

▶ **Find** Westminster Underground station, SW1A 2JR (51.501394, -0.124844). Walk 80m (260ft) to Westminster Bridge. The statue stands at the entrance to the bridge with the London Eye on the other side of the river in the foreground.

51.500803, -0.121852

Middle Temple Gardens, Holborn
Trees, roses, river and temples. Savour the scene of Shakespeare's meeting between Richard Plantagenet and John Beaufort, which sparked the Wars of the Roses. The garden's real story is stranger than fiction. They were part of the headquarters of the Knights Templar until the band was dissolved in 1312. The gardens were taken over by the Knights Hospitallers until Henry VIII seized them in 1540. They passed to English barristers in 1608, and remain the HQ of the British legal profession.

▶ **Find** Temple Underground station, Victoria Embankment, WC2R 2PH (51.511293, -0.114367). Facing the Thames, walk L along the river 240m (790ft) to the National Submarine War Memorial. The park is opposite.

51.511186, -0.110313

THAMES PATH EAST (TIDAL)

SMITHS OF WAPPING

Food service under the motto 'Famous for fish'. Close to Wapping Overground station and Tower Bridge Underground station, and features floor-to-ceiling windows with river views.

Smiths of Wapping, 22 Wapping High St, London E1W 1NJ

www.smithsrestaurants.com

020 7488 3456

THE PROSPECT OF WHITBY

One of London's oldest pubs, next to the Shadwell Basin. Spectacular views over the Thames, including from the beer garden and first-floor balcony and terrace.

The Prospect of Whitby, 57 Wapping Wall, Wapping, E1W 3SH

020 7481 1095

BREAD STREET KITCHEN AND BAR

Restaurant alongside the riverside FP with toilet access.

Bread Street Kitchen and Bar, 44 Narrow Street, Limehouse, E14 8DJ

www.gordonramsayrestaurants.com/the-narrow

020 592 7950

Top TEN Tower of London

One of England's most iconic buildings, epitomised by the phrase 'sent to the Tower'. Its reputation for torture and death is partly based on the execution of seven people here; most deaths took place to the N of the Tower at the equally notorious Tower Hill, where more than 100 people were executed over a 400-year period. Sit under the shade or shelter of trees in the shadow of Tower Bridge. Direct water access 500m (⅓ mile) W along the shore via concrete steps.

▶ **Find** Tower Hill Underground station, EC3N 4DJ (51.510679, -0.0765322). Walk 275m (900ft) to the Thames and around the vast Tower building set back from the shore.

51.506904, -0.075556

Foreshore, Wapping

Foreshore is accessible at low tide by various stairs along the N bank of the Thames. The foreshore is a mixture of sand, mud and rock. Hire a kayak at Shadwell Basin.

▶ **Find** The Prospect of Whitby (see left). Turn R onto the Thames path just past the pub and down to the small beach.

51.507389, -0.050315

London Museum Docklands, W India Quay

Museum covering the history of the River Thames over 500 years. Built in warehouses on the Isle of Dogs, not far from Canary Wharf. Entry is free.

▶ **Find** W India Quay DLR station, E14 4EE (51.507049, -0.0205117). Walk around the N Dock to the museum. There are numerous car parks around Canary Wharf.

51.507581, -0.024036

Island Gardens, Greenwich

Views of Greenwich from tree-lined green next to Greenwich Foot Tunnel.

▶ **Find** Mudchute DLR station, E14 9ZT (51.491861, -0.015079). Exit on the E Ferry Rd and walk R 500m (⅓ mile) to Manchester Rd. Turn L another 220m (720ft) before turning R again onto Douglas Path down to the River Thames, the tunnel and the gardens. The café in the park is open most days.

51.486814, -0.007696

THE GRAPES

 Riverside terrace for seafood and ales.

76 Narrow Street, E14 8BP

www.thegrapes.co.uk

020 7987 4396

THE WHITE CROSS, RICHMOND

 Famous for being wonderful, and by the water.

The pub dates back to 1780 and was originally called the Waterman's Arms. Built on the site of a Franciscan friary dissolved by Henry VIII in 1534. Remains of the friary are incorporated within the extensive cellars. Serves favourites such as beer-battered fish and chips, sausage and mash, homemade pies and burgers.

Surrey, Riverside House, Water Ln, Richmond TW9 1NR

www.thewhitecrossrichmond.com

020 8940 6844

THE SHIP

 Pub beside an old cobbled ramp down to the stony foreshore. Overlooks the London Boat Race finishing line. Best at high tide when the waters lap up to the Rd.

The Ship, Mortlake, 10 Thames Bank, London SW14 7QR

www.greeneking.co.uk/pubs/greater-london/ship

020 8876 1439

Bow Creek Ecology Park (formerly Limmo Peninsula Ecological Park), Blackwall

Little island of woodland close to the E bank of Bow Creek. It's actually a bend in the river made up of streams, ponds and meadows. Best in summer when the wildflowers are out.

51.511543, 0.003195

Obelisk, Old Deer Park, Kew/Richmond

Now sadly eroded and defaced, this small obelisk lies on the original Meridian Line that ran through the King's Observatory in the Old Deer Park. The clocks in the Houses of Parliament used to be set in time with this Meridian Line until Greenwich Mean Time took over as the timekeeping benchmark in the 1880s.

51.464492, -0.314617

Kew Gardens, Kew

Vast wood by the Thames, part of one of the largest botanical garden collections in the world.

▶**Find** Kew Gardens station, Station Approach, Kew, TW9 3BZ. Park entrance is a 440-yard walk. Also walk 1.9km (1.2 miles) along the riverbank from the obelisk (see above), turn R if facing the river.

51.479492, -0.295444

Terrace Gardens, Richmond

Richmond Bridge

THE WHITE HART

Famous SW13 sunsets. Built in 1662 (and rebuilt in 1899) on the banks of the river, it features trees, terraced balconies, foreshore and steps down to the water.

The White Hart, The Terrace, Mortlake, Richmond, SW13 0NR

www.whitehartbarnes.co.uk

02088 76 5177

THE DUKE'S HEAD

This Putney pub sits at the start of the Oxford and Cambridge University Boat Race.

8 Lower Richmond Rd, Putney, SW15 1JN

www.dukesheadputney.com

020 8788 2552

ST MARY'S CHURCH/PUTNEY PANTRY

Historic church where, in August 1647, Oliver Cromwell and his New Model Army set up headquarters to hold their first Parliamentary conference, known as the 'Putney Debates'. The pantry inside the church grounds offers wonderful home-cooked food – cakes, pies, tarts and hot meals.

St Mary's Church, Putney High St, SW15 1SN

www.putneypantry.com

020 8789 1137

Leg O Mutton, Richmond upon Thames
Good place to see bats – over the disused Rez, along 800m (½ mile) stretch of river front. Also known as 'Lonsdale Road Reservoir'.
▶ **Find** where Gerard Rd meets Lonsdale Rd in Barnes. From the parking lay-by (51.476725, -0.249377), and facing the river, walk R along the FP 400m (1,310ft) until you are between the Rez and the river.

51.483972, -0.247702

Barnes Towpath, WWT London Wetland Centre, Richmond upon Thames
More than 40 rare native black poplars line what is arguably the most beautiful wooded section of the tidal Thames. These trees are thought to be the last remnants of a wild species, as DNA tests have shown they are genetically rare. Eleven of the 40 are genetically unique. Many of the trees are female, which is also extremely rare. Only 10 per cent of the UK population is female.

51.477943, -0.226857

Putney Bridge towards Fulham

THE SHIP
 Pub refreshments and food on the banks of the Thames since 1786. Also London craft beers, premium ales. Five-minute walk from Wandsworth Town station.

41 Jews Rd, Wandsworth, London, SW18 1TB

www.theship.co.uk

02088 709667

FIUME, WANDSWORTH
 "Fiume" is the Italian word for 'river'. A large Mediterranean piazza-style terrace sits right on the bank of the waterside. Great views of the Thames from the outdoor terrace.

Sopwith Way, Circus W Village, Battersea Power Station, SW8 5BN

www.fiume-restaurant.co.uk

020 3904 9010

THE BLACK CAB COFFEE CO
 Riverside hot drinks, pancakes and snacks. Great coffee and vegan food.

1 Riverlight Quay, London SW11 8AU

www.theblackcabcoffeeco.com

02074 988760

WWT London Wetland Centre, Barnes
Watch bitterns, parakeets, sparrowhawks and sand martins. A wetland over 100 acres of disused reservoirs on a loop in the Thames. Hides, plus a café, daily tours and specialist talks.

www.wwt.org.uk/wetland-centres/london/

51.479400, -0.227272

Wandsworth Park, Putney Bridge Rd, Wandsworth
Avenue of trees riverside and cycling on the river wall. Moorings. The 8ha park has 350 species of tree.

www.wandsworth.gov.uk/parks

51.463506, -0.206144

St Mary's Church, Battersea
Beautiful riverside church. Famous as the last resting place of an American military officer who in 1780, during the American Revolutionary War, defected to the British. He led the British army in battle against the very men he had once commanded.

www.stmarysbattersea.org.uk

51.476649, -0.175402

NATIONAL TRAILS

THAMES PATH EAST (TIDAL)

RIVERSIDE CAFE

 By the water, with views of Big Ben on the other side of the river. Hot food and drinks.

Lambeth Pier, Lambeth Palace Rd, Lambeth, SE1 7SG

02074 017575

THE FOUNDER'S ARMS

 Located beside Tate Modern and Blackfriars overground station. Brunch, lunch and dinner on the terrace.

52 Hopton St, Bankside, SE1 9JH

www.foundersarms.co.uk

020 7928 1899

PREMIER INN

 Budget accommodation close to the riverbank and 320m (1,050ft) from London Bridge station and trains to Brighton. Ask for a quieter room.

34 Park St, Bankside, SE1 9EF

www.premierinn.com

02070 892580

 Top TEN

The London Peace Pagoda, Battersea Park

Symbolic architecture in a serene location, with views over Chelsea Embankment. One of 80 peace pagodas in the world.

51.481980, -0.159067

Gabriel's Wharf, Bankside

One of the few places past Tilbury where you can find proper sand at low tide. Somewhere to either get onto the water or the shore or just sit around.

➤ **Find** Blackfriars overground station, EC4R 2BB (51.511843, -0.103740). Walk across the bridge to the S side of the river and turn R to find beach 400m (1,310ft) away.

51.508464, -0.108914

London Bridge, Southwark

Watch sunrise over the greatest river city in the world. This bridge is the river link between the City of London and Southwark.

➤ **Find** London Bridge station, SE1 3QX. Bridge is a 5-min walk. It can take much longer to cross with a camera in your hand on a clear dawn, winter or summer – because there are so many great photos to take.

51.506890, -0.088229

Statue of the Sphinx at Cleopatra's Needle

THE OLD THAMESIDE INN

 Pub a short stroll from Clink St, Borough Market, Winchester Walk and London Bridge station.

Pickfords Wharf, Southwark, SE1 9DG

www.nicholsonspubs.co.uk

020 7403 4243

THE ANGEL

 Pub with good-priced ales. Best river views of Tower Bridge are upstairs.

101 Bermondsey Wall E, Rotherhithe, SE16 4NB

02073 943214

THE MAYFLOWER PUB

 The oldest pub on the Thames has one of the greatest stories. Enjoy a candlelit restaurant in the decked jetty. You may spot the original 1620 mooring point of the Pilgrim Fathers' Mayflower ship. Indoors, while warming yourself by the open fire, imagine who may have been sitting in your seat 400 years ago.

117 Rotherhithe St, Rotherhithe, SE16 4NF

www.mayflowerpub.co.uk

020 7237 4088

Cleopatra's Needle

Woolwich Foot Tunnel, Greenwich

The Thames Path starts/ends at the entrance to a tunnel, surrounded by the sounds of industry and river traffic, and E of the Thames flood barrier. It is as far from the passive springs that form the Thames source as it's possible to get. Not pretty to the eye here. But a trail that passes the UK's best restaurants, most important historic places and oldest trees, and cascades like a metaphorical waterfall into the most important path in England: The England Coast Path. From here, everything is possible and discoverable.

➤**Find** Waterfront Leisure Centre, Woolwich High St, London, SE18 6DL, and the entrance to the Woolwich Foot Tunnel where the Thames Path meets the ECP.

51.494305, 0.062876

ST CHRISTOPHER'S INN GREENWICH HOSTEL

 Backpacker hostel right next to Greenwich station. Good access for Greenwich Park and river FP. Prices include breakfast.

189 Greenwich High Rd, Greenwich, SE10 8JA

www.st-christophers.co.uk/london/greenwich-hostel

02088 583591

THE CUTTY SARK

 Pub claiming to offer the best fresh fish dishes in Greenwich. Try the Greenwich seafood pot for a treat.

4–6 Ballast Quay, Greenwich, SE10 9PD

www.cuttysarkse10.co.uk

020 8858 3146

Teddington Lock to Kew Bridge

WILD THINGS TO DO BEFORE YOU DIE

EXPLORE the oldest pub on the river

VISIT England's most iconic tower

STAND under one of more than 40 rare native black poplars

TOUCH a peace pagoda

DRINK IN the views of the Thames

WALK a tree-lined avenue

LOOK for peregrines over Westminster Bridge

TOUCH the statue to Boudicca

TASTE the best food and wines

DINE al fresco by the river

Top TEN

 ▶ **St Brides Haven**, Snorkel through kelp forests.
51.753757, -5.186160

 Wooltack Point Deer Park, Look for seal pups, and views over Skomer and Skokholm.
51.738563, -5.252845

 Musselwick Beach, Forage for mussels, dog whelks and spider crabs hiding in seaweed or cliff ends.
51.73476074349705, -5.209911069743792

 Marloes Sands, Look for leatherback turtles. Their arrival coincides with that of thousands of jellyfish.
51.721485, -5.212591

 Little Castle Head Lighthouse, Britain's best ria. Foraging super site for glasswort and sea purslane. Taste salt air around a natural rock arch of limestone. Best at full tide.
51.610219, -4.998488

 The Cauldron, Balance above the Devil's Cauldron: an abyss of fury, theatre and wonder.
51.611733, -4.991220

 Freshwater E, Taste sea rocket and prickly saltwort around the dunes.
51.644783, -4.862379

 King's Quoit Burial Chamber, A Neolithic burial dolmen, 6,000 years old.
51.640804, -4.806016

 Lydstep Caverns Beach, Explore the best beach and caverns in Pembrokeshire. Only accessible at low tide.
51.644780, -4.766206

 ⓞ **Green Bridge, Angle**, Taste salt air around a natural rock arch of limestone. Best at full tide.
51.610219, -4.998488

Mount Sion

PEMBROKESHIRE COAST PATH SOUTH

BEST FOR: MOTHER NATURE

Turtles, ospreys, limestone cathedrals

START: BROAD HAVEN   FINISH: AMROTH

Pembrokeshire is the most important wildlife zone in Britain. Turtles, whales and ospreys all float on currents of watery air around the southern parts of the National Trail.

Guillemot stacks, offshore puffins, mussel streams, dog whelks, winkles and limpet caves. Nature caters for almost every human need: food, shelter, water and, best of all, curiosity. If surfing at Tenby is your thing, the chance to look for anemones as big as dinner plates while foraging for oysters on the way home is multitasking at its best.

To really see the wild, sit still, even if on a surfboard. For a long while. Better still, wild camp on a wooded beach or shelter in the porch of a prehistoric cave. Europe's biggest deep-water port is surrounded by some of these wildest spaces.

New Haven is the best example of a ria in Britain, and the largest estuary in Wales. Otters, dolphins and porpoises feed here.

Swim in seaweed, salt marsh and creek. Dunes and cliffs are laden with both sand martins and swifts.

THE GALLEON INN

Family-run pub with beer garden and beachfront seating. First-floor seating views over Broad Haven beach.

35A Enfield Rd, Broad Haven, Haverfordwest, Pembrokeshire, SA62 3JW

www.thegalleoninn.com

01437 781157

PENDYFFRYN MANOR B&B

One of the best B&Bs on the path. 90m (295ft) from the beach.

2 Settlands Hill, Little Haven, Pembrokeshire, SA62 3LA

www.pendyffryn-guesthouse.co.uk

01437 781863

The Settlands

Pembrokeshire Coast Path South start/end, Broad Haven

The Pembrokeshire Coast S path starts/ends in Broad Haven, opposite the beach. Always busy, it's a good place to think about the unique solitude and isolation of the path ahead, with its limestone cliffs and stacks, and its sinkholes, tides and deep-water ports. But also about the seafood and plant foraging, places to hide, and the cross and stone remnants of Britain's early Christian past.

▶**Find** Marine Rd car park, Broad Haven, SA62 3JR (51.779673, -5.102634).

51.779957, -5.102757

Little Haven Beach, Broad Haven

Walk around rock formations and caves over low-tide sand. Shallow around the shore. Good for snorkelling.

▶**Find** Marine Rd car park, SA62 3JR (51.77960, -5.102642). Walk to the shore and NT, and turn L, walking SW to the site.

51.774903, -5.109066

Top TEN St Brides Haven, Marloes and St Brides

Explore the kelp forests on both sides of the bay while snorkelling. Look for pollocks and wrasses. Prawns, crabs and lobsters between rocks. Many dolphins visit this sand and rock cove. Good at low tide for sea anemones fishing with venomous tentacles in rock pools.

▶**Find** St Brides Cross car park, SA62 3AJ (51.753444, -5.184616), and loos. Facing the coast, turn L and walk 45m (150ft) to cove.

51.753757, -5.186160

St Bridget's Church, St Brides

Touch the Celtic crosses in the graveyard. Wooden rafts, sunbeams and pews in the church. Lots of energy and calm.

51.753757, -5.184997

NATIONAL TRAILS

TY NANT

B&B in old fishing village of St Brides Bay. No pets. Little Haven beach is good for swimming.

10 Wesley Rd, Little Haven, Pembrokeshire, SA62 3UJ

www.littlehavenguesthouse.com

07485 179455

WEST HOOK FARM CAMPING

Small campsite with clean basic facilities. The campsite fields overlook St Brides Bay.

W Hook Farm, Marloes, Pembrokeshire, SA62 3BJ

www.westhookfarm-camping.co.uk

01646 636424

RUNWAYSKILN

Unique, vibrant place for food and simple accommodation.

Marloes Sands, Marloes, Pembrokeshire, SA62 3BH

www.runwayskiln.co.uk

01646 636545

Top TEN — Wooltack Point Deer Park, Marloes and St Brides

Look for seal pups and views over Skomer and Skokholm. Choughs are common on walk down to Marloes sands. Puffins nest offshore Skomer and Skokholm. Boat trips are available from April to August. Good for dolphin-spotting.

51.738563, -5.252845

Top TEN — Musselwick Beach, Marloes and St Brides

Beach only accessible after high tide. Lots of rock climbing and clear pools. Forage for mussels and dog whelks. Fish for bass, conger, pollock and mackerel.

▶Find Martin's Haven NT car park, Martin's Haven, SA62 3BJ (51.734381, -5.244624). Walk W onto the FP that connects to the NT and walk 1km (⅔ mile) to the point. Loop back along the coast FP to rejoin the NT S.

51.73476074349705, -5.209911069743792

Gateholm Island, Marloes and St Brides

Stargaze on a prehistoric island settlement. Grass meadows of wildflowers. Only accessible at low tide, so take care not to get stranded. Easy scramble from the W side from Marloes beach. Virgin sands, blue water and good fishing.

51.718961, -5.231637

Marloes Sands

POINT FARM CAMPSITE, DALE

 Small campsite. Each pitch has its own fire pit, with logs and charcoal available to buy. Small motorhomes (max 6m (20ft)), but no caravans. One of the first campsites to be awarded the Green Key environmental standard award in recognition of its approach to environmental management.

Point Farm, Dale, Pembrokeshire, SA62 3RD
www.pointfarmdale.co.uk
01646 636842

COCO'S BRASSERIE AT DALE YACHT CLUB

 Tapas dine in or takeaway. Views over Dale Beach. Try the seafood platter.

Coco's Brasserie at Dale Yacht Club, Dale, Pembrokeshire, SA62 3RD
www.facebook.com/profile.php?id=1000 57620 582213
07967 352456

THE GRIFFIN

 Watch catch of the day being pulled from the shore. Lobster, crab, sea bass dishes and more. Claims to be the last pub standing where once there were 15.

Dale, Pembrokeshire, SA62 3RB
www.griffindale.co.uk
01646 636227

Marloes Sands, Marloes
Look for leatherback turtles. Their arrival coincides with that of thousands of jellyfish. The turtles can grow to 1.8m (6ft). Find fossils around the soft sand and clear water. The rock formations and pipes are good.

51.721485, -5.212591

Westdale Bay, St Ann's Head
No access, that's why it's good. Fort is a few metres S and castle is a little E.

51.7083366280365, -5.187035193101779

Cobblers Hole, St Ann's Head Lighthouse
A wonderwall of rock. Look for the different colours as light shines on St Ann's Head inlet, with 100ft walls of different shades.

51.681621, -5.175172

Watwick Bay, Dale
Spider crabs hide in seaweed or cliff ends. They are easier to see in calm weather, when the water is clear. You'll be alone with sand and solitude. Much care needed as access is not always possible and can be dangerous. Limpets and winkles round the rocky edges to forage.

51.692619, -5.160892

Dale Point, Dale
Move along a 1.6km (1 mile) wooded boreen from S end of Dale Beach to Dale Point.
➤ Find Dale Beach car park (51.709478, -5.169583) and walk 90m (295ft) to beach.

51.704494, -5.163201

Pickeridge, Dale
Forage along a tidal lagoon. Best at low tide. Wild thyme and kale along this 2.4km (1½ miles) BW, half of which spans Milford Haven's rock and gorse seawall. Good for beachcombing. More fun than Dorset's Chesil Beach.

51.718225, -5.170480

Watch House Bay, St Ishmaels
Stony black beach. Very little access, so isolated and quite wild.

51.715294, -5.134854

NATIONAL TRAILS

Herbrandston Church

ECO ESCAPE CAMPSITE
Wild pitches from an off-grid site. Hay meadow or woodland pitches for tents and motorhomes. Fire pits, barbecues, toilets and hot showers.

Venn Dairy Farm, Waterston Rd, Milford Haven, Pembrokeshire, SA73 1DN

www.eco-escape.co.uk/camping
07898 353592

^{TOP TEN} Little Castle Head Lighthouse, St Ishmaels
Britain's best ria. Foraging super site for glasswort and sea purslane. Full of spring flowers. Port of Milford Haven and Stack Rock Fort can be seen from here. Dolphins and porpoises occasionally follow shoals of fish into the estuary.

51.717181, -5.109676

 ### Sandy Haven Stepping Stones, Herbrandston
Taste wild strawberries found around the dunes. Explore the low tide crossing of salt marsh and muddy creeks.

51.724566, -5.105412

 ### Kilroom, S Hook Fort
Look for edible seaweed and occasional oysters. Lava seaweed is best from Christmas until June. You may also find gutweed.

51.711354 -5.086307

 ### Conduit Beach, Milford Haven
Colourful anemones feed around the rocky pools.
▶**Find** Nelson Quay car park, Milford Haven SA73 3AZ (51.713898, -5.040536). Walk to the dock and, facing the water, turn R and keep walking W 1km (⅔ mile) to the site.

51.708288, -5.049117

Milford Haven

THE ALUMCHINE RESTAURANT

 Restaurant at Neyland Yacht Club with views over the River Cleddau. Specialises in Italian, fish and steak dishes.

Neyland, Pembrokeshire, SA73 1QA

www.thealumchine.co.uk

01646 600267

THE FERRY INN

Nautical-themed inn with river views and good food.

Pembroke Ferry, Pembroke Dock, Pembrokeshire, SA72 6UD

www.facebook.com/theferryinn/?locale=en_GB

01646 839334

TRAVELODGE PEMBROKE DOCK

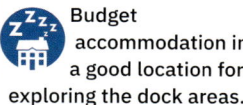 Budget accommodation in a good location for exploring the dock areas.

Pier Rd, Pembroke Dock, Pembrokeshire, SA72 6TR

www.travelodge.co.uk/hotels/296/Pembroke-Dock-hotel

08719 846299

WATERMANS ARMS

 Restaurant directly on the Mill Pond. Views of Pembroke Castle and the surrounding castle pond, just over the Mill bridge.

2 The Green, Pembroke, Pembrokeshire, SA71 4NU

www.watermansarmspembroke.co.uk

01646 682718

Saint Tudwal's Church, Milford Haven

Juvenile ospreys occasionally fly over the church in late summer looking for mullet. They migrate back to Africa. Great views from here of Europe's biggest deep-water port.

51.706755, -4.960982

Sykemore, Pennar, Pembroke Dock

Look for – or avoid – adders along the grass and wood canyon down to Pembroke River. They prefer to escape, so make lots of noise to announce yourself.

51.682691, -4.944415

Neyland Marina, Neyland

Listen for nightingales in April on the wooded walk past the marina.

▶ **Find** Marina/Brunel Quay car park, Station Rd, SA73 1LS (51.705764, -4.944605), and walk N 1km (⅔ mile) to woodland.

51.713085, -4.943756

Pembroke Castle, Pembroke

Touch the castle, birthplace of Henry VII of England, on the rocky edge of Milford Haven Waterway. The mill pond a was originally a defensive moat around the northern side of the castle, while its tidal waters powered the corn mill that supplied the castle and the town.

51.677264, -4.921494

Giant's Tap, Monkton, Pembroke

A giant, fun tap outside bluebells woods.

51.671683, -4.936395

Goldborough Pill, Hundleton

Look for wild angelica in summer where wood meets water. The large compound umbels of white or greenish-white flowers are similar to the deadly giant hogweed and hemlock. Used in folklore for stomach upsets and indigestion.

51.670991, -4.974397

NATIONAL TRAILS

PEMBROKESHIRE COAST PATH SOUTH 109

CASTLE FARM CAMPING AND SELF-CATERING

 Small family farm, camping field and self-catering accommodation. Showers, electric, toilets and outdoor washing-up.

Angle, Pembroke, Pembrokeshire, SA71 5AR

www.facebook.com/Castlefarm.angle

07584 476547

WAVECREST CAFE

 Café is on the coast path and sandy West Angle Beach. Rock pools and good swimming.

W Angle Bay, Pembroke, Pembrokeshire, SA71 5BE

www.wavecrestangle.co.uk

01646 641457

 ### The Devil's Quoit, burial site, Angle

Look for the collapsed burial chamber and disused pits close to the wind-blown dunes of Broomhill Burrows. The fallen capstone is on private land but can be seen from the path.

51.660275, -5.057346

 ### Freshwater W, Angle

Best beach in Pembrokeshire. Rock pools, sand dunes and adders to look for or avoid.

➤ **Find** B4319 car park, SA71 5AH (51.662841, -5.060659). Dunes to the rear of the car park E and beach to W.

51.662732, -5.067057

 ### Flimston Chapel, Castlemartin

Listen for razorbills and guillemots that nest in the sea caves along this bit of coast. The chapel is set inside the Castlemartin military firing range, so access can be limited.

51.620639, -5.000409

 ### Ermigate Ln, Stackpole and Castlemartin

Look for alexanders, sea radish and wild mint along a 2.4km (1½ miles) Ln. The path tracks S down to the coast path, where it joins a 4.8km (3 miles) BW past Bullslaughter Bay, between Elegug Stacks and St Govan's Chapel.

51.624086, -4.995120

Pembrokeshire Castle

GUPTON FARM CAMPSITE

 50 pitches for tents and campervans, and five bell tents a short walk from beach at Freshwater W.

Gupton, Pembroke, Pembrokeshire, SA71 5HW

www.nationaltrust.org.uk/holidays/wales/gupton-farm-campsite

01646 661332

Top TEN Green Bridge of Wales, Angle

Taste salt air around a natural rock arch of limestone. Best at full tide when the immovable cathedral of rock collides with waves.

51.610787, -4.999463

Elegug Stacks, Angle

Nature's standing church. Guillemots nest on the two limestone stacks, just offshore, from early spring. Also peregrine falcon, razorbill, kittiwake, fulmar and petrel.

➤Find Stack Rocks car park, Pembroke SA71 5HS (51.612268, -4.997060). Follow NT to shore, 140m (460ft).

51.611686, -4.996068

Top TEN The Cauldron, Elegug Stack Rocks, Flimston

Balance above the Devil's Cauldron: an abyss of fury, theatre and wonder. A rocky plug hole that falls down to a bottomless pit.

➤Find Elegug Stacks (see above) and walk along the NT E 500m (⅓ mile) to the site.

51.611733, -4.991220

The Green Bridge

110 NATIONAL TRAILS

PEMBROKESHIRE COAST PATH SOUTH

Mount Sion

PARKE FARM CAMPING, PARKE FARM

A farmhouse campsite. Toilets, showers, communal fridge/freezer, on-site shop. Fire pits and starter pack options can be added to booking. Electric pitches are 6 amp.

Merrion, Pembroke, Pembrokeshire, SA71 5DU

www.parkefarmcamping.co.uk

01646 450452

Huntsman's Leap, Stackpole and Castlemartin

Look for the giant crevice gash in the limestone cliffs. Legend claims a huntsman leapt across the chasm on his horse, but died of fright. The cliffs are separated by around 3m (10ft) at their narrowest. Much care needed.

▶**Find** St Govan's Chapel (see below) and walk 500m (⅓ mile) W on the NT.

51.598457, -4.944127

St Govan's Chapel, Bosherston

Chapel hanging over the cliffs. Named for a hermit who lived here in the 6th century. Steep steps down rocky path.

▶**Find** St Govan's Head car park, Bosherston SA71 5DR (51.599540, -4.936767). Walk S 180m (590ft) to the chapel steps.

51.598391, -4.937767

Church Rock, Saddle Point

Surfers and kayaks paddle out to this iconic rock island surrounded by beaches and cairns. Beware tides and offshore winds.

▶**Find** Broad Haven Beach S car park, Pembroke, SA71 5DR (51.607137, -4.924981). Facing the sea, walk 275m (900ft) to the coast overlooking Broad Haven.

51.606219, -4.914517

ST GOVAN'S INN
 Camping, food and rooms close to the Bosherston Lily Ponds. Brings together much of what's best about the S coast path.

Bosherston, Pembroke SA71 5DN
www.facebook.com/StGovansInnBosherston
01646 661792

BOSHERSTON CAMPSITE
 Back to basics… but what's not to like between woodland, mere pond and dunes.

Bosherston Camping, Buckspool Farm, Bosherston, Pembrokeshire, SA71 5DP
www.rj-roberts.wixsite.com/bosherston
07770 869972

 ## Saddle Point, Sandy Pit, Stackpole and Castlemartin
Touch the cave pool – a special place to spend more than a few hours.

51.608769, -4.915062

 ## Devil's Quoit, Stackpole and Castlemartin
Standing stone surrounded by a Bronze Age complex and dunes. Many finds have been discovered beneath the sand. Explore the dunes all over Broad Haven for flora and fauna.

51.617916, -4.917746

 ## Barafundle Bay Beach, E Trewent
One of the best beaches in Pembrokeshire. Backed by pine trees, with cliffs on all sides.

51.618162, -4.904169

 ## Stackpole Quay, E Trewent
Peaceful melting between humans and nature. Small settlements, jetties, creeks, landing places and piers blend with the shore and wild. Worth a few hours to explore.
▶**Find** Stackpole car park, SA71 5LS (51.625038, -4.903797). Walk 275m (900ft) E to the coast.

51.62381639120141, -4.900349617770014

 ## Freshwater E, Lamphey
Top TEN
Find sea rocket and prickly saltwort around the dunes. Popular with surfers.
▶**Find** Freshwater E car park, Trewent Hill, SA71 5LY (51.644635, -4.871273), on the SW edge of the beach dunes.

51.644783, -4.862379

 ## King's Quoit Burial Chamber, Manorbier
Top TEN
Neolithic burial dolmen, 6,000 years old. Megalithic slab on top of what is considered one of the UK's best surf beaches. The beach faces SW, with a reef break on the bay's R side.
▶**Find** Manorbier Beach car park, Manorbier, SA70 7SY (51.644926, -4.799152). Walk 800m (½ mile) W past the beach to site.

51.640804, -4.806016

 ## Church Doors Cove, Manorbier
Touch rock arch and cliffs with more beauty than a Gothic church carved by master masons. Best at sunset on a low tide.
▶**Find** YHA Manorbier car park, SA70 7TT (51.644304, -4.775781), and walk along the coast path to the site.

51.642658, -4.774015

NATIONAL TRAILS

EAST TREWENT FARM, COTTAGES AND B&B

 B&B and self-catering cottages a short walk from Freshwater E beach.

E Trewent Farm, Cottages and B & B, Stackpole Rd, Pembrokeshire,

www.easttrewentfarm.co.uk

01646 672127

PARK HOTEL

 Hotel with views over N beach and harbour.

Direct access to beach, gardens, clifftop terraces and heated outdoor pool. Restaurant serving breakfast, and dinner (pre-booking only); afternoon tea in the Garden Bar.

N Cliffe, Tenby, Pembrokeshire, SA70 8AT

www.parkhoteltenby.com

01834 842480

Lydstep Caverns Beach, Manorbier

TOP TEN

Possibly the best beach and caverns in Pembrokeshire. Only accessible at low tide.

51.644780, -4.766206

The Burrows, Tenby Golf Club, Penally

Walk barefoot along the sand burrow shoreline to Tenby.

▶**Find** Penally station, SA70 7PS (51.658964, -4.722083). Exit station and walk NE to cross the rail bridge, and then walk SE over the golf course and dunes to find the NT.

51.662367, -4.711324

St Catherine's Fort, Castle Hill, Tenby

Steep steps, beach views and Tenby Castle. The Dennis Café looks right over the beach.

▶**Find** N Beach car park, SA70 8AG (51.678483, -4.702617). From the Tenby N beach walk S, either along the beach Rd or N beach, 1.6km (1 mile) to S Beach. Best early morning at low tide.

51.670551, -4.691802

Tenby, N Cliffe, Brynhi

Surf, surf, surf. N beach is better than S.

▶**Find** N Beach car park (see above).

51.680527, -4.698572

Huntsman's Leap

MEADOW FARM CAMPSITE, TENBY

 Campsite on top of the Tenby N cliff, with views over Tenby beaches and harbour. Minimum of two-night stay, or three-night bank and summer holidays.

Northcliffe, Tenby, Pembrokeshire, SA70 8AU

www.meadowfarmtenby.co.uk

01834 818500

TREVAYNE FARM CARAVAN & CAMPING PARK

 Woodland tents pitch without electricity. Also campervan pitches over Carmarthen Bay. Farm shop for milk, bread, eggs and local seasonal produce.

Monkstone, Saundersfoot, Pembrokeshire, SA69 9DL

www.trevaynefarm.co.uk

01834 813402

 ### Monkstone Point, Saundersfoot
Look for waterfalls and pool just N of the beach and point. Best in September. Low-tide beach surrounded in rock formations, sand and bracken-laden woodland.

51.697550, -4.683322

 ### Rhode Wood, Swallowtree Gardens
Twisted pine and oak woodland over pill and sand. Like walking a Jurassic landscape.
➤Find Saundersfoot Harbour, SA69 9HE (51.710844, -4.699296 and walk 1.2km (¾ mile) S into the woodland on the NT.

51.701386, -4.693812

 ### Saundersfoot, Amroth
Best beach walk in Pembrokeshire is 8km (5 miles) long... at low tide.
➤Find Milford St car park, SA69 9NG (51.710361, -4.700897807367561). Walk NE 275m (900ft) to harbour and beach.

51.725923, -4.674057

St Govan's Chapel

WISEMAN'S BRIDGE INN

B&B and camping by the beach. Beer garden that extends right down to the beach. The shores here were the stage for rehearsals of the D-Day landings during the Second World War.

Wiseman's Bridge, Saundersfoot, Pembrokeshire, SA69 9AU
www.wisemansbridgeinn.co.uk
01834 813236

Finish/start, The Water's Edge, Amroth

The Pembrokeshire Coast Path starts/ends beside the rocky beach at Amroth. The place is quiet, and a fitting end to a trail that manages to combine the busiest industry and port traffic with an overwhelming sense of loneliness, isolation, and oneness with nature. The wild along this coast is probably best epitomised not by dolphins or deer, but by rock stacks and sinkholes. These are treacherous and wonderful places, ringing with the sound of seabirds, waves and wind. The limestone cliffs and pillars are the best in the world. This path, and its overwhelming lack of human interludes, might be the closest it's possible to get to nature.

▶**Find** Amroth car park, Amroth, Narberth, SA67 8NQ (51.731974, -4.662580). Walk to the shore a few metres and, facing the water, turn L and walk E 1km (⅔ mile) either along the coast Rd or the beach.

51.734024, -4.647306

WILD THINGS TO DO BEFORE YOU DIE

LOOK for leatherback turtles

BALANCE above the Devil's Cauldron: an abyss of fury, theatre and wonder

SWIM in kelp forest

LOOK for seal pups

FIND spider crabs in seaweed

SMELL salt air around a natural rock arch of limestone

TASTE sea rocket and prickly saltwort around the dunes

TOUCH a Neolithic dolmen

EXPLORE the best caverns in Pembrokeshire

Top TEN

 ◯ Cemaes Head, Watch minke whales from the highest sea cliff in Pembrokeshire.
52.115859, -4.729312

 Ceibwr Bay, Listen to the chaotic clips of sand martins calling on the wing.
52.078121, -4.761575

 The Witches Cauldron, Look for the collapsed cave at Traeth Bach.
52.071638, -4.770807

 Aberfforest Beach, A stream and waterfall to bathe feet, surrounded by seaweed.
52.019345, -4.878692

 Dinas Head, Look for humpback whales and orcas from the best viewing point along the entire Pembrokeshire coast.
52.032833, -4.908891

 Strumble Head Lighthouse, Listen to choughs around a remote lighthouse.
52.029338, -5.072026

 Carreg Samson, Touch stone pillars under a Neolithic capstone roof.
51.958517, -5.132952

 Melin Trefin Mill, Ruin with a view. Waterfalls, springs and caves.
51.948548, -5.153629

 Blue Lagoon Caves, Explore a natural harbour with aqua water. Secret caves and a redundant slate mine.
51.937541, -5.208943

 ◯ Druidston beach, A cavers' paradise, and the best low-tide beach in Pembrokeshire.
51.812012, -5.104991

PEMBROKESHIRE COAST PATH NORTH

BEST FOR: BLUE LAGOON CAVES

Graceful whales, caves, magic springs

START: ST DOGMAELS   FINISH: BROAD HAVEN

Of all the wonders of the natural world, there are three phenomena that capture human attention more than any other: cetacea, fire and caves.

Cetaceans, the family of mammals that includes dolphins and whales, favour the most rugged coastline in Britain.

As the wildest coast comes peppered in caves, it would be rude to not light at least one fire on a beach below the tideline to celebrate the Pembrokeshire triad.

Caves were valued by our ancestors the way we celebrate cathedrals and their fonts today.

St Davids Cathedral, Iron Age hillforts and Bronze Age round barrows are a nice touch of human engineering inserted into the Pembrokeshire wilderness we share with sea mammals. The vegetable world contributes a great deal too, with wild strawberries in the dunes and fat hen growing out of the cave edges along with sea kale, angelica and oraches.

Inevitably, our ancestors protected, stole and fought for these places. Don't be surprised to find dry caves above the waterline close to or under the many castles and hillforts associated with waterfalls and springs. Fortification isn't about fighting. It's about defence from those you stole from, or those who want to steal what you hold most precious: shelter, warmth and fresh water for your family.

Nolton Haven

BASIC SAFETY

- Caves and tunnels pose a risk – seek local advice before entering or exploring.
- Visit caves and tunnels on calm days.
- Always wear a helmet in case of banging head on overhangs, falling rocks or other hazards.
- Do not explore deep caves or tunnels without back-up torches.
- Beware caves that contain pipework, streams or flowing water that might be used by water companies as emergency flush for large amounts of water.
- Beware of becoming trapped in a cave on either a high or low tide if it suddenly floods quickly.
- Do not enter mine tunnels without professional assistance or advice.
- Use only bona fide tour groups with life jackets, wetsuits and helmets if carrying out sea cave explorations.

THE FERRY INN
Waterfront pub. It's a bit special.
Poppit Rd, St Dogmaels, Cardigan, Pembrokeshire, SA43 3LF
www.theferryinn.co.uk
01239 615172

Start of Pembrokeshire Coast Path N, The Moorings, St Dogmaels

The Pembrokeshire Coast N path starts/ends squeezed between a boat ramp and a jetty onto the estuary of the River Teifi. Houses line the bottom of the hillside that sweeps down to the water. It's as good a setting as any of the trails – riverside to the R, green hills to the L. If you can arrive a day early, a boat tour is a must. Dolphins, porpoise, seabirds and caves.
▶**Find** the T-junction where The Moorings meets the B4546, St Dogmaels, Cardigan, SA43 3GF.

52.088779, -4.682120

Poppit Sands, St Dogmaels

Listen to the sound of waves blowing over River Teifi dunes. This water/sand landscape is as good as anything along the trail.
▶**Find** Poppit Sands Beach car park, St Dogmaels, Cardigan, SA43 3LN (52.104034, -4.698969). Cross the Rd and over the dunes to the beach.

52.104594, -4.696950

Top TEN Cemaes Head, St Dogmaels

Look for minke whales from the highest sea cliff in Pembrokeshire.
▶**Find** Cardigan car park, SA43 3LP (52.110592, -4.725754). Walk back to NT and turn L, and head N 800m (½ mile) to site.

52.115859, -4.729312

PEMBROKESHIRE COAST PATH NORTH 119

TEIFI WATERSIDE HOTEL

 Garden by the waterside, and 13 sea-facing bedrooms over Poppit Sands.

Poppit Sands, Poppit, Cardigan, Pembrokeshire, SA43 3LN

www.teifiwatersidehotel.co.uk

01239 612085

NEWPORT SANDS

 Sea views, café, restaurant and rooms.

Newport Links Golf Course, Golf Course Rd, Newport, Pembrokeshire, SA42 0NR

www.newportsands.co.uk

01239 820244

Cwm-yr-Eglwys Bay

Top TEN Ceibwr Bay, Nevern
Listen to the chaotic clips of sand martins calling on the wing. They nest along these cliffs. Also nesting fulmars above the small beach.
▶ **Find** car park at Cardigan, SA43 3BW (52.068058, -4.747465). Exit the car park and turn R onto Rd and then follow the Rd L down to FP and trees. Walk from car to NT on coast is 1.6km (1 mile).

52.078121, -4.761575

Top TEN The Witches Cauldron, Ceibwr Bay
Look for caves around Ceibwr Bay, just S of Foel Hendre. The collapsed cave at Traeth Bach, the Witches Cauldron, is one of the best known.

52.071638, -4.770807

Morfa Head, Nevern
Move along the rocky crop of gorse and heather. Wide S views of Newport Sands and bay, all the way to Dinas Head.

52.039835, -4.846159

Newport Beach, Nevern
Look for dolphins offshore of this stunning beach. Rock pools and caves to explore too.
▶ **Find** Newport Sands car park, Feidr Pen-Y-Bont, Nevern, Newport, SA42 0NR (52.030793, -4.838264) and walk down to beach.

52.031452, -4.839287

St Brynach's ruin

TŶ CANOL FARM CAMPSITE

Family-run campsite with sea views. Open all year.

Tŷ Canol Farm, Newport, Pembrokeshire, SA42 0ST

www.facebook.com/newportcamping

01239 820264

🌊 River Nevern, Parrog, Newport

Where fresh water marries sea. Nothing quite like it. Walk the low-tide sand, but beware of incoming tides and sinking sand.

52.022584, -4.842981

🏅 Top TEN Aberfforest Beach, Newport

Inhale the sea air around a secluded beach. There is a stream and waterfall to bathe feet. Lots of seaweed in summer.

52.019345, -4.878692

🏅 Top TEN Dinas Head, Dinas Cross

Look for humpback whales and orcas from the best viewing point along the entire Pembrokeshire coast.

▶ **Find** Pwllgwaelod Beach car park, SA42 0SE (52.021601, -4.909059), and walk 1.6km (1 mile) N on the NT along the coast.

52.032833, -4.908891

🙌 St Brynach's Church, Dinas Cross

Church ruin and graveyard beside the beach.

52.023555, -4.894980

NATIONAL TRAILS

PEMBROKESHIRE COAST PATH NORTH

THE OLD SAILORS

Small pub at the foot of the gorge down to the beach. Fish finger sandwiches are a favourite.

Sailors Safety, Pwllgwaelod Beach, Dinas Cross, Newport, Pembrokeshire, SA42 0SE

www.facebook.com/theoldsailorsdinascross?locale=en_GB

01348 811486

Pwllgwaelod Beach, Feidr Fawr

Paddle in shallow water. Good rock formations to explore if the water is uninviting. Short walk to Dinas Head, with views towards Fishguard.

▶**Find** Sailors Safety car park, Dinas Cross, Newport SA42 0SE (52.021058, -4.907624). Exit car park to the W and beach is 140m (460ft). Alternatively, exit the car park E and walk the wooded FP 1km (⅔ mile) to the E end of Dinas Island.

52.02151573172775, -4.90956801133382

Fishguard Fort, Fishguard and Goodwick

Small fort, large cannons and big views. Fishguard Harbour walk is as impressive as the fort views over the bay.

▶**Find** Fishguard Fort car park, A487, Lower Town, Fishguard, SA65 9NB (51.999289, -4.969618). Exit car park N and walk 180m (590ft) to Castle Point.

52.001274, -4.970717

THE HIDE PEMBROKESHIRE CAMPING & GLAMPING

Off-grid non-electric site, surrounded by tall trees. Sea views and a bird hide.

Only 500m (⅓ mile) from the path down a Ln.

The Hide, Dinas Cross, Newport, Pembrokeshire, SA42 0YB

www.thehidepembrokeshire.co.uk

07887 406714

Fishguard Harbour, Quay St, Fishguard and Goodwick

Listen to jumping fish. The most relaxing rest place in Pembrokeshire is at sea level – sitting on the stone wall on Quay St. Best on a calm day when the water is still. Yacht Club Café (on the quay) is a good place to get a cuppa.

▶**Find** Harbour car park, A487, Lower Town, Fishguard SA65 9NB (51.995154, -4.968717). Facing the water, walk to the R around the quay.

51.997930, -4.971725

THE SHIP INN

Small pub just off the harbour, with lots of history and memorabilia on the walls to look and learn from.

3 Newport Rd, Lower Town, Fishguard, Pembrokeshire, SA65 9ND

www.fishguardbay.com/explore/dine/the-ship-inn

01348 874033

Aber Draw Waterfall

YHA PWLL DERI

Incredible views, but easy to miss the turning when walking. Great volunteer managers and quite modern. Well-equipped self-catering kitchen. Tends to close outside of peak season, but make sure you visit if you get a chance.

Castell Mawr, Trefasser Cross, Trefasser, Goodwick SA64 0LR

www.yha.org.uk

0345 371 9536

GARN ISAF

B&B, self-catering and camping. Good base for St Davids and access to path.

Abercastle, Haverfordwest SA62 5HJ

www.garnisaf.com

01348 831838

Carnfathach Summit Views, Pencaer

Look for basking sharks from one of the NT's best coastal summits. Waterfalls and woodland just to W make this is good place to explore.

▶**Find** Fishguard and Goodwick station, Goodwick, SA64 0DG (52.004181, -4.994752). Exit the station and walk N towards New Hill and the NT. Follow path 4km (2½ miles) to site.

52.023311, -5.007745

Carreg Wastad Point, Pencaer

Touch the monument erected in 1897 to mark the unsuccessful French invasion a hundred years earlier, in 1797. The large stone is at a point with the best N views up the Cardigan coast. The stone, inscribed in Welsh and English, marks where Britain was last invaded – on this occasion, more than 1,000 of Napoleon's men, landed here and caused some havoc.

52.023582, -5.023889

Strumble Head Lighthouse, Pencaer

Top TEN

Listen to choughs around a remote lighthouse. Look for dolphins, heather, gorse and seals. The sea is exceptionally clear here.

▶**Find** Strumble Head car park, Pencaer, SA64 0JL (52.028993, -5.070462). Exit the car park W and walk 90m (295ft) to the coast.

52.029338, -5.072026

Carreg Samson

PEMBROKESHIRE COAST PATH NORTH   123

TRELLYN WOODLAND CAMPING

 Incredible site. Campfires, free firewood, touring park and glamping.

Each pitch has its own covered campfire.

Abercastle, Haverfordwest, Pembrokeshire, SA62 5HJ

www.trellyn.co.uk

01348 837762

THE SHED BISTRO

 Fish and chip bistro on the path by the sea. Famous for its own-caught local fish and shellfish landed daily on the quay in front of the bistro.

56 Llanrhian Rd, Porthgain, Haverfordwest, Pembrokeshire, SA62 5BN

www.theshedporthgain.co.uk

01348 831518

 ### Garn Fawr Fort, Pencaer
Minor detour, major upside. Inhabited for at least 6,000 years. Feel the cold wind they felt back then in winter. It was most recently a hillfort.

▶ **Find** Garn Fawr car park, Goodwick, SA64 0JJ (52.007937, -5.062972). Exit the car park W and walk 275m (900ft) to the site.

52.008194, -5.067492

 ### Abermawr Beach, Pencaer
Paddle around low-tide sand. Pebbles at high tide. Bluebell woodland and streams surround the walk down.

51.969452, -5.083846

 ### Carreg Samson, Pencaer
Stone pillars support a capstone of Neolithic design. Legend says the stones were placed here by St Samson, who lost a finger in the process. The finger is said to be buried at the top of Ynys-y-Castell, the islet at the entrance to nearby Abercastle cove.

51.958517, -5.132952

 ### Melin Trefin Mill, Llanrhian
Ruin with a view. Waterfalls, springs and caves.

▶ **Find** Porthgain car park, Haverfordwest, SA62 5BL (51.947819, -5.180974). Walk N onto the coast path. Turn R, facing the sea, and walk E, 3.2km (2 miles).

51.948548, -5.153629

 ### Traeth Llyfn, Llanrhian, St Davids
Look out for seals that come here to sunbathe.

▶ **Find** Abereiddy Beach car park, Abereiddy, SA62 6DT (51.936556, -5.205594). Walk N on the NT, 1.6km (1 mile) to site. Metal stairs down to beach.

51.94268815046005, -5.198495713627593

 ### Blue Lagoon Caves, Porthgain
Better than a scene from Garland's novel The Beach. A natural harbour with aqua water. Secret caves and mystery. Best on a calm, warm day in winter. The old slate mine that has been reoccupied by nature makes this place even more special.

51.937541, -5.208943

 ### Porth y Dwfr Spring, St Davids
Look for the grey dorsal fins of porpoises hunting for fish beneath diving gannets. This is a 9.65km (6 miles) stretch of remote FP, splintered by freshwater springs.

51.915001, -5.259394

Porthstinian

YHA ST DAVIDS
 Converted farmhouse at Whitesands Bay for swimming, surfing, coasteering, climbing, riding and walking. A 1.6km (1 mile) detour from the path but via the Carn Llidi Bychan burial chambers (51.904242, -5.290303), so what's not to like.

Llaethdy, Whitesands Bay, St Davids, Haverfordwest, Pembrokeshire, SA62 6PR

www.yha.org.uk/hostel/yha-st-davids

03453 719141

PENCARNAN FARM CAMPING & CARAVAN PARK
 Camping on a 96-acre working farm. The site extends down to Porthsele beach, on Pembrokeshire's most westerly point. Look toward St George's Channel, which connects with the Irish sea to the N and the Celtic Sea to the S. A static caravan field and two camping fields overlook Whitesands Bay. Two more camping fields set back away from the bay have views towards Ramsey Island.

Pencarnan, St Davids, Haverfordwest. Pembrokeshire, SA62 6PY

pencarnanfarm.co.uk

01437 720580

Coetan Arthur Dolmen, St Davids
Touch a Neolithic tomb of megaliths. The stones support a capstone that was placed on this wild, rocky peninsula as a beacon, thought to be at least 5,000 years old. Like most of these burials, it comes with a view best seen at night. Porthmelgan Beach below is worth exploring.

51.904777, -5.308353

Whitesands, St Davids
Sandy but busy. Surf beach. Rent surf and body boards. Like all of this coast, wet suits needed.
➤**Find** RNLI St Davids Lifeboat Station car park, St Justinian, SA62 6PY (51.878784, -5.307081). Exit the car park W and walk N along the coast 3.2km (2 miles) to the site.

51.895595, -5.296004

RNLI St Davids Lifeboat Station, St Justinians
Trips to Ramsey Island to see razorbills and puffins. Explore the story of St Justinian and his chapel, the remains of which are seen from the path.
➤**Find** RNLI St Davids Lifeboat Station car park, St Justinians, SA62 6PY (51.878784, -5.307081).

51.879120, -5.308858

Ramsay Island, St Davids
One of the most isolated FP stretches, around 11.2km (7 miles) between St Justinians and St Non's Retreat. Looking over Ramsey Island and Shoe Rock.

51.861161, -5.317861

NATIONAL TRAILS

PEMBROKESHIRE COAST PATH NORTH 125

RHOSSON GANOL CARAVAN AND CAMPING SITE

 Dog-friendly and barbecues allowed. 40 grass pitches for touring caravans, campervans and tents.

St Davids, Haverfordwest SA62 6PY

www.pembrokeshire-camping.co.uk

07498 462543

RHOSSON CAMPSITE

 Basic, low-key site since the 50s. The campsite is mainly left to run itself.

Rhosson Farm, St Justinians, St Davids, Haverfordwest, Pembrokeshire, SA62 6PY

www.rhosson.co.uk

01437 720285

PORTHCLAIS FARM CAMPSITE

 Small family-run campsite within a walk of St Davids. Rated as one of the UK's best campsites.

St Davids, Haverfordwest, Pembrokeshire, SA62 6RR

www.porthclaiscampsite.co.uk

07970 439310

 ### Porthclais Harbour, St Davids

Huge boat ramp down to the water. Fee for kayaks. Good kayaking in harbour, best when tide is out. Lime kilns and other historic features are worth exploring.

51.867895, -5.280488

 ### St Non's Chapel and Well, Ffynnon Wen

Inside the chapel ruin, find a Celtic cross engraved on a pillar stone. Another stone with a Celtic cross and four sun rays can be found at Caerfai Bay. The site is now claimed as the birthplace of St David, the patron saint of Wales, allegedly born AD 500.

➤**Find** Ffordd Caerfai car park, St Davids SA62 6QT (51.872733, -5.256537). Facing the sea, turn R and walk SW, 1.2km (¾ mile) to site.

51.872535, -5.268116

 ### Caerfai Bay Fort, Caerfai Camp

Wildflower meadow over Caerfai Bay. Lots of caves, but much care needed getting down. Great views.

➤**Find** Ffordd Caerfai car park, St Davids, SA62 6QT (51.872733, -5.256537). Exit the car park L and walk 90m (295ft) to the beach.

51.869244, -5.251184

St Justinian

GLAN-Y-MÔR CAMP SITE, SAINT DAVID'S

 Small campsite for tents, campervans and caravans. Toilets, hot showers, dish-washing area.

On-site catering van. Surfboard, wet suit and paddleboard hire. Fire pit hire and log cabins.

Caerfai Rd, Saint David's SA62 6QT

www.glan-y-mor.co.uk

01437 721788

CAFE ON THE QUAY

 Licensed café on the quay. Light lunches, cakes and ice cream.

Trinity Quay, Solva, Haverfordwest, Pembrokeshire, SA62 6UQ

www.facebook.com/profile.php?id=100057090805905

01437 721725

HARBOUR INN

 Dog-friendly pub overlooking the harbour.

31 Main St, Solva, Haverfordwest, Pembrokeshire, SA62 6UT

www.harbourinnpubpembrokeshire.co.uk

01437 720013

 ### Solva Lime Kilns, Solva Harbour, Haverfordwest

Sheltered beach and heritage. Kilns are beautiful, set back in the natural harbour inlet against the cliff face.

➤**Find** Solva Harbour car park, Solva, SA62 6UT (51.873994, -5.189494). Facing the water, exit the car park on L side and walk through coastal woodland 500m (⅓ mile) to site.

51.872627, -5.190609

Dinas Fawr, Solva

Look up to one of the darkest skies on the path. The peninsula is as far as it gets from light pollution.

➤**Find** Solva Lime Kilns (see above) and keep walking N then E along the coast path, 3.2km (2 miles) to the site.

51.861427, -5.180767

Newgale Sands

NEWGALE FARM CAMPSITE

 Basic toilets, no showers but vast views.

Newgale Farm, Newgale, Haverfordwest, Pembrokeshire, SA62 6AS

www.campingandcaravanningclub.co.uk/campsites/uk/pembrokeshire/haverfordwest/newgalefarm

07779 506742

NEWGALE CAMPSITE

 Basic or electric pitches by the beach. Dog-friendly. Established in 1935. Van provides pizzas and burgers.

Newgale, Haverfordwest, Pembrokeshire, SA62 6AS

www.newgalecampsite.co.uk

07539 906611

Porthmynawyd beach, Brawdy

Paddle on a secret beach. Sand and pebbles. Craggy climbs and rock pools.

Find Dinas Fawr (see left) and keep walking N and then E, 400m (¼ mile) along the coast path to the site.

51.862728, -5.157622

Pointz Castle Springs, Brawdy, Newgale

Listen to birdsong on a spring-laden FP. This river valley once provided fresh water to Pointz Castle.

▶**Find** Porthmynawyd beach (see above). On exit, rather than following the coast path, take the FP NE into the wooded valley to follow the springs (51.866415, -5.156879). FP leads out onto main Rd 800m (½ mile) away, but there really isn't anywhere to park.

51.869715, -5.152996

Newgale Beach S, Newgale

Collect shells on the shingle sand as the tide goes out. Beach is 3.2km (2 miles) long, but it feels much shorter if beachcombing.

▶**Find** Newgale car park, Welsh Rd, SA62 6BD (51.853019, -5.122937). Beach is opposite, so arrive early.

51.851484, -5.124683

Sibbernock Point, Newgale Sands

Move along a 1.6km (1 mile) stretch of beach Rd and boreen along Newgale Sands.

▶**Find** Maidenhall National Trust car park, Haverfordwest, SA62 6BD (51.839031, -5.110945), and walk S onto beach Rd.

51.847971, -5.119667

Nolton Haven beach, Nolton Haven

Paddle low-tide rock pools, sand and vast caves.

▶**Find** Welsh Rd car park, SA62 3NH (51.825115, -5.107198 and walk straight down to the beach. Low tide best. Listen to a roaring cave from the overhead path 275m (900ft) N.

51.823599, -5.110661

Druidston Beach, Haverfordwest

The clue is in the name. A cavers' paradise. But perhaps the best beach in Pembrokeshire when the tide is out. The sweeping sandy Druidston beach is topped by two natural arches, a priest's vault and caves.

▶**Find** Nolton Haven beach (see above) and walk 1km (⅔ mile) S.

51.812012, -5.104991

Maidenhall Point

THE DRUIDSTONE HOTEL

Hotel and cottage accommodation in 20 acres of grounds on the sea's edge over St Brides Bay. Food, drink, music, sea, beach.

Nr Druidston Haven, Welsh Rd, Haverfordwest, Pembrokeshire, SA62 3NE

www.druidstone.co.uk

01437 781221

Harold Stone, The Havens, Broad Haven

Touch the standing stone, between gorse and scrub.
➤**Find** Marine Rd car park, SA62 3JR (51.779594, -5.102646), walk to the shore and NT. Facing the water, turn R and walk N, 1km (⅔ mile).

51.790183, -5.103348

Pembrokeshire Path N start/end, The Havens, Broad Haven, SA62 3NB

The Pembrokeshire Coast N path starts/ends in Broad Haven overlooking the sea from the Enfield Rd boat ramp. Walk down onto the beach in bare feet to feel sand. Having navigated some of the wildest coast in Britain, this is a good place to finish. A calm resort to rest and to consider what has gone: whales, caves, magic springs, the sound of seabirds, secret beaches as well as the most breathtaking limestone cliffs and stacks in the world.
➤**Find** Marine Rd car park, SA62 3JR (51.779594, -5.102646).

51.779957, -5.102757

Solva Harbour

WILD THINGS TO DO BEFORE YOU DIE

WATCH minke whales from the highest sea cliff in Pembrokeshire

LISTEN to the chaotic clips of sand martins

LOOK for a collapsed cave

BATHE feet in seaweed and stream

LOOK for humpback whales

TOUCH mysterious stone pillars

WASH in a waterfall

EXPLORE secret caves

VISIT a druid beach

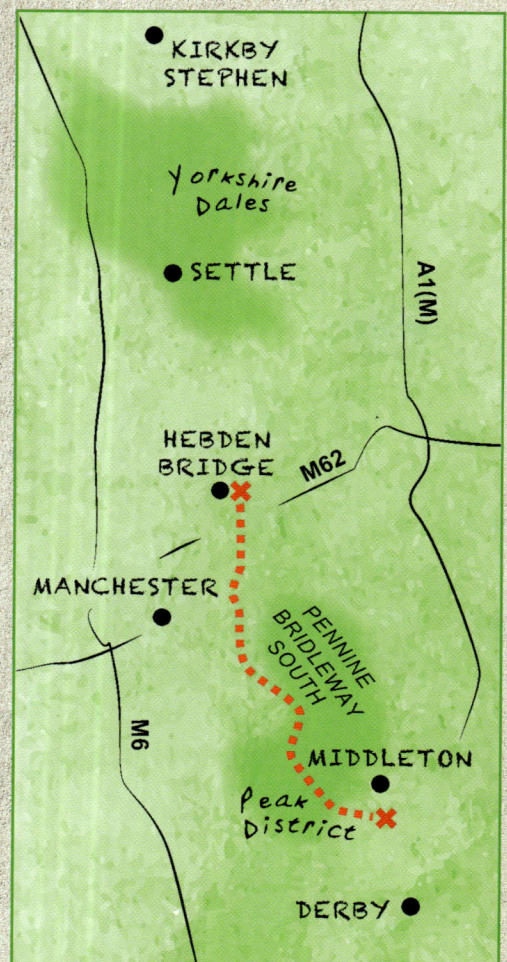

Top TEN

 Harboro Rocks, Look over Carsington Water from a cave site famous for remains.
53.094578, -1.641437

 **Chee Dale**, Look for climbers on the limestone cliffs.
53.255557, -1.815632

 Lantern Pike, Taste crowberries, which can be found among the driest blanket peats of Lantern Pike in late winter and early spring.
53.392355, -1.961820

 Robin Hood's Picking Rods, Touch mysterious stone blocks.
53.414975, -1.991725

 Higher Swineshaw Rez, Inhale the cold mountain around the peaks that make some of the toughest walks on the trail.
53.492652, -1.995863

 Saddleworth Moor parking, Smell wildflowers along waterside and moor between sinkholes and bogs.
53.608037, -2.017474

 Top of Pike, Walk a track that Lancashire millworkers made during the cotton famine of 1861–65.
53.651886, -2.210903

 Cowpe Low, Stargaze over Cowpe Rez. Views over Pendle and Yorkshire Dales.
53.681848, -2.268836

 Lumbutts Water Tower, Move around the tower and mill dam, against the backdrop of Stoodley Pike Monument.
53.707665, -2.067466

 Stoodley Pike Monument, Climb a spiral staircase of 39 stone steps carved into the landscape, with great views.
53.714305, -2.041542

PENNINE BRIDLEWAY SOUTH

BEST FOR: CYCLING

Stone tombs, lake bats, disused rails

START: MIDDLETON   FINISH: HEBDEN BRIDGE

The southern part of the Pennine Bridleway is dominated by three things: bikes, cotton-grass and blanket bog.

In between the soft mires and forest ravines are limestone heaths, cliff and crag, all of which can be visited in half a day by pedal over hard track. For those on horseback, the ability to move confidently without fear of the path ending before nightfall is a rare gift in 21st-century England.

While nature passes quickly over the BW, it is the human mills, factories, bridges and culverts that provide the access.

Upland heathland burnt for grouse is full of crowberry, bilberry and heather. The upland rides through oak and ash woods into conifer and pine plantations. They all provide variety and shelter from harsh weather.

There are caves to find, clean rivers to wash in and ride, and drystone walls and flower-rich grasses to sit on.

Human activity is never far from the isolated mires when on a horse or bike.

Stepping stones inevitably become an occasional problem on detours, so it's a good idea to pack light or carry detachable panniers.

The freedom of bike over BW is comparable to kayaking, if for no other reason than it's a rare treat to overload weight onto a vessel or vehicle.

Middleton Top

MINNINGLOW MEADOWS, MATLOCK

A campsite on a working farm. Tents, caravans and motorhomes. On-site fishing lake.

Minninglow Grange, Pikehall, Matlock DE4 2PR

www.facebook.com/minninglowcamping/?locale=en_GB

07544 771805

Start of Pennine BW, The Moor, Rise End

The Pennine Way BW S path starts/ends at the Middleton Top Visitor & Cycle Hire Centre exit, with views over Wirksworth and Carsington Water. The cycle centre epitomises what lies ahead. More than 322km (200 miles) of BW, GW, country Ln, Rd and boreen. It's an invitation to choice. Whether to walk, ride a horse or ride a bike. There is nothing else like it in Britain. A yellow brick Rd adventure of wilderness, industry, stone tombs, lakes, rivers, reservoirs and disused railways lines.

▶Find Middleton Top Visitor & Cycle Hire Centres, Rise End, DE4 4LS. (53.093562, -1.589962)

53.093273, -1.590105

Hopton Tunnel, Hopton

Feel the magic around an old railway tunnel.

53.090249, -1.606139

Top TEN Harboro Rocks, Brassington

Move up to 379m (1,243ft) above sea level for views over Carsington Water. Ice Age remains were found in Harboro Cave. Burial ground nearby.

▶Find Wirksworth Dale car park, Matlock, DE4 4HA (53.088812, -1.652648). Exit the path and travel E along the Rd 460m (1,500ft) to find FP on the R. Follow FP to Manystones Ln and turn R 275m (900ft) until FP on L. Follow FP onto Pennine Way and cross onto FP up onto rocks.

53.094578, -1.641437

FIVE WELLS CAMPSITE

Barn accommodation beside a Neolithic tomb in the Peak District National Park. The famous Five Wells are just to the E. No showers, but a working farm with loos and running water.

Five Wells Farm, Flagg, Buxton SK17 9RB

www.facebook.com/p/Five-Wells-Campsite-100070083924561/

07918 675322

Minninglow Hill, Brassington

Feel how tranquil it is among trees around tombs and barrows. The site is Neolithic (about 5,500 years old) but was used into the Bronze Age. The path here is an old railway line.

53.112525, -1.688692

Chee Dale, Wormhill

Top TEN

Look for climbers on the limestone cliffs. The views make this a worthwhile detour of about 1.6km (1 mile). Explore Tunstead Quarry.

▶ Find Millers Dale car park, Wormhill, SK17 8SN (53.256286, -1.794397). Exit car park and get onto the dismantled railway line. Follow the line 1.6km (1 mile) W to the river FB.

53.255557, -1.815632

Chee Dale Stepping Stones, Wormhill

The scent of rocks, water and wildlife around a limestone gorge. The River Wye is impressive. Balance around slippery scrambles and climbs – but care needed, especially when wet.

▶ Find Chee Dale (see above) and follow the river walk E 500m (⅓ mile) from the river FB.

53.252643, -1.819269

Disused railway line bridge, Blackwell in the Peak

Move along part of the old London to Manchester line, renamed the Monsal Trail. Well worth half a day or more along the river and rail section.

▶ Find Chee Dale Stepping Stones (see above) and keep travelling W on the line.

53.250850, -1.832256

Monk's Dale, Wheston

Look for sparrowhawks along the valley of trees. A minor detour W of the path.

53.272529, -1.801608

Wheston Cross, Wheston Bank

Smell the sweet scent of maple trees in spring and autumn. The site was historically used for speeches and open court hearings.

53.284769, -1.803600

Charles, King and Martyr Church, Buxton

Touch the walls of what was a 'Gretna Green' for runaway couples. The church was outside of ecclesiastic law until a law change in 1804.

53.309829, -1.830808

HAYFIELD CAMPING AND CARAVANNING CLUB SITE

 Camping on the River Sett. Good access to Kinder Scout. Accommodates backpackers, bikepackers and motorhomes.

Kinder Rd, Hayfield, High Peak SK22 2LE

www.campingandcaravanningclub.co.uk/campsites/uk/derbyshire/high-peak/hayfield-camping-and-caravanning-club-site/

01663 745394

THE SPORTSMAN INN

 Dog-friendly pub in the village at the bottom of Kinder Scout. Log fire and a beer garden.

Kinder Rd, Hayfield, Derbyshire, SK22 2LE.

www.thesportsmaninn.co.uk

01663 741565

 ### Rushup Ln, Chapel-en-le-Frith
A 1.6km (1 mile) boreen from Whitelee (53.328143, -1.852400) to Rushop Hall (53.339092, -1.863380) via Rushup Ln. Leads to closed boreen and burial ground to Roych Clough (below Tom Moor Plantation).

53.333722, -1.855020

 ### River Sett, Kinder Bank
River and valley views. Most importantly a car park base for Kinder Scout, but it's a long walk.
➤**Find** Bowden Bridge car park, 165 Kinder Rd, SK22 2LJ (53.378997, -1.928813). Walk to Kinder Rd and follow NE to site.

53.381523, -1.928249

 ### St Matthew's Church, Hayfield
Flowering gardens beside the water. The bells are famous for being both irritating or inspiring, depending on your mood.

53.379444, -1.945857

 ### Low Gate Ln, Birch Vale
Listen for Canada geese. Good views from the stone wall track over the Rez.

53.379906, -1.965435

Lantern Pike, Primrose Vale (Top TEN)
Taste crowberries, which can be found among the driest blanket peats of Lantern Pike. Sweeter after frost in late autumn or early winter. Views over Kinder from 373m, but it's quite a climb.

53.392355, -1.961820

Wormhill

PENNINE BRIDLEWAY SOUTH   135

Walkerwood and Brushes Rez

THE WALTZING WEASEL B&B

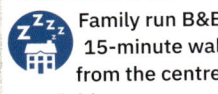 Family run B&B a 15-minute walk from the centre of Hayfield.

8 New Mills Rd, Birch Vale, High Peak, Derbyshire, SK22 1BT

www.the-waltzing-weasel-bed-breakfast.derbyshire-uk.com/en

01663 743402

Robin Hood's Picking Rods, Stockport
Top TEN

Touch mysterious stone blocks. Man-made for sure, because nature doesn't carve round pillars that fit sockets in a stone base. Thought to have been carved in the 9th century, they may have been a single stone column that has broken and been remounted. Theories on their origin range from an ancient marker for a druid sacrifice site, to Robin Hood using the place for target practice. Popular cyclists' route.

53.414975, -1.991725

Lees Hill, Hollingworth, Tameside
Look for merlin and views over Swineshaw Rez.

53.491358, -1.986959

Higher Swineshaw Rez, Hollingworth
Top TEN

Inhale the cold mountain air around the peaks and mountain views. Some of the toughest walks on the trail up here.

53.492652, -1.995863

Cowbury Green, Carrbrook
Taste hazelnuts in autumn along this tree-lined waterside walk.

53.506190, -2.013759

Gaddings Dam

THE SADDLEWORTH HOTEL

 Posh stopover in 4-star hotel with wide valley and Rez views.

Huddersfield Rd (A62), Delph, Oldham, Greater Manchester, OL3 5LX

www.saddleworthhotel.co.uk/

01457 871888

THE RAMS HEAD INN

 Moorland views; a 450-year-old inn with log fire, log stoves, real ale. Farm shop stocks pork pies, wine, bread and more. Sandwiches, takeaways and main meals.

Ripponden Rd, Denshaw, Saddleworth OL3 5UN

www.ramsheaddenshaw.co.uk

01457 874802

 ### Noonsun Hill, Mossley
Mix bilberries in with granola for a ready meal. They can sometimes be found between heather and peat patches on Moor Edge Rd.
▶**Find** Dysarts Arms, Mossley, Huddersfield Rd, Mossley, Ashton-under-Lyne, OL5 9BT. Facing the pub, turn L and walk 10m (30ft) to the FP on the R. Follow the FP 365m (1,200ft) and turn R on the NT. Walk another 180m (590ft) to the site.

53.523387, -2.020871

 ### Saddleworth Museum & Gallery, Uppermill
Local history museum over four floors. Somewhere to lose some time when the weather turns foul.
www.saddleworthmuseum.co.uk

53.546933, -2.007770

 ### Standedge, Brun Moore
Where the Pennine BW meets the Pennine Way.

53.583452, -1.978089

 ### Roman Fort, Castleshaw
Touch the fort ruin, which marks a once important route from London to Chester.
▶**Find** Waters Ln car park, Delph, OL3 5LX (53.579457, -2.007247). Exit the car park and walk Rd N along Castleshaw Lower Rez. Follow Rd for 800m (½ mile), arching R, to fort.

53.583617, -2.003310

 ### Dirty Ln, Castleshaw
Move along a 2.4km (1½ mile) boreen from Standedge Foot Rd (53.585868, -1.983324) to Bleak Hey Nook Ln (53.582366, -1.998855) to Dirty Ln (53.584255, -2.003954) to Castleshaw Top Bank (53.586685, -2.007919) beside Upper Rez.

53.584289, -2.004355

NATIONAL TRAILS

PENNINE BRIDLEWAY SOUTH   137

HOLLINGWORTH LAKE CARAVAN PARK

Caravans and motorhomes only. Not a bad base if exploring the trail on day trips from here. Barbecues and shop on-site.

Rakewood Rd, Rakewood, Littleborough, Greater Manchester, OL15 0AS

www.hollingworthlake caravanpark.com

07498 970972

Top TEN Saddleworth Moor, Denshaw

Smell wildflowers along waterside and moor. Beware hidden sinkholes and bogs. The views (400m) make it easy to get distracted on Saddleworth Moor. The Pennine Way passes the E side of this Dark Peak area.

▶ **Find** Dowry Rez N (53.598530, -2.020092) and walk N on NT, 1.6km (1 mile) to site.

53.608037, -2.017474

Norman Hill Rez Falls, Bleakedgate Moor

Touch the water as it runs from Norman Hill into Piethorne Rez. Good views from Norman Hill. Lots of blanket bog and cotton-grass.

53.611785, -2.049852

Rakewood Viaduct, Rakewood

The alchemy of steel on the M62 being carried over the meandering Longden End Brook is impressively mediated by the engineering of the Rakewood Viaduct. It's not on a par with anything constructed by Isambard Kingdom Brunel, but is impressive nonetheless. The viaduct was built in 1966 and opened to motorway traffic in 1971. Parking (53.623142, -2.083776).

53.620991, -2.081184

Hollingworth Lake, Dearnley

Touch the wood carvings around the lake. The lake circuit takes about 90 minutes – a 800m (½ mile) detour from the trail.

▶ **Find** Hollingworth Country Park, Rakewood Rd, Littleborough, OL15 0AQ for car park, which is 90m (295ft) from the waterside.

53.631874, -2.091230

Mossley

Lumbutts

THE WINE PRESS

Views over Hollingworth Lake from the N shore. Traditional English food. Three courses, a light lunch or just coffee.

93 Hollingworth Rd, Littleborough OL15 0AZ

www.sanrocco.co.uk/the-wine-press

THE SUMMIT INN
Somewhere to use as a work station while planning your next trip. Wi-Fi, sandwiches and drinks.

140 Todmorden Rd, Littleborough, Greater Manchester, OL15 9QX

www.thesummitinn.com

01706 379500

 ### Summit of Rochdale Canal, Clough
Smell elderflowers in May while walking the canal path. It's a relaxing break from the chore of navigating compass and map.

53.665773, -2.081502

 ### Higher Slack Brook Nature Reserve, Wardle
Listen for owls at dusk. The bird hide is good for watching migrating birds. Farm ruin and mines nearby.
▶ **Find** Watergrove car park, Wardle, OL12 9NJ (53.655599, -2.135186). Follow the NT 1.6km (1 mile) N around the water to the site.

53.664406, -2.139738

 ### Top of Pike, Rooley Moor
Top TEN
Walk the 'Cotton Famine Road' made by unemployed Lancashire millworkers during the cotton famine of 1861–65. The ruin of what was the Moor Cock Inn at Rooley Moor Brow dates to the 1930s. There were dozens of quarries in this area, with workers using the pub. Peak is 398m (1,305ft) for good views.

53.651886, -2.210903

 ### Old Tom's Wood, Rydings
Sense the history around a hidden ruin and woodland walks.
▶ **Find** Higher Slack Brook Nature Reserve (see above) and follow the NT to the S for 1.2km (¾ mile).

53.661407, -2.145123

PENNINE BRIDLEWAY SOUTH 139

HARGREAVES ARMS

B&B and pub in the Lumb Valley. Good for budget travellers who want access to the Pennines. Real ale and lagers.

910 Burnley Rd E, Rossendale, Lancashire, BB4 9PQ

www.thehargreavesarms.co.uk

01706 215523

THE TOP BRINK INN, TODMORDEN

Family-owned free house and food shop between Hebden Bridge and Todmorden. Countryside pub on the trail. Dog-friendly.

Top Brink, Lambutts, Todmorden, W Yorkshire, OL14 6JB

www.topbrink.com

01706 812696

 ### Waugh's Well, Rossendale
A 800m (½ mile) detour from Black Hill. Waugh's Well was built to commemorate local poet Edwin Waugh (1817–90) and looks over Scout Moor Rez and across towards Holcombe Moor.
Waugh, sometimes known as the 'Lancashire Burns', became famous for sketches. His first book, *Sketches of Lancashire Life and Localities*, was published in 1855.

53.672162, -2.260632

 ### Cowpe Moss, Pennine BW, Boarsgreave
Stony peak along the Rossendale Way with views over Cowpe Rez.

53.671826, -2.243197

 ### Cowpe Lowe, Hugh Mill
Stargaze over Cowpe Rez. Wild and wonderful place with good views over Pendle and Yorkshire Dales. There's a bench at the 440m (1,440ft) summit.

53.681848, -2.268836

 ### Lumbutts Water Tower, Todmorden, Calderdale
Move around the tower and mill dam. From Lumbutts Rd, see Stoodley Pike Monument silhouetted against the backdrop of the tower.

53.707665, -2.067466

Langfield Common

OLD CHAMBER FARM AND CAMPING

 1.6km (1 mile) detour E from the trail.

Spencer Ln, Hebden Bridge, W Yorkshire, HX7 6JG

www.oldchambercamping.com/

07814 321606

FOX AND GOOSE

Community pub with character. W Yorkshire's first co-operative pub serving ale, pork pies, vegan pasties, barista coffees and cake.

7 Heptonstall Rd (A646), Hebden Bridge, W Yorkshire, HX7 6AZ

www.foxandgoose.org

01422 648052

 Top TEN

Stoodley Pike Monument, Todmorden

Climb a spiral staircase of 39 steps, accessed from the N side. The stone monument commemorates the defeat of Napoleon and was completed in 1815, after the Battle of Waterloo. It's a detour, but the views are worth it.

▶ **Find** Withens Clough car park, Hebden Bridge, HX7 5TS. Exit the car park W and walk the FP along the Rez, continuing for 2.4km (1½ miles) until it joins the Pennine Way. Turn N on the NT and walk 1.6km (1 mile) to the site.

53.714305, -2.041542

Rochdale Canal Bridge, Callis Wood

The Pennine BW S path starts/ends at the Rochdale Canal. Like the cycle hire centre start, the canal epitomises what has gone and what is to come. A transit avenue through 21st century commerce butted up against prehistoric wild, where some of the cleanest rivers in England run alongside once toxic industry, bat roosts, bridges and disused railway lines.

▶ **Find** the Callis Wood/Rochdale Canal bridge where the Pennine BW meets the A646, Hebden Bridge.

53.734091, -2.044666

Rochdale Canal, Callis Wood

Wormhill

WILD THINGS TO DO BEFORE YOU DIE

TOUCH mysterious stone blocks

INHALE cold mountain air

SMELL moor flowers

WALK a track made by hungry millworkers

STARGAZE over a reservoir

LOOK over Carsington Water from a cave

WATCH climbers on the limestone cliffs

TASTE crowberries

MOVE around a tower and mill dam

CLIMB a spiral staircase of 39 steps

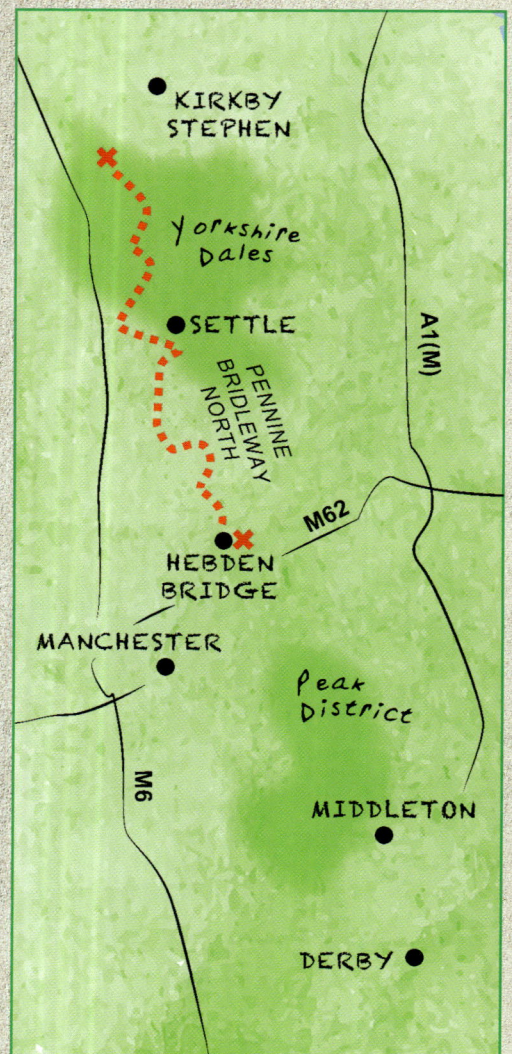

 Standing Stone Hill, Standing stones surrounded by purple moor grass.
53.768846, -2.075862

 Sheddon Clough, Look for long-eared owls over a lunar landscape of windswept moors.
53.761468, -2.162448

 Wold Fell, A rare platform of rock: limestone pavement.
54.260985, -2.321704

 Stainforth Force Waterfall, Watch salmon jumping upstream around waterfall and sunshine.
54.099888, -2.280593

 Clapper Bridge, Walk over an 800-year-old packhorse bridge.
53.848765, -2.103801

 Shake Holes Caves and Wood, Walk around caves, wood and holes in a valley between limestone pavements.
54.108495, -2.324730

 Snaizeholme, Look for red squirrels in Snaizeholme woodland.
DL8 3AX

 Great Knoutberry Hill, Packraft the tarns on the highest peak in Yorkshire.
54.279588, -2.326417

 Wild Boar Fell, Touch the Stone Men of the Fell: a set of large standing cairns.
54.384239, -2.373964

 Cranberry, River Eden, Listen for otters along the upper reaches of the Eden. A rare chance to walk the quiet

Gisburn

PENNINE BRIDLEWAY NORTH

BEST FOR: BOREENS

Limestone pavements, water caves, old railways

START: HEBDEN BRIDGE FINISH: COTE MOOR

The northern part of the Pennine Bridleway has the best boreens in Britain. We could debate that dramatic waterfalls and limestone pavements are more important. But the ability to move at a snail's pace along a tiny, single-track path with a grass mohican is one of the most enjoyable pleasures in the National Trail pantheon.

A boreen is a country lane that is unpaved, and is too narrow for two cars to pass. Most have a wild-flower edge along either side.

The prevalence of these little lanes along the Pennine BW is largely thanks to the number of country houses with parkland, linked to the mills and factories their owners once staffed. These roads were originally created for deliveries when the stately classes made a shilling by running goods in and out of Daddy's drive. The roads grassed over with the emergence of second and third homes abroad, and IT trading. The circle of life is wonderful like that.

River Calder, Callis Wood

WHITE LION HOTEL

Pub, restaurant, hotel. Homemade food since 1657. Hebden Bridge's largest beer garden. Ten en-suite rooms.

Bridge Gate, Hebden Bridge, W Yorkshire, HX7 8EX

www.whitelionhebdenbridge.co.uk/

01422 842197

PACK HORSE INN

A whitewashed moorland inn. Popular with walkers and cyclists on both the Pennine Way and the BW.

Widdop Rd, Widdop, Hebden Bridge HX7 7AT

www.thepackhorseinn.co.uk

01422 844614

Rochdale Canal Bridge, Callis Wood
The Pennine BW N path starts/ends at the Rochdale Canal and tracks up and over the Yorkshire Dales. The Pennine BW S path is made of gritstone N and limestone S. This northern path is a larger and more varied version of the last. It's like exploring a kaleidoscope after looking through a microscope. Not better, just different. Water caves, caverns, limestone cliffs, raptors, grouse, limestone pavements and rare woodland, prehistoric tombs and mile upon mile of secluded boreen.
▶**Find** the Callis Wood/Rochdale Canal bridge where the Pennine BW meets the A646, Hebden Bridge.

53.734091, -2.044666

Winter's Ln, Blackshaw
A 1.6km (1 mile) boreen from Mount Olive Chapel Cemetery (53.735672, -2.050892) to Marsh Ln (53.742243, -2.053970) to Bow Ln (53.744171, -2.055943) via Winter's Ln.

53.738899, -2.050776

Land Farm Garden, Colden
Explore a unique garden. Only open several times in summer under the National Garden Scheme Yorkshire. Lilies and other rarities of the wild in a cultivated part of the Pennines.

53.756837, -2.069550

NATIONAL TRAILS

PENNINE BRIDLEWAY NORTH 145

OAKENBANK GLAMPING

Glamping close to the Lancashire/Yorkshire border. A 800m (½ mile) detour from trail.

Lower Oakenbank Farm, Trawden, Lancashire, BB8 8PS

www.facebook.com/oakenbankglamping/

07745 535217

PARSON LEE FARM GLAMPING

Farmhouse in 64-acre grounds surrounded by grouse moors and streams. 300m detour.

Parson Lee Farm, Wycoller, Trawden, Lancashire, BB8 8SU

07444 695715

Top TEN Standing Stone Hill, Blackshaw, Calderdale
Standing stones surrounded by purple moor grass via a short detour. Beware boggy ground inbetween the heather.

53.768846, -2.075862

Top TEN Sheddon Clough, Mereclough
Look for long-eared owls over a lunar landscape of windswept moors. These hills were once used to mine limestone boulders left behind by glaciers.

53.761468, -2.162448

Cant Clough Rez, Worsthorne Moor
Cormorants fish here. Good for birds generally. Explore the industrial archaeology at the Shedden lime works.

53.773764, -2.161269

Heptonstall Moor, Stone
Step over boggy top moor where the BW meets the iconic Pennine Way.

53.773493, -2.082218

Gorple Rez, Heptonstall Moor
Listen for grouse around the waterside trail and stone walls. Surrounded by rocky crags and moorland.

53.779093, -2.086246

Widdop Rez, Wadsworth
Sanctuary for Canada geese, short-eared owls and cuckoos in spring. Frog lay spawn around the edges in March.

▶**Find** Widdop Rez car park, HX7 7AZ (53.791712, -2.095981). Exit the car park on the W side and walk 90m to the waterside.

53.791372, -2.098288

Gisburn

BLACK LANE ENDS TAVERN

 Traditional and isolated pub on the hills above Skipton and Colne. Specials board is good value.

Skipton Old Rd, Colne, Lancashire, BB8 7EP

www.blacklaneendstavern.co.uk

01282 863070

THE CRAVEN HEIFER INN

 Hotel is 500m (⅓ mile) S of trail. Bike hire in the village.

400 Colne Rd, Kelbrook, Lancashire, BB18 6TF

www.thecravenheiferinnkelbrook.co.uk

53.898740, -2.150947

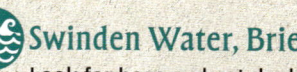 Swinden Water, Briercliffe

Look for barn owls at dusk around the FB over Swinden Water.
➤ **Find** Hurstwood Rez path (53.781323, -2.167865) and follow the NT path N.

53.793816, -2.150858

Will Moor, Trawden Forest

Listen for curlews that breed high on these heather moors. Move over blanket peatland on the way to the peak at 343m (1125ft).
➤ **Find** Thursden Scenic Spot (53.816738, -2.140502) and walk 1km (⅔ mile) N on the NT.

53.822380, -2.133516

Clapper Bridge, Wycoller Hall, Colne

Top TEN

Walk over an 800-year-old packhorse bridge. The hall ruins blend into the quiet village. Purple flowers grow in the beck at springtime.

53.848765, -2.103801

Knarrs Hill, Pendle

Look for the white flowers of marsh saxifrage in the fens and swamps around Knarrs Hill. The plant has been used for centuries by traditional herbalists for sore throats and skin irritations. Climb the hill to grassy views at 334m.

53.878374, -2.098930

Gisburn Old Rd, Blacko

A 1.6km (1 mile) boreen from White Moor (53.885847, -2.208539) to Weets Hill (53.895787, -2.220128) via Sandyford over grass and shrub heath.

53.891276, -2.212663

Stainforth Force Waterfall

PENNINE BRIDLEWAY NORTH 147

ANCHOR INN SALTERFORTH

 Pub beside the Leeds & Liverpool canal. Food and coffee.

Salterforth Ln, Barnoldswick, Lancashire BB18 5TT

www.theanchorinnsalterforth.co.uk/index

01282 850055

Dog Hill Brow, River Ribble

 ### Weets Hill, Gisburn Old Rd, Blacko
Stargaze over the Ribble Valley between Pendle Hill and the Southern Pennines. The hill is 397m but it's mostly dry walking from Barnoldswick.

53.899454, -2.218828

 ### Leeds & Liverpool Canal Bridge, Barnoldswick, Pendle
Grass-centred boreen beside Lower Park Marina.

53.912139, -2.174461

 ### New Ing Hill, Coal Pit Ln, Gisburn, Ribble Valley
A 2.4km (1½ mile) tree-lined boreen from Coal Pit Ln (53.914352, -2.237126) to Westby Hall Farm (53.928133, -2.263674) via New Ing Hill.

53.924216, -2.244069

 ### Castle Haugh, Newsholme
Explore a wooded castle mound. The Norman motte and bailey is surrounded by broadleaf and yew trees.

53.952755, -2.260558

 ### Cow Bridge, Long Preston, Wigglesworth
Paddle raft to shale islands and riverbanks. The stone-walled river bridge is beside a giant ash tree.

54.008485, -2.264792

 ### The Edge, Long Preston
1.6km (1 mile) boreen view over Ribble Valley, from Long Preston (54.020171, -2.254082) to High Barn (54.034916, -2.263861) via The Edge.

54.027706, -2.260029

Malham Tarn

THE WHITE BULL
Traditional inn with rooms and access to the Yorkshire Dales. Detour 800m (½ mile) N of the trail into this Lancashire village.

Main St, Gisburn, Lancashire, BB7 4HE

www.thewhitebull-gisburn.co.uk

01200 411181

THE BUCK COUNTRY PUB
Curries, burgers, pastas and steaks, or hot and cold sandwiches.

Kiln Ln, Paythorne, Clitheroe, Lancashire BB7 4JD

www.buckcountrypubpaythorne.co.uk

01200 445488

MAYPOLE INN
A 17th-century village inn of the Dales with rooms. Special offers available for multi-night stays.

Maypole Inn, Main St, Long Preston, Skipton, N Yorkshire, BD23 4PH

www.maypole.pub

01729 841066

THE GOLDEN LION
A 17th-century coaching inn for rooms or meals.

Duke St, Settle, N Yorkshire, BD24 9DU

www.goldenlionsettle.co.uk

01729 822203

Mitchell Ln, Settle
Move across heather moor and bog. This is a breeding ground for upland birds. A 2.4km (1½ mile) boreen from Long Preston (54.020171, -2.254082) to Hunter Bank (54.048637, -2.260577) via Mitchell Ln.

54.058116, -2.263578

Scaleber Force, Settle
Feel spray from the 12-metre (40-foot) waterfall that crashes down a limestone gorge. The fall drops into a deep pool and feeds into the River Ribble, beside Scaleber Wood.

54.059116, -2.244613

Grizedale Caves, Upper Settle
Look for hunting peregrine around the disused mine shafts, caverns, caves and rocky ledges. The 6.4km (4 miles) path between Scaleber Force and Malham Cove is an adventurers' paradise, much of it over limestone pavement. Local courses in rock climbing and more at Malham.

54.072222, -2.193549

Winskill Stones, Langcliffe
A 1.6km (1 mile) boreen from Leys Barn (54.083500, -2.261843) to Upper Winskill (54.094289, -2.262179) via Winskill Stones over limestone pavement.

54.089419, -2.254592

NATIONAL TRAILS

PENNINE BRIDLEWAY NORTH   149

KING WILLIAM THE FOURTH GUEST HOUSE

Bike-friendly B&B, with parking for bikes and secure storage. Also bike-washing facilities and tools, track pump and bike stand.

High St, Settle, N Yorkshire BD24 9EX

www.kingwilliamthefourthguesthouse.co.uk

01729 268152

CRAVEN HEIFER HOTEL

Yorkshire Dales home-cooked food and bedrooms. Open fire and river views.

Main Rd, Stainforth, Settle, N Yorkshire, BD24 9PB

www.cravenheiferstainforth.co.uk

01729 822435

Top TEN Stainforth Force Waterfall, Little Stainforth

Watch salmon jumping upstream. Move along the river to a waterfall. Stainforth Bridge is a 17th-century packhorse crossing over the River Ribble. Locals wild swim here, although the water can be fast-flowing. Knights Table is a short walk.

▶ **Find** Main Rd parking, Stainforth, BD24 9PQ (54.101035, -2.275964). Exit the car park onto the main B6479 and walk N 230m (750ft) to the railway bridge on the L. Cross the bridge and then cross the Stainforth Bridge after another 275m (900ft) (there is limited parking here). Take the FP S along the riverside and walk 140m (460ft) to the site.

54.099888, -2.280593

Banks Barn, Little Stainforth

A 3.2km (2 miles) boreen from Stainforth Force Waterfall (54.102292, -2.278435) to Swarth Moor (54.117592, -2.301254) via Winskill Stones.

54.106532, -2.289851

Thwaite Ln, Austwick

A 2.4km (1½ mile) boreen from Norber Sike (54.117175, -2.346277) to Thwaite Plantation (54.120189, -2.382343) via Long Tram Plantation.

54.117628, -2.363369

Top TEN Shake Holes Caves and Wood, Feizor

Caves, woods and holes in a valley between limestone pavement on either side.

54.108495, -2.324730

Malham Tarn

KNIGHT STAINFORTH HALL CAMPING & CARAVAN PARK

 Campsite for tents and motorhomes on the River Ribble. Also holiday homes and cottages. This is a 45-acre estate of Knight Stainforth Hall, once owned by the Knights Templar.

Little Stainforth, Settle, N Yorkshire, BD24 0DP

www.knightstainforth.co.uk

01729 822200

SILLOTH HOUSE CAMPSITE

 By the waterway, family-run campsite in the Yorkshire Dales. Shower block, toilets and electricity. Popular with trail cyclists.

Silloth House, Austwick, Lancaster, LA2 8DH

www.silloth-house.co.uk

07854 368832

The Lake, Ingleborough Hall Outdoor Education Centre, Clapham

Touch the waterfall and trees along this river walk.

▶**Find** Yorkshire Dales National Park car park, Clapham, LA2 8EQ (54.118713, -2.390797). Exit the car park to the W and walk N on Church Av. Follow the path 365m (1,200ft) to St James' Church, on Clapham Beck. Follow the BW out of the church to the R, and walk E to either join the NT after 550m (1,800ft) or turn L into the woodland to find The Lake. Falls are to the N end.

54.120322, -2.387487

Ingleborough Cave, Clapham cum Newby

Balance between springs and caves on the edge of limestone pavement. A stream runs alongside the path. The path passes caves. Payment is needed to enter the caves. Hard hats are provided.

▶**Find** The Lake (see above) and NT and walk 1.6km (1 mile) N.

54.135108, -2.374953

River Ribble Bridge, Fawber

Look for brown trout around the bridge over the River Ribble.

54.172633, -2.313789

Cave Hill, Calf Holes/Dry Lathe Cave

Explore caves and look for bats around the 400m peaks.

54.195925, -2.302220

Pennine Way and BW meet, Cam Houses

The meeting of paths is always charged with energy. Feel the passing of people, their purpose and their stories.

54.243557, -2.268378

Top TEN
Wold Fell, Dent, Westmorland and Furness

Limestone pavement over a 558m (1,830ft) peak.

54.260985, -2.321704

Dent Fell

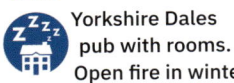

THE GAME COCK INN

Yorkshire Dales pub with rooms. Open fire in winter.

The Green, Austwick, Lancaster, LA2 8BB

www.gamecockinn.co.uk

01524 251226

Low Stennerskeugh

Great Knoutberry Hill, Westmorland and Furness
Top TEN

Packraft the tarns on the highest peak in Yorkshire. At 672m (2,200ft), the views are impressive. Packrafting this high is a rare and unique experience.

54.279588, -2.326417

Arten Gill Viaduct Falls, Arten Gill Viaduct, Dent

Nature and architecture meet on the W side of Dent Fell. The viaduct has 11 arches and is 35m (117ft) high. Blocks of Dent 'marble' and local limestone were used to build the arches. The limestone is full of fossils.

54.268064, -2.345299

Stone House Bridge, Dent

Look for brown trout and lamprey around a famous waterside crossing bridge.
▶ **Find** the river bridge by Stone House, LA10 5RL.

54.268411, -2.353378

Galloway Gate, Garsdale

A 4.8km (3 miles) boreen from Swallow Hole (54.287575, -2.340325) to Garsdale Station (54.321478, -2.328699) via Garsdale Coal Pits.

54.302072, -2.330735

Dandry Mire/Moorcock Viaduct, Garsdale Head, Westmorland and Furness

Architectural engineering meets moor at Moorcock Viaduct.

54.325354, -2.319668

Johnston Gill Waterfall, Hawes

Paddle in a small waterfall on the River Ure, beneath Cobbles Hill Bridge.

54.333129, -2.308509

Great Knoutberry Hill

THE TRADDOCK
Stopover for people walking the dales. Rooms and afternoon teas. Ten course tasting menu for foodies.

Austwick, Settle, Yorkshire Dales, LA2 8BY

www.thetraddock.co.uk

01524 251224

River Ure Cave, High Abbotside
Explore the cave, and look for rare plants and bats, just S of the river crossing.

54.361874, -2.325697

Jingling Sike Cave, High Abbotside
Look for white-clawed crayfish around a cave that takes its name from the stream.

54.364647, -2.327796

The High Way, High Abbotside
A 8km (5 miles) GW from Johnston Gill (54.341061, -2.300183) to the River Eden Thrang (54.398973, -2.335526) via Jingling Sike Cave.

54.363611, -2.327561

Hell Gill Bridge, High Abbotside
Get down into the spinal canal of rocks that form a tunnel prop for the bridge. Many plants around the water of Hell Gill Beck under sunlight and moss. Good place to hide. Spooky at night.

54.366952, -2.330303

Eden Sike Cave, Mallerstang, Hawes
Look for bats around this limestone cave of Eden Sike stream. Hellgill Waterfall is 300m and to the S (54.363933, -2.342233).

54.367176, -2.339077

Wild Boar Fell, Mallerstang
Touch the Stone Men of the Fell: a set of large standing cairns. At 708m, this is not a place to come in bad weather. A 3.2km (2 miles) detour, there and back (just over 1 mile each way), from the BW at High Dolphinsty (54.394603, -2.361981), with views of Howgill Fells.

54.384239, -2.373964

PENNINE BRIDLEWAY NORTH 153

THE SPORTSMANS INN

Food and rooms overlooking the River Dee. Popular with hikers. Locally sourced food and hand-pulled cask ales.

Cowgill, Dent, Cumbria, LA10 5RG

www.thesportsmansinn.com

01539 625282

THE MOORCOCK

Country B&B with licensed tearoom. Good food and beer.

Garsdale Head, Sedbergh, Cumbria, LA10 5PU

www.the-moorcock.co.uk

07960 930047

Top TEN Cranberry, River Eden, Westmorland and Furness

Look for otters along the upper reaches of the Eden. This is a rare chance to walk the quiet riverbank. Short detour and riverside walk after crossing Thrang Bridge. The main BW bridge is here (54.392548, -2.337501), with a waterfall and a short walk W on BW here (54.393088, -2.344307).

54.402500, -2.340752

Long Gill, Kirkby Stephen

The sunken water crossing on Hashygill Moss leads into a nesting area for golden plover and lapwing. Short-eared owls hunt here.

54.400411, -2.378705

Cote Moor, Ravenstonedale

The Pennine BW N starts/ends without a fanfare, like a host who has politely asked you to leave a two-day party. What lies ahead or behind is the UK's best limestone pavement, crossings over 21 major rivers, red deer, red squirrel, merlins and hen harriers, tombs and hundreds of boreens and caves and even more clifftops. Oh… and lots of bats.

▶ **Find** the Fat Lamb Country Inn, Crossbank, Ravenstonedale, Kirkby Stephen, CA17 4LL. Head S on the A683 for 800m (½ mile). The trail starts on Cote Moor at the junction to the L (E) signposted 'Street Stennerkeugh'.

54.409124, -2.405258

WILD THINGS TO DO BEFORE YOU DIE

LOOK for long-eared owls over a lunar landscape

CLIMB up to limestone pavement

WATCH salmon jumping upstream

FIND standing stones surrounded by moor

WALK around caves below limestone pavement

PACKRAFT the tarns on the highest peak in Yorkshire

TOUCH the Stone Men of the Fell

LISTEN for otters on the River Eden

LOOK for peregrine around disused mines

WALK an 800-year-old packhorse bridge

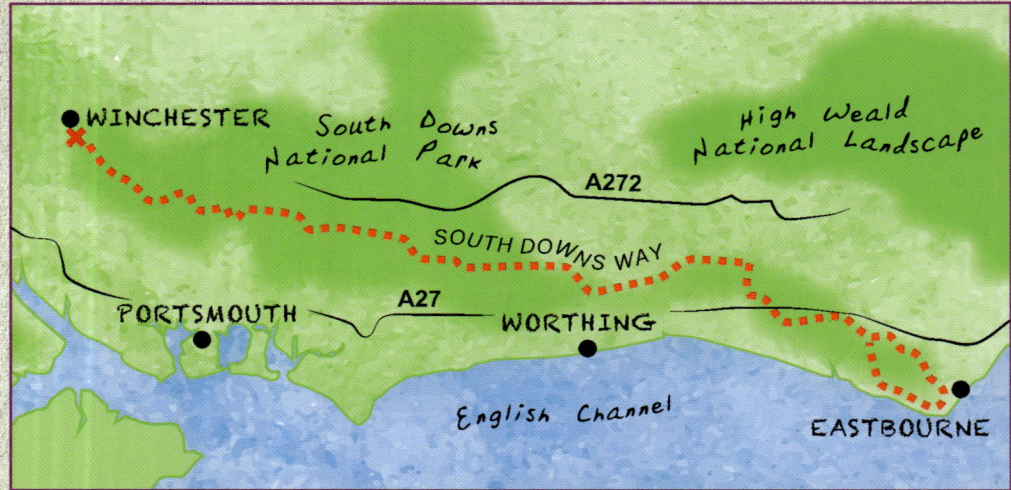

 ▶ Beachy head Cliffs, Tramp along the greatest 19km (12 miles) walk in the world from Eastbourne to Alfriston.
50.735804, 0.235174

 Cliff End Lagoon, Listen to dunlin and redshank birds feeding around the lagoon.
50.759491, 0.151966

 The Long Man of Wilmington, Look for the largest human in Western Europe. The Dodd man is naked and holds two posts.
50.810843, 0.188423

 Ditchling Beacon, Stargaze from the highest point (250m/820ft) on the S Downs.
50.905556, -0.115078

 Devil's Dyke, Explore the largest dry chalk valley in the county, a vast natural ditch, wildflowers and butterflies.
50.882953, -0.204918

 Rook Clift, Inhale the scent of one of the rarest woods in England: an ancient large-leaved lime woodland, on chalk, fed by ravine springs.
50.957509, -0.834603

 Chanctonbury Ring, Walk a mass of beech trees planted on an Iron Age hillfort.
50.896759, -0.381160

 Bignor Hill, Touch the remnants of an ancient yew tree on Bignor Hill. The tree sits between wild garlic and views over the Arun valley.
50.910012, -0.602819

 Cocking chalk stream, Paddle a rare chalk stream and explore the plants that grow there. An 800m (½ mile) detour N from the path.
50.946777, -0.757855

 ▶ Beacon Hill Burial, Look for any of 13 species of wild orchid that grow here on steep grass slopes.
50.998514, -1.141900

SOUTH DOWNS WAY

BEST FOR: WILDFLOWERS
Trout, white cliffs, yew

START: WINCHESTER   FINISH: EASTBOURNE

A 'whale-backed' spine of chalk through Kent and Surrey supports hundreds of species of flowers and grasses. Half of all the orchid species native to Britain live in this area.

Small fragments of rare sand and white heath. But it gets better than that. You will find more than 60 plant species per square foot: within a space the size of a mouse mat.

Some of the most edible plants live underneath majestic beech hangers.

The South Downs is not a typical wooded canopy. Most of the trees have gone. What's left is remarkable. Primitive large-leaved lime woodland, yew woodland and mature elms. In between the woods and downs are rivers — the most colourful at the Seven Sisters, the iconic snake view of Cuckmere Haven, down to Beachy Head.

Dark night skies, bats and the rarest of flowers.

Harting Down

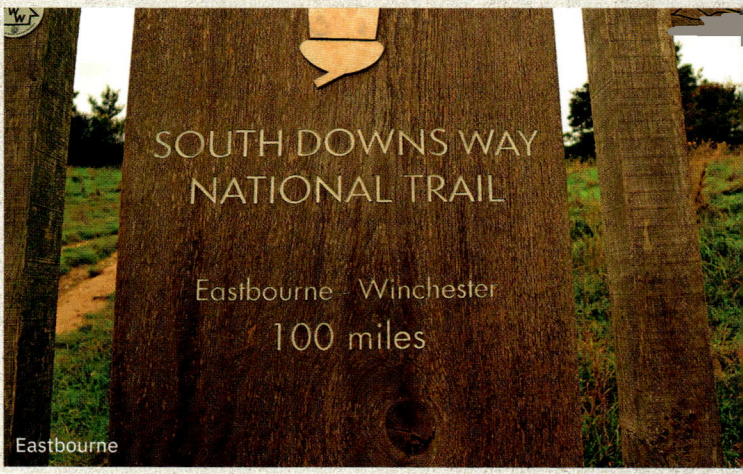
Eastbourne

THE BEACHY HEAD

Food with a view over the S Downs and towards the Belle Tout lighthouse and English Channel. Cask ales, wines and British gin in the garden or by log fires.

Beachy Head Rd, Beachy Head, Eastbourne, E Sussex BN20 7YA

www.vintageinn.co.uk/restaurants/south-east/thebeachyheadeastbourne#/

01323 728060

Dukes Dr meets Foyle Way, Eastbourne
The South Downs Way starts/ends with what is arguably the greatest and most scenic path in the world. This 'whale-backed' spine of chalk follows a line from white cliffs, beach and chalk water through trout-laden rivers, yew trees and a virtually treeless meadow of spring flowers and heath. The path starts as it ends, a climb onto a ridge of remarkable wilderness, views and clean air.
▶ **Find** where Dukes Dr meets Foyle Way, Eastbourne, BN20 7XN

50.752108, 0.267090

Well Combe, Holywell
Taste hawthorn blossom in spring from chalk down. Plenty of scattered scrub to find shade. See as far as Dungeness. Can be bleak up here in winter.
▶ **Find** Heathy Brow car park, Beachy Head Rd, BN20 7XY (50.7464712, 0.2556355). Exit the car park and walk across the Rd to meet the NT in 180m. Walk 800m (½ mile) NE to the site.

50.750504, 0.263930

Beachy Head Lighthouse, Holywell
Look for soaring kittiwakes. They nest on the chalk cliffs above the iconic red and white lighthouse. Belle Tout lighthouse is to the W and Birling Gap to the E.
▶ **Find** Beachy Head W car park, Beachy Head Rd, BN20 7YA (50.740004, 0.2470693). Exit the car park to the S and walk onto the coast path. Walk 320m (1,050ft) W to views over the lighthouse.

50.738089, 0.250137

SOUTH DOWNS WAY   157

THE CUCKMERE INN
Food with marshland views. Gardens and a gated entrance on to Exceat Bridge over the River Cuckmere.

Exceat Bridge, Cuckmere Haven, Seaford BN25 4AB

www.vintageinn.co.uk/restaurants/south-east/thecuckmereinn seaford#/

01323 892247

Beachy Head Cliffs
Move along the greatest 19km (12 miles) walk in the world. The cliffs are a nesting site for fulmars. Also a famous suicide spot, with its own chaplaincy team. Look for the flat wave-cut platform, best seen when the tide is out.
➤**Find** the path, 45 minutes from central London by train.

50.735804, 0.235174

Birling Gap, E Dean and Friston
Paddle the milky white seawater stained by the chalk cliffs. Alternatively, stay on top of the cliffs to use the viewing platform. There are geological information boards. The shore is good for rock pools and beachcombing.
➤**Find** Birling Gap and the Seven Sisters car park, Beachy Head Rd, BN20 0AD (50.743466, 0.202069).

50.742507, 0.200742

Cliff End Lagoon, Seaford
Listen to dunlin and redshank feeding around the lagoon. The beach is a 600m (⅓ mile) detour. It was an important landing place for smugglers in the Middle Ages.

50.759491, 0.151966

Cuckmere Canal, Seaford
Listen for brown trout feeding on flies in summer. Canada geese and Bewick's swans overwinter here. Herons and cormorants feed in summer.
➤**Find** Seven Sisters car park, Litlington Rd, BN25 4AD (50.7764250.151577). Exit parking to the S and keep walking across the Rd and 180m (590ft) to the river view.

50.769642, 0.148757

Seven Sisters Cliff End

BO-PEEP FARMHOUSE,

Country B&B in a Sussex Downs hamlet on the trail. Doubles and a twin; full English breakfast included. The farmhouse was once the home of the English painter Roger Fry.

Bopeep Ln, Alciston, Polegate, E Sussex, BN26 6UJ

www.bopeepfarmhouse.co.uk

01323 871299

YHA S DOWNS, LEWES

Bedrooms, bell tents, camping pods and Landpods in the grounds. Hostel was opened by Queen Elizabeth II in 2013. Self-catering kitchen, lounge and café.

Itford Farm, Beddingham, Lewes, E Sussex, BN8 6JS

www.yha.org.uk/hostel/yha-south-downs

03453 719574

THE ABERGAVENNY ARMS

A 15th-century country pub serving home-cooked food. Popular with walkers on the Way.

Newhaven Rd, Rodmell, Lewes, E Sussex, BN7 3EZ

www.abergavennyarms.com

01273 472416

Friston Forest, Cuckmere Valley
Smell the pine forest at its best in spring when surrounded with flowers. The path curves to the N past the edge of the forest.

50.781665, 0.157152

Cuckmere River, Alfriston
Look for the blue flash of a kingfisher. The ditches and drains are full of dragonflies. Seals sometimes swim upriver at high tide.

50.801190, 0.153922

Windover Hill, Wilmington
Smell downland flowers. This is the top of the old coach Rd from Eastbourne to Alfriston.
➤**Find** S Downs Way lay-by, Polegate, BN26 5RH (50.811689, 0.162670). Head E onto the NT and walk 1.6km (1 mile) on the BW to the site.

50.808116, 0.186400

The Long Man of Wilmington, Wilmington
Look for the largest human in Western Europe. The man is naked and holds two posts. A depression on the top E of the Long Man are the remains of the Neolithic flint mines.

50.810843, 0.188423

Firle Beacon Long Barrow, Firle
Big burial site and 360-degree views. Share the space with paragliders and hang-gliders on the thermals.
➤**Find** Bo Peep car park, BN26 6UJ (50.826176, 0.120128). Exit car park to the NW and walk 1.6km (1 mile) along the NT and BW to the site.

50.833595, 0.108004

River Ouse, Southease Bridge, Lewes
Junction busting with energy, that defies time and space. Riverside FP S and N, E bank or W bank. A church sits just over the water.
➤**Find** Firle Beacon car park, S Downs Way, BN8 6LR (50.833587, 0.083187). Exit the car park W and travel the NT and BW 4.8km (3 miles) to the river, via White Lion and Red Lion ponds.

50.830015, 0.025984

Monk's House, Rodmell
Author Virginia Woolf's 16th-century country home. Browse rooms, outdoor writing hut and gardens. Pre-booking essential.
www.nationaltrust.org.uk/visit/sussex/monks-house

50.838615, 0.016577

SOUTH DOWNS WAY 159

HOUSEDEAN FARM CAMPSITE

 Camping on a working farm. S Downs views. Campfires allowed.

Housedean Farm, Brighton Rd, Lewes, E Sussex, BN7 3JW

www.housedean.co.uk

07919 668816

THE HALF MOON

 Pub classics: gammon, egg and chips, pork belly, butternut squash curry and seafood specials.

www.thehalfmoonplumpton.co.uk

Ditchling Rd, Plumpton, Brighton, E Sussex, BN7 3AF

01273 890253

Seaford Head

Plumpton Plain, Plumpton Bostall
Graveyard, mounds and enclosure (50.896014, -0.053438) to S.

50.897194, -0.069469

Ditchling Beacon, Ditchling Bostall
Stargaze from the highest point (250m) on the S Downs. Find two dew ponds 500m (⅓ mile) W along the path.
▶**Find** Ditchling Beacon car park, BN6 8XD (50.901491, -0.105065). Exit car park to the W and walk 365m (1,200ft) along the NT and BW to the site.

50.905556, -0.115078

Clayton Windmills, Pyecombe
Look for the famous windmills on the horizon, known as 'Jack and Jill'. Views over the Brighton coast and N Downs.
▶**Find** Windmills car park, Clayton, BN6 9PG (50.905557, -0.1480785).

50.905377, -0.147475

Cuckmere River

THE PLOUGH PYECOMBE
 Family-run free house. Food and drink in the bar, restaurant or garden. Hikers and dog-walkers use the front patio area.

London Rd, Pyecombe, Brighton, E Sussex, BN45 7FN

www.theploughpyecombe.co.uk

01273 842796

THE WILDFLOWER CAFE
 Caravan kitchen for breakfasts and sourdough sandwiches.

Saddlescombe Farm, Saddlescombe Rd, Brighton, E Sussex, BN45 7DE

www.facebook.com/WildflourSouthDowns/?locale=en_GB

07821 604198

 ### Summer Down, Newtimber
Look for blue butterflies. Chalk hill blue and Adonis blue are common on this boreen walk.

50.885355, -0.196676

 ### Devil's Dyke, Poynings
Top TEN
The largest dry chalk valley in the county, a vast natural ditch with wildflowers and butterflies. Find Devil's Dyke car park, Devil's Dyke Rd, Brighton BN45 7FH.

50.882953, -0.204918

 ### Rook Clift, Elsted
Feel your way around one of the rarest woods in England: an ancient large-leaved lime woodland, on chalk, fed by ravine springs. Inevitably, rare insects and flowers are here too, most notably the cheese snail. Rook Clift is part of a primitive ash and beech woodland that spreads 8km (5 miles) S to the Yew Forest of Kingley Vale. (50.890831, -0.832836) and Wildhams Wood (50.916077, -0.834803).

50.957509, -0.834603

 ### Edburton Hill Castle, Edburton
Touch the old motte and bailey castle between Perching Hill and Edburton Hill.

50.885153, -0.241521

NATIONAL TRAILS

YHA TRULEIGH HILL

 Hostel just inland of coastal towns of Shoreham, Brighton, Hove and Worthing. Large grounds. Campfires, pond and nature areas.

Shoreham-by-Sea, W Sussex, BN43 5FB

www.yha.org.uk/hostel/yha-truleigh-hill

03453 719047

THE FRANKLAND ARMS

 Steaks, sausage and mash, fish pie and fry-ups. Large beer garden, and pet-friendly.

3 London Rd, Washington, Pulborough, W Sussex, RH20 4AL

www.thefranklandarms.com

01903 891405

WASHINGTON CARAVAN & CAMPING PARK

 Campsite at the foot of the S Downs, overlooked by Chanctonbury Ring. Open all year for electric hardstanding and grass-pitched caravans and campervans. Pitches for 80 tents.

London Rd, Washington, Pulborough, W Sussex, RH20 4AJ

www.washcamp.com

07746 698206

Beeding Hill Boreen, Horsham

Move along a 3.2km (2 miles) metal and gravel track between Edburton Hill and Anchor Bottom.

▶ **Find** Beeding Hill car park, S Downs Way, BN44 3TF (50.874459, -0.284533). Exit the car park to the NE and follow the NT and BW 1.6km (1 mile) to mid site.

50.880399, -0.268837

River Adur, Horsham

Look for cormorants feeding in the river and the drainage ditches. FP walk both S and N on E bank and W bank.

▶ **Find** the A283 car park, Steyning, BN44 3TN (50.874876, -0.299716). Exit the car park S and walk 365m (1,200ft) along the Rd to find the NT on the R. The trail shortly turns R to the river FB.

50.870979, -0.301890

St Botolph's Church, Steyning

Explore a Saxon church with medieval wall paintings. The main gate to the church is a recreation of an old Sussex design – a Tapsel gate, only found in Sussex.

50.870471, -0.305100

Annington Hill, Horsham

Move along a BW and boreen between the River Adur and Cross Dyke. The Downs Link path runs N along a disused railway line and links the S Downs Way with the N Downs Way.

50.870405, -0.329447

Top TEN Chanctonbury Ring, Wiston Bostal, Wiston, Horsham

A mass of beech trees planted on an Iron Age hillfort. It was also occupied by the Romans, who used the site as a temple. Disused pits to the W.

50.896759, -0.381160

River Ouse Peak

AMBERLEY BLACK HORSE

Award-winning restaurant and hotel. Homemade fishcakes, hand-dived scallops, fillet steak and fish of the day.

High St, Amberley, Arundel, W Sussex, BN18 9NL

www.amberleyblackhorse.co.uk

01798 831183

SOUTH DOWNS BUNKHOUSE

Beds for walkers and cyclists who want warm, comfortable accommodation at budget price. Houghton Farm is an arable and dairy farm. The bunkhouse is a converted barn.

Houghton Farm, Houghton, Arundel, BN18 9LW

www.southdownsbunkhouse.co.uk

01798 831100

THE GEORGE & DRAGON

Good food and real ales in one of the oldest pubs in Sussex. Dates back to 1276, and King Charles II may have stopped here in 1651 when escaping after his defeat at the Battle of Worcester.

Houghton, Arundel, W Sussex, BN18 9LW

www.thegeorgeanddragonhoughton.co.uk

01798 831559

Highden Hill Cross Dyke, Washington

Move around earthworks and burial sites. There's not much to see, but good for wildflowers and grasses.

➤**Find** Wiston Estate car park, Washington, RH20 4AZ (50.897114, -0.408075). Exit the car park W and walk S to cross the A24 London Rd. Keep following the NT and BW 1km (⅔ mile) to the site.

50.896197, -0.422013

Amberley Mount, Rackham

Listen to skylarks over open access chalk grassland. There's a burial site and views from the top.

➤**Find** Kithurst Hill car park, Storrington, RH20 4HW (50.902437, -0.479219). Exit the car W and walk along the NT and BW 3.2km (2 miles) to the site.

50.902527, -0.518522

River Arun, Houghton Bridge, Amberley

Listen to waterfowl from the new Brighton bridge over the river. FP walk N on both E and W bank.

➤**Find** Amberley train station, Houghton Bridge, BN18 9LR (50.896670, -0.541854). Exit the station to the N and follow the trail and river path 500m (⅓ mile) to the FB.

50.896748, -0.543369

Coombe Wood, Bury Hill

Look for fungi among the giant fallen trees. Walk the BW lined with hazel and grassy flowers. Much beech with holly around the wooded fringes.

50.898015, -0.568308

Chanterbury Ring

MANOR FARM CAMPSITE

Camping 100m off the trail. Farm shop and log cabin.

Hillbarn Ln, S Downs Cocking, Midhurst, GU29 0HS

www.manorfarmcocking.co.uk/camping.html

01730 814156

Harting Down

Westburton Hill Woodland, Bignor
Watch pearl-bordered fritillary butterflies feeding along the woodland rides.

50.909960, -0.594275

Bignor Hill, Bignor
Top TEN

The remnants of an ancient yew tree on Bignor Hill. The tree sits among wild garlic with views over the Arun Valley.

50.910012, -0.602819

Sutton Down, Slindon
Listen to barking deer in autumn along the downs and woodland margin. Stane St connects Chichester with London along this BW walk.

▶ **Find** Bignor Hill car park, S Downs Way, RH20 1PQ (50.908279, -0.616529). Exit the car park to the W and walk on the NT and BW 1.6km (1 mile) to the site.

50.909184, -0.636603

Combe Bottom, Heyshott Down Round Barrow Cemetery, Singleton
Explore a burial site dated to 1500 BC. The down is important, littered in tumuli and cross dykes. Cremations pots found here dating to Bronze Age and earlier.

50.940843, -0.711080

THE WHITE HART

 Old village pub with home-cooked meals and comfortable guest rooms.

The Street, S Harting, Petersfield, W Sussex, GU31 5QB

www.the-whitehart.co.uk

01730 825124

POUND ORCHARD B&B

 Stylish and modern B&B. Breakfast comes with coffee, tea, cereals, Dorset mueslis, sourdough toast.

Church St, E Meon, Petersfield, Hampshire, GU32 1NH

www.poundorchard bnb.co.uk

07957 592589

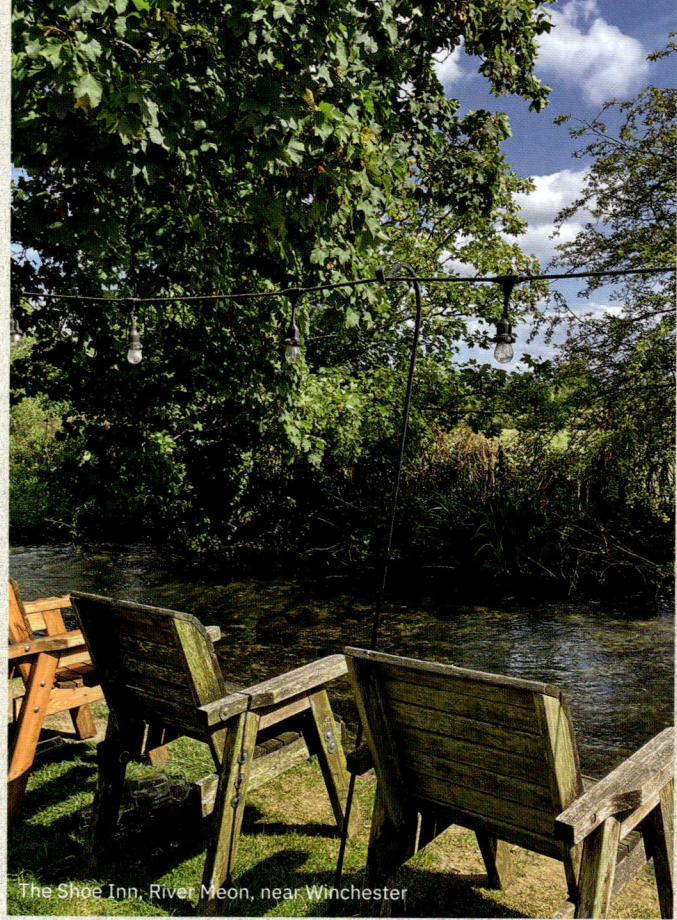

The Shoe Inn, River Meon, near Winchester

Cocking chalk stream, Crypt Farm, Cocking

Top TEN

Paddle a rare chalk stream and explore the plants that grow here. A 800m (½ mile) detour N from the path.

➤**Find** Cocking Hill car park, GU29 0HT (50.943134, -0.755742). Exit the car park to the W and walk 230m (750ft) to the GW on the R. Take the R turn and walk away from the NT for 500m (⅓ mile) to the site.

50.946777, -0.757855

Linch Ball, Newfarm Plantation, Bepton

Walk barefoot over a meadow of grass and clover. A 1.6km (1 mile) boreen crosses the site from Didling Hill to Cocking via Linch Ball. The peak reaches 248m (814ft) and is an old burial mount.

50.949474, -0.793779

NATIONAL TRAILS

SOUTH DOWNS WAY

WHITEWOOL FARM
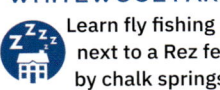
Learn fly fishing next to a Rez fed by chalk springs. Yurts also available. Meon Springs is considered one of Hampshire's best fly fisheries.

E Meon, Petersfield GU32 1HW

www.meonsprings.com

01730 823429

THE SHOE INN

Coffee made using the local Hampshire Pantry coffee beans. Riverside garden with views of Old Winchester Hill. Food from local suppliers, served in front of open log fires during autumn and winter.

Shoe Ln, Exton, Hampshire, SO32 3NT

www.theshoeexton.co.uk

01489 877526

 ## The Devil's Jumps, Elsted and Treyford
Feel the steep climb up to a Bronze Age tomb. Views as far as the Isle of Wight.

50.949182, -0.827030

 ## Beacon Hill Fort, E Harting
Catch a glimpse of tidal water off Chichester Harbour to the SW. Look out for orange berries of climbing bryony among hawthorn. They are extremely poisonous but the roots were used for medicine in ancient times. Feral pigeons feed in the stubble.

50.959197, -0.851913

 ## Harting Down, E Harting
Look for deer from the top of a 230m chalk valley. The S-facing slopes of the down are one of the few habitats in Britain warm enough to support the Adonis blue butterfly.

▶Find the Harting Down car park, off the B2141, GU31 5NG (50.956940, -0.876095). Exit the car park to the E and walk on the NT or BW over Harting Down towards Beacon Hill 2.4km (1½ miles away).

50.959860, -0.866368

 ## Butser Hill Burial, Langrish
Move along one of the most dramatic sections of path surrounded by chalk grass, woodland and field mushrooms. Explore the burial ground at the 270m (885ft) peak.

▶Find Queen Elizabeth Country Park car park, Petersfield, GU32 1QR (50.974768, -0.988151). Exit the car park E and, walking away from the NT, swing N for 800m (½ mile) towards the site.

50.977818, -0.980100

 ## Old Winchester Hill, Exton, Petersfield
Iron Age hillfort, surrounded by woodland and views.

▶Find Old Winchester Hill car park, Droxford Rd, Petersfield, GU32 1HW. Exit the car park S to find the NT. Follow it S and then W for 2km (1¼ miles) to the site.

50.980948, -1.088896

 ## Disused railway line, Exton, Winchester
Look for hares around the BW N and S. The line is almost 24km (15 miles), from Fareham to W Meon.

50.986624, -1.112067

HOLDEN FARM CAMPING & CAFE

Family campsite with fire pit pitches surrounded by farmland. Part of the National Park Dark Skies.

Holden Farm, Cheriton, Alresford, Hampshire, SO24 0NX

www.holdenfarm.co.uk

07599 553740

River Meon Bridge, Exton, Warnford

Paddle in a chalk stream. The crossing leads to a riverside track to St Peter and St Paul's Church. A remarkable headstone shows the Angel of Death summoning the scholar from his books.

50.987340, -1.119311

Top TEN
Beacon Hill Burial, Beacon Hill Nature Reserve, Exton

Look for any of 13 species of wild orchid that grow here on steep grass slopes.

▶**Find** Beacon Hill car park, SO32 3LG (51.001668, -1.148550). Exit the car park SE along the edge of the woodland and walk 500m (⅓ mile) along the NT and BW to the site.

50.998514, -1.141900

Lomer Village, High Dell Farm, Exton

Touch a prehistoric settlement that existed until the medieval era. Explore mounds in the ground and the old village pond (51.005540, -1.153448).

51.006860, -1.156107

Skull gravestone, St Peter and Paul's Church, Exton

SOUTH DOWNS WAY

Telegraph Hill, Chilcomb

Burial site with views over Winchester. Leads into Gypsy Ln.
▶**Find** Cheesefoot Head car park, Winchester, SO24 0HU (51.046500, -1.246389). Exit the car park W and walk 120m (390ft) NW on the Rd to meet the NT. Turn L and walk W along the trail and BW for 190m (590ft) before turning N and following the path 800m (½ mile) to the site.

51.049952, -1.257629

Winchester City Mill, Winchester

The S Downs Way starts/ends in a remarkable statement of time, the former Saxon capital of Wessex, beside the River Itchen. It's no more or less profound than Hadrian's Wall, Offa's Dyke or King Charles III ECP. Just another reminder that for all our mongrel past and likely future, it's less about those that rule or have ruled and more about good company, chalk streams, scrumping next to a long barrow under a cloudless sky on a warm June night.
▶**Find** the Winchester City Mill, Bridge St, Winchester, SO23 0EJ, beside the river.

51.061021, -1.307938

WILD THINGS TO DO BEFORE YOU DIE

TRAMP the greatest 19km (12 miles) walk in the world: from Eastbourne to Alfriston

TOUCH the remnants of an ancient yew tree

LOOK for the largest human in Western Europe: the Dodd man

STARGAZE from the highest point on the S Downs

EXPLORE the largest dry chalk valley in the county

INHALE the scent of a rare wood

LISTEN to birdsong at dusk on a tidal lagoon

SEE a mass of beech trees on an Iron Age hillfort

PADDLE a rare chalk stream and explore the plants that grow there

LOOK for 13 species of wild orchid on grassy slopes

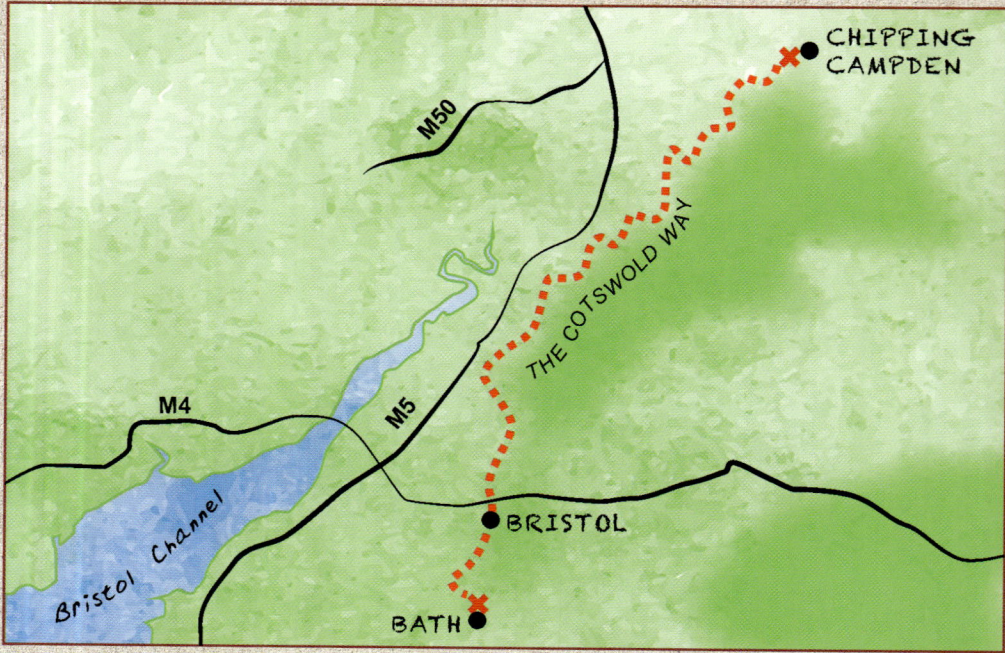

Top TEN

- ▶ **Burhill Iron Age Hillfort**, Explore overgrown mounds of trees and shrubs around a fort ruin.
  52.025597, -1.877453

- **Belas Knap Long Barrow**, Touch a 5,000-year-old gravesite.
  51.928376, -1.979574

- **Lineover Wood**, Smell wild garlic in spring around large-leaved lime trees.
  51.870531, -2.017629

- **Severn Springs Pub**, Read the stone: "HIC TUUS O TAMESINE PATER SEPTEMCEMINUS FONS". Believed to be one of the sources of the River Thames.
  51.851021, -2.048040

- **Little Sodbury Wood Fort**, Explore ramparts more than 2,000 years old.
  51.541578, -2.346836

- **Devil's Chimney**, Find the single, finger-like limestone chimney above the disused quarry.

- **Nympsfield Long Barrow**, Explore a 6,000-year-old barrow. Artefacts, human remains and flint tools have all been found here.
  51.710266, -2.299572

- **Source of the River Frome**, Look for the source of the Frome.
  51.510479, -2.344186

- **Cleeve Hill Wash Pool**, Touch the waterpool beside the River Isbourne. The highest point on the trail.
  51.935734, -2.006441

- ◉ **Kelston Roundhill**, The best view of Bath. Also see Bristol and the Severn Bridge.
  51.405790, -2.417704

COTSWOLD WAY

BEST FOR: LIME FOSSILS AND HISTORIC PLACES

Ashrams, orchids, limestone

START: CHIPPING CAMPDEN   FINISH: BATH

Sit alone at the Thomas Cromwell monument over the ruins of the Cistercian abbey, or peer into the 5,000-year-old grave of 30 people, to feel the separation and distance from the past.

The Cotswold Way is dominated by that thing we can't comprehend. Time. It is frozen into the fossilised limestone that shapes everything in the valleys below the trail: the cottages, the stone walls, the post offices, the school buildings. It's as offensive as a society of Stepford Wives.

Limestone fossils remind us of what we feel but can't understand. To stand on a hillfort over the Cotswold hills, it's impossible to imagine what life was like 2,500 years ago. It's beyond the scope of our current intellect. We mastered time in the past – but it's a secret lost or stolen to the CE epoch.

The city of Bath, Bath Abbey, manicured yew trees, Neolithic stone circles, Mesolithic, Bronze Age henges, and 17 Iron Age hillforts. They stand along the scarp valley and ridge. A reminder that something is missing, but is almost within arm's reach. It's a dizzying but worthwhile walk.

Broadway Tower

THE BROADWAY HOTEL

 A 16th-century inn with 19 bedrooms, and three cottages. Open fires and all-day food.

The Green, High St, Broadway, WR12 7AA

www.broadway-hotel.co.uk

01386 852401

THE LYGON ARMS

 A 600-year-old hotel that has hosted royals and rebels. Afternoon teas, meals and posh rooms.

High St, Broadway, WR12 7DU

www.lygonarmshotel.co.uk

01386 852255

 ## Chipping Campden Market Hall, Chipping Campden

The Cotswold Way starts/ends at an ornately scribed pavement plaque outside Market Hall, Chipping Campden, Gloucestershire. It's a town worthy of some time, not least for the church and its many rows of trees and views.

▶**Find** Market Hall, High St, Chipping Campden, GL55 6AJ

52.050724, -1.780680

 ## Dover Hill, Weston Subedge

Move along tree-lined avenues for views over the Vale of Evesham. Somewhere to appreciate the edge of the Cotswold escarpment.

▶**Find** Dover's Hill car park (52.054473, -1.801993), Weston Subedge, Chipping Campden, GL55 6UW. Exit the car park NNE and walk 140m (460ft) to the scarp edge and views.

52.055084, -1.802238

St James Church, Chipping Campden

BUCKLAND MANOR

Hotel and award-winning restaurant with produce from the Vale of Evesham. Afternoon teas with champagne on the terraces, or by the fire.

Broadway, Worcestershire, WR12 7LY

www.bucklandmanor.co.uk

01386 852626

NORTH FARMCOTE B&B

B&B on a working family farm for sheep and cereals. Single and double rooms. Visit the herb garden – 30 varieties of chilli peppers, plus Vietnamese coriander, mints, sages, thymes, basil, bergamot and many more.

N Farmcote, Winchcombe, Gloucestershire, GL54 5AU

www.northfarmcote.co.uk

01242 602304

Market Hall, Chipping Campden

The Kiftsgate Stone, Weston Subedge
Touch the Neolithic moot stone on the Mile Dr. The stone is hard to find between plants on the edge of Weston Park.
▶ **Find** Fish Hill car park, WR12 7LD (52.030579, -1.826359). Exit the car park N and follow the NT NEE across Buckle St for 2.8km (1¾ miles) to site.

52.049007, -1.804327

Burhill Iron Age Hillfort, Buckland
Top TEN
Explore a fort ruin. Overgrown mounds with trees and shrubs, but all the better for that. The fort once covered 3 hectares (7.4 acres). Short detour via FP from Way. St Michael Church, Buckland, Broadway, WR12 7LY is 500m (⅓ mile) from the fort.

52.025537, -1.877453

The Stanton Guildhouse, Stanton
Enrol in summer schools in arts and crafts in the wild. This 'ashram' was set up in 1973 by Mary Osborn after she met Mahatma Gandhi in the 1930s. She was interested and inspired by retreats he founded in wild spaces in India. Gandhi's belief centred on the idea that there is a 'spiritual' aspect to the simplest of human activities, especially when using traditional skills and basic materials. Gandhi's philosophy encouraged Osborn to turn her home into a centre dedicated to traditional crafts. The centre has continued after her death.

52.00601444120923, -1.8946486612218183

Church of St Michael and All Angels, Broadway
Touch the ancient cross on a walk up towards the church. The large yew trees make this a special place.

52.022232, -1.882331

CLEEVE HILL HOTEL

Inhale clean air from a hotel at the peak of the Cotswolds, with views over the Malvern Hills. Home-baked cookies or cakes in the honesty bar are a nice touch.

Cleeve Hill, Cheltenham, Gloucestershire, GL52 3PR
www.cleevehillhotel.co.uk
01242 672052

Cromwell's Seat, Beckbury Camp, Wood Stanway
Stand at the spot where Thomas Cromwell watched Hailes Abbey burn following the dissolution. The valley views against a woodland are always cool in summer. The limestone monument sits on the edge of a hillfort known as 'Beckbury Camp'.

51.967975, -1.909880

Hailes Abbey, Hailes, Nr Winchcombe
Touch the cloister ruins of the Cistercian abbey, which dates from 1246. A little church is next door. The museum is also worth a look and good for a cuppa.

51.968916, -1.926664

Belas Knap Long Barrow, Winchcombe
Explore a 5,000-year-old gravesite. More than 30 people were found buried in the four chambers. Look for cowslips around the edges of the barrow.

51.928376, -1.979574

Cleeve Hill Wash Pool, Southam
Touch the waterpool beside the River Isbourne. The highest point on the trail. A rare moment on a trail that is almost devoid of water, other than man-made dew ponds. Good views over Cheltenham.
▶ **Find** Cleeve Hill Common car park, Southam, GL52 3NF (51.922305, -2.0102494), for easy access.

51.935734, -2.006441

Cleeve Ring Settlement, Cleeve Hill, Southam
Smell wildflowers in summer. Views over the Malvern Hills. Golf club for food and drinks.
▶ **Find** Cleeve Hill N car park, Southam, GL52 3PW (51.9218761, -2.010232). Exit the car park S and walk 1km (⅔ mile) SSW across the common to the site.

51.937813, -2.023493

The Memorial Tree, Tewkesbury
Move around the top of the fort, for views from a perfectly positioned bench (51.929062, -2.019713).

51.929177, -2.020079

Bill Smyllie's Reserve, Tewkesbury
Listen to finches and long-tailed tits over gorse-lined sandy track.

51.916143, -2.014281

The Lynches Wood, Weston Subedge

UPPER HILL FARM B&B

B&B on the edge of Cleeve Common. Flagstone flooring, wooden beams and exposed stone walls.

Beechfield House,
Upper Hill Farm,
Whittington, Cheltenham,
Gloucestershire, GL54 4EU

www.upperhillfarm.co.uk
01242 235128

Dowdeswell Wood and Rez, Charlton Kings

Look for roe deer that feed in this spruce woodland. The edges are bordered in hazel, elder and ash. Parts of the forest are extremely thick and dark, making it a good place to find shelter from heat or rain. Good for kingfishers as the woodland is fed by many springs. The River Chelt feeds into the Rez at the S end of the wood. Native white-clawed crayfish in the Rez.

51.877494, -2.019455

Top TEN Lineover Wood, Dowdeswell

Find and touch large-leaved lime trees and beech. These limes are rare in England. The woods are also full of wild garlic in spring. Other rare plants include angular Solomon's seal and lily-of-the-valley. Red, roe and fallow deer graze in the wood.

51.870531, -2.017629

Ravensgate Hill, Pegglesworth

Look for purple toadflax on the uphill walk. Used in folklore as a herbal wash for skin complaints and inflammation. Find the bench at the top of Ravensgate Hill for big views.

51.864857, -2.029188

Top TEN Seven Springs, Coberley

Read the stone: "HIC TUUS O TAMESINE PATER SEPTEMCEMINUS FONS". Here, O Father Thames, is your sevenfold spring. Believed to be one of the sources of the River Thames. Steps fall down among the trees to the Seven Springs. Best in spring when bluebells and wild garlic are out. Also common spotted and pyramidal orchids.

51.851112, -2.050498

STAR GLAMPING

Camping without the hassle of tent pegs or rain, specifically for people with disabilities. Right on the trail. The National Star group objective is to help people with disabilities realise their potential as active citizens in control of their lives.

Ullenwood Manor Rd, Ullenwood, Cheltenham, Gloucester, GL53 9QU

www.nationalstar.org/visit-us/starglamping

01242 527631

Dover's Hill

Devil's Chimney, Shurdington
Top TEN

Find the single, finger-like limestone chimney above the disused quarry. Burials, barrows and a hillfort show how important this place was, and is. The ruins and geology match the big skies and Cheltenham views from a plateau of orchids and butterflies.

▶**Find** Daisy Bank car park, Shurdington, Cheltenham, GL53 9QQ (51.868629, -2.0743859). Exit the car park S and walk across the Rd to the FP, which runs S to the NT. After 800m (½ mile) meet the NT and turn R, walking W towards the site, 320m (1,050ft) away.

51.864246, -2.077291

Salterley Grange, Shurdington

Pine woodland bordered by a stone wall.

▶**Find** Hartley Ln car park, GL53 9QJ (51.857917, -2.0797785). Exit the car park E and join the NT after 90m (295ft). Turn R and walk S to join the Rd. Follow the NT E and then SW for 800m (½ mile) towards the site.

51.855249, -2.077423

Crickley Hill, Nr Birdlip, Coberley

Look for purple devil's-bit scabious. The ancients used the plant as important medicine for leprosy, flu, tickly coughs and adder bites. The Brecon Beacons can be seen on a clear day. Crickley Hill Fort predates the Iron Age.

▶**Find** Crickley Hill car park, Cotswold Way, GL4 8JY (51.845523, -2.105225) for easy access by Rd.

51.845876, -2.103736

COTSWOLD WAY 175

THE ROYAL GEORGE HOTEL

 Dog-friendly bedrooms in 26 acres of land, with Cotswold views.

Birdlip, Gloucester, Gloucestershire, GL4 8JH

www.greenekinginns.co.uk/hotels/gloucestershire/royal-george-hotel

01452 862506

Barrow Wake, Birdlip

Barrow is long gone under the Rd but the wooded views over the Severn Valley predate the 5,000-year-old burial.

▶ **Find** Barrow Wake car park, off the A417, GL4 8JX (51.837352, -2.100843). Exit the car park at the midpoint to the NW to find the viewpoint.

51.836570, -2.101797

Witcombe Wood springs, Great Witcombe

Listen for water. Pine and beech wood is full of springs, particularly around the centre of the wood.

51.822262, -2.123669

Cooper's Hill Wood, Brockworth

Move over grass-plateau views after a N climb on the path.

▶ **Find** Cooper's Hill car park, Gloucester, GL3 4SB (51.825125, -2.167724). Exit the car park S to find the NT and follow the path 800m (½ mile) W and then S to find the site.

51.828822, -2.159846

Mary's Church, Painswick

Touch ornate yew trees, clipped into straitjackets, but cleverly year-marked. A festival of 99 yews, they say. If only the curators could allow one or two to grow wild. Snowdrops in late winter.

51.785680, -2.194852

Church of St Michael and All Angels, Stanton

ST MICHAEL'S RESTAURANT AND B&B

 Rooms and restaurant overlooking the St. Mary's Church yews. Walk the narrow streets among medieval cottages of what was once part of the flourishing wool and cloth trade.

Victoria St, Painswick, Stroud GL6 6QA

www.stmichaelsbistro.co.uk

01452 812712 (B&B); 01452 203306 (restaurant)

THE VINE TREE INN, RANDWICK

 Good views, beer garden and food. Roast chicken and curries are among top dishes.

Randwick, Stroud, Gloucestershire, GL6 6JA

Maitlands Wood, Painswick

Look for butterflies and orchids at the entrance to Maitlands Woodland. The site is a disused quarry that has been returned to nature. An unusual horseshoe-shaped boreen runs for 3.2km (2 miles) from St John the Baptist Church, Edge, Stroud down the W side of Maitlands Wood, and then back up to link with Haresfield hillfort.

51.781083, -2.223322

Haresfield Hill boreen, Haresfield

Boreen detour (that link with previous boreen) from Cliff Wood (51.783315, -2.244299) to Haresfield hillfort (51.778387, -2.250665), via Harefield Camp (51.775932, -2.244814). The single track loops 2.6km (1.6 miles) S, around Broadbarrow Green, and links at both ends with the Cotswold Way. Haresfield Beacon has views as far as the Severn Bridge, Wye and the Welsh border.

51.778624, -2.260867

Teffa Bear Cave, Standish

Explore the cave beneath Haresfield Mount.

▶**Find** Haresfield Hill car park, Standish GL6 6PP. Exit the car park S to find the NT, then turn R, and follow the trail for 500m (⅓ mile) SWW to find the top. The cave is 140m (460ft) S.

51.773040, -2.250218

Standish Cross Dyke, Standish

Move over an Iron Age cross dyke. You'll find it halfway along a boreen, Robbers Rd, in Standish Wood. The single-track boreen is no longer open to traffic as it has been gated. It remains open to horse riders and walkers as a 1.6km (1 mile) BW from Ash Ln, at the S end of Standish Wood (51.757656, -2.256907), to Randwick Rd (51.764001, -2.245902). Cross dykes date from the Bronze Age, usually to mark boundary lines. They are often found on drove roads or tracks associated with hillforts. Prehistoric camps and Haresfield hillfort are situated less than 1.6km (1 mile) N of the cross dyke in the upper regions of Standish Wood. Robbers Rd marks the boundary line for Standish Parish and Randwick and Westrip Parish.

51.762078, -2.251904

Standish Wood Long Barrow, Randwick

Best in spring when the beech woodland is full of wood anemone, cowslip and bluebell. Look for orchids in late spring. Robber's Rd is a prehistoric burial site of barrows and tumuli set on a rocky outcrop of dense woodland.

51.760273, -2.256289

COTSWOLD WAY 177

GATEKEEPERS LODGE

 Gatekeepers Lodge for two people. Bike storage. Outdoor dining area, BBQ in the secret courtyard.

Upper St, Dyrham, Nr Bath, Somerset, SN14 8HN

www.gatekeeperslodge.co.uk

51.479091, -2.375774

 Stroudwater Canal, Kings Stanley, Stroud
Canalised walk W of Ebley, almost 1.6km (1 mile) long, lined with beech and hazel.

51.739705, -2.266525

 Pen Hill Wood, Nympsfield
Feel dappled sunshine on skin in a woodland of giant beech and pine. Wood anemones, celandine and snowdrops in early and late spring.

51.720153, -2.266422

 Top TEN Nympsfield Long Barrow, Frocester
Explore a 6,000-year-old barrow. Artefacts, human remains and flint tools have all been found here. Another barrow 1.6km (1 mile) S (51.698714, -2.305985).
▸**Find** Coaley Peak car park, off the B4066, GL11 5AU (51.7104523, -2.298707). Exit the car park to the N and the site is 45m (150ft) to the N.

51.710266, -2.299572

 Uley Long Barrow, Coaley
Squeeze inside with a torch and some imagination. A pig-tusk pendant and human remains were found inside. The site has been dated to be at least 6,000 years old.

51.698738, -2.305963

Humblebee Wood, Winchcombe

Belas Knap

WOODLAND HOUSE B&B

 B&B with bike storage and laundry. Double and single rooms.

13 Woodland Ave, Dursley, Gloucestershire, GL11 4EW

www.woodlandhousebnb.co.uk

01453 298773

🌳 Cam Long Down, Cam

Smell the scent of a bluebell-laden wood in spring. Hillside woods and Cam Peak. Possible to see the Severn Estuary, Gloucester, Malvern Hills and even the Black Mountains.

▶**Find** Cam Peak car park, Springhill, GL11 5HH (51.693287, -2.338469). Exit the car park to the S across and up to Cam Peak 365m (1,200ft) away. Once at the peak, take the FP E for 275m (900ft) to join the NT and BW. Keep walking E for 800m (½ mile) to reach the peak.

51.694114, -2.328291

🌙 Drakestone Point, Stinchcombe

The climb to the monument is worth it for views of S Wales and Tyndale Monument.

▶**Find** Stinchcombe Hill car park, Dursley, GL11 6AQ (51.683823, -2.371725). Exit the car park to the W and follow the NT W for 800m (½ mile) to the site.

51.681337, -2.381801

🌙 Brackenbury Ditches Hillfort, N Nibley

Touch fort ramparts 800m (½ mile) S of William Tyndale Monument, along this beech and hazel woodland walk. Tyndale translated the New Testament into English.

51.652094, -2.364597

Wotton-under-Edge, Coombe

Move along a 1.6km (1 mile) boreen from Holywell, Stroud, to Wotton-under-Edge, Stroud. Blackquarries Hill, Holywell (51.642740, -2.337602) is metal Rd, path to Tor Hill is grassy (51.637917, -2.329300).

51.638949, -2.322965

Wortley Hill, Wotton-under-Edge
This Jurassic-style valley path is both daunting and impressive, with steep banks on either side of Wortley Hill.

51.628468, -2.330202

St Adeline's Church, Little Sodbury
Touch the carved wood inside the church. The churchyard is full of flowers in spring and swallows in summer.

51.547768, -2.351484

Little Sodbury Wood Fort, Horton
Move around ditches and ramparts that are more than 2,000 years old. This 10-acre hillfort is on grass meadow. Used by the Saxons after the Romans left.

51.541578, -2.346836

Source of the River Frome, Sodbury
Look for the Frome (51.510952, -2.345559) – the source is just to the SE a few metres.

51.510479, -2.344186

Dyrham Park, Dyrham, Nr Bath
Woodland walk of hazel and pine. Views of Severn Bridge, Pen y Fan and the Brecon Beacons. Mansion estate with gardens, lakes and deer park.

51.481577, -2.377373

Holy Trinity Church, Cold Ashton
Holy Trinity Church is at the end of a grass-lined boreen track.

51.453026, -2.359714

Cooper's Hill

HILL FARM

 B&B a day's walk 14.5km (9 miles) from Bath and on the Cotswold Way. Cook your own English breakfast from fresh produce provided. Evening meals and picnic lunches available.

Greenway Ln, Cold Ashton, Chippenham, SN14 8LA

www.hillfarmbath.com

01225 891952

Dyrham Park

Sir Bevil Grenville's Monument, Charlcombe, Bath
Read up on the memorial marking the Civil War Battle of Lansdown Hill of 1643. Information boards give details. Also interesting for the beech trees.

51.431892, -2.399929

 ### Kelston Roundhill, Kelston
The best view of Bath. You can also see Bristol and the Severn Bridge in the distance.

51.405790, -2.417704

 ### Kingston Parade, York St, Bath
The Cotswold Way starts/ends with a carved stone disc outside Bath Abbey, although it is a better place to finish rather than to start. The city embodies much of what the trail is: a historic exploration of trade, culture and human nature. Orchids and stone circles. Limestone hillforts and sanctuaries. History and ancient roads.

▶ **Find** Kingston Parade, York St, Bath, BA1 1NG.

51.380924, -2.359002

Belas Knap Long Barrow

WILD THINGS TO DO BEFORE YOU DIE

FIND a limestone chimney

SMELL wild garlic in a lime woodland

VISIT a 5,000-year-old gravesite

MOVE around 2,000-year-old ramparts

LOOK for the source of the Frome

FEEL a waterpool at highest point of the trail

STAND over the best view of Bath

EXPLORE a fort ruin

TOUCH ornate yew trees

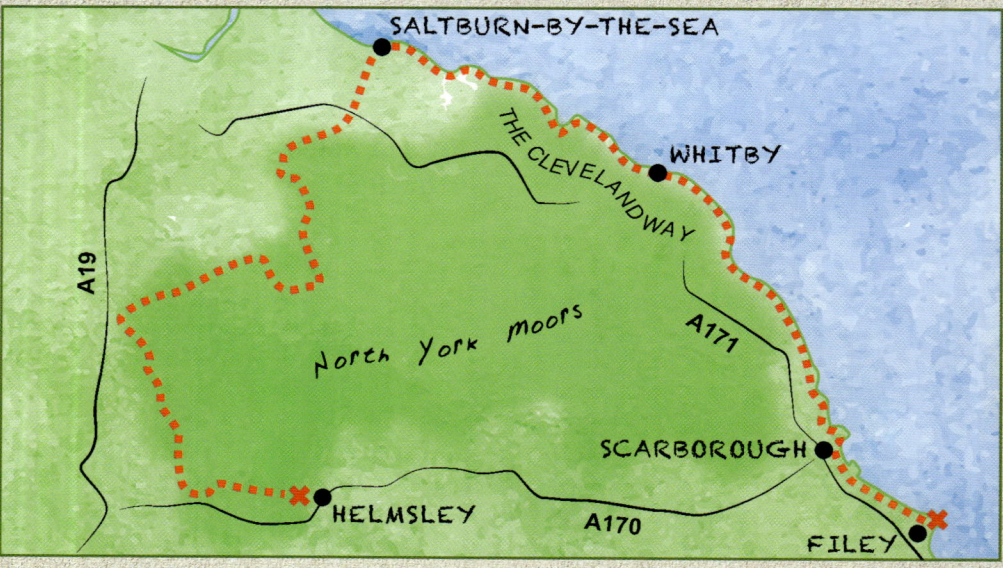

 **Top TEN**

 ▶ **Fairies Parlour (cave),** Look for bats around a cave at dusk.
54.245462, -1.222554

 Windypit Tumulus, Touch mounds and ditch of an Iron Age hillfort built into the limestone.
54.263352, -1.225067

 Wainstones, Stand at the foot of huge sandstone blocks that form the Wainstones. Some of the best views over the N York Moors are from Hasty Bank.
54.424417, -1.138531

 Greenhow Bank BW, Wait to spot giant eagle owls hunt E of Wainstones.
54.423717, -1.068591

 Round Hill, The highest point in the N York Moors.
54.405696, -1.085942

 Ingleby Incline, Scramble up one of the toughest climbs on the path.
54.417667, -1.068074

 Roseberry Well, Climb Yorkshire's Matterhorn for views over N York Moors and over Middlesbrough to the sea.
54.505460, -1.106874

 Guisborough Wood Springs, The largest woodland on the Cleveland Way is pine and broadleaf trees over heather.
54.521019, -1.039548

 Boulby Mines, Spend some time around one of the best places in UK to see bats. Ten species of bat live along the trail, several of them here.
54.562405, -0.825423

 ▶ **The Coomb,** Look for seals from the cliff platform.
54.404615, -0.489340

Greenhow Plantation

CLEVELAND WAY

BEST FOR: BIRDS AND BATS

Yorkshire Matterhorn, heather, bat caves

START: HELMSLEY   FINISH: FILEY BRIGG

The Cleveland Way is a pagan marriage of love and convenience, the only trail that cohabits with three other National Trails.

It is the polygamous nature of the path that makes it special in the pantheon of 'pagan' unions. Wainwright stole what he considered the best 14 miles of the Cleveland Way to yoke it with his life's love, the Coast to Coast trail.

The Cleveland Way forms another match at Filey Brigg with a second mistress: the Wolds Way. And then there's the England Coast Path from Saltburn to... yep, Filey. A handsome threesome.

YHA HELMSLEY

Award-winning hostel, surrounded by some good independent cafés, bookshops and galleries.

Carlton Ln, Helmsley, N Yorkshire, YO62 5HB

www.yha.org.uk/hostel/yha-helmsley

03453 719638

THE FEATHERS HOTEL
A 16th-century coaching inn for overnight and dinner. Open fires in winter, courtyard in summer. Seasonal menus; local sourced ingredients.

Market Pl, Helmsley, N Yorkshire, YO62 5BH

www.feathershotelhelmsley.co.uk

01439 770275

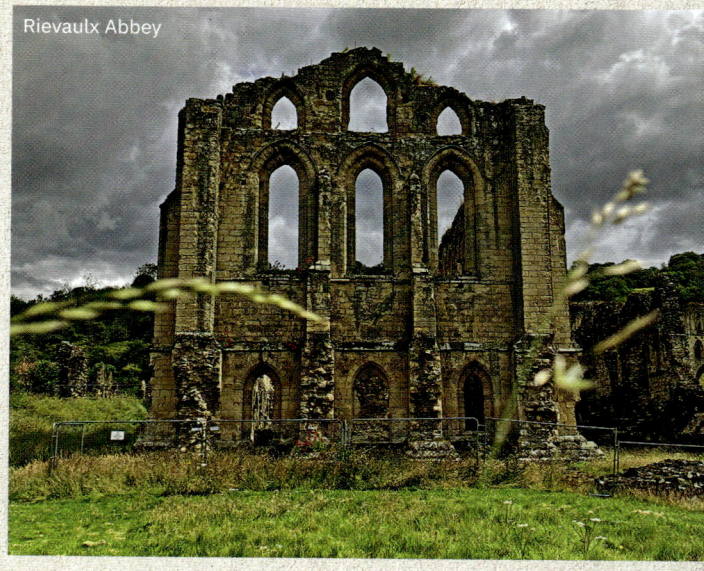

Rievaulx Abbey

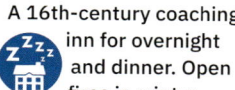 **Cleveland Way/High St, Helmsley**
The Cleveland Way starts/ends in a market square, on the soft edge of the Yorkshire Moors. The moors' edge defines the trail, from stalls to beach. Heather, bat caves and giant owls. The peak of the Yorkshire Matterhorn is almost as iconic as the moors.
➤Find Cleveland Way car park, 17 Cleveland Way, Helmsley, YO62 5AZ (54.246889, -1.064966). Exit car park to the N and walk E towards the start site.

54.246556, -1.061236

 Helmsley Castle, Castlegate
Pass the castle ruin as you leave the town. It's worth an hour or more. Best at dawn in spring for photos and wildflowers. Look for the hiding places and castle stories.

54.245631, -1.066407

Rievaulx Bridge, Rievaulx
Paddle barefoot down to the water to walk over the stony riverbed. Abbey detour is less than 1.6km (1 mile) N. Ruins of the 800-year-old Rievaulx Abbey are beautifully framed by the wooded river valley. A good place to relax.
➤Find Rievaulx Abbey car park and visitor centre, YO62 5LB (54.257302, -1.118775). Exit the car park S and follow the Ln 800m (½ mile) to the bridge site.

54.251118, -1.120601

NATIONAL TRAILS

Church of St Michael, Cold Kirby

Knights Templar church. It was taken over by the Knights Hospitallers when the Templars had their lands seized. The font is 12th-century, albeit the current church was rebuilt in the 19th century.

54.253483, -1.182671

White Horse Hill Figure, Kilburn High and Low

The largest and most northerly of England's horse figures, surrounded by woodland views, at the S end of Sutton Bank. The work of local schoolmaster John Hodgson and 30 volunteers, who dug it out in 1857. A very recent addition to the prehistoric 'horse' sculptures around Britain, but still impressive. There are more than 100 steps. Feels like more when climbing into the wind. Wildflowers surround the site.

54.224981, -1.211834

Sutton Bank National Park Centre, Sutton Bank

Walks, bike trails and lots of area information.
01845 597426 https://www.northyorkmoors.org.uk/things-to-do/attractions/sutton-bank-national-park-centre (01845 597426)

54.240873, -1.208560

Sutton Bank Tumuli, Hambleton

Burial ground and bench views over Happy Valley. Many wildflowers in May.
▶**Find** Sutton Bank car park, off A170, YO7 2HJ (54.240952, -1.210908). Exit car park SW down the Ln to join A170. NT and FP is across the Rd. Follow the trail 550m (1,800ft) SE.

54.236453, -1.208420

Carlton Moor

THE GOLDEN LION

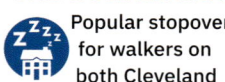

Popular stopover for walkers on both Cleveland Way and C2C. Classic pub food, real ales and wines. Comfortable and stylish rooms.

6 W End, Osmotherley, Northallerton, N Yorkshire, DL6 3AA

www.goldenlionosmotherley.co.uk

01609 883526

THE QUEEN CATHERINE HOTEL

The UK's only Queen Catherine Hotel. Family-owned pub for food and rooms on the N York Moors. Pub history dates back more than 300 years.

7 W End, Osmotherley, Northallerton, N Yorkshire, DL6 3AG

www.queencatherinehotel.co.uk

01609 883209

Sutton Brow, Sutton-under-Whitestonecliffe

Wooded plantation of high drama. Denser and darker than a boat trip into Joseph Conrad's soul. The sides of Sutton Bank are the western entrance to the formidable N York Moors.

54.240687, -1.214213

Garbutt Wood, Sutton-under-Whitestonecliffe

Broadleaf woodland for deer and birds. Gormire Lake is worth a detour on W edge of wood. There are only four natural lakes in Yorkshire… this is one of them. The other three include Malham Tarn.

54.244002, -1.226467

Fairies Parlour (cave), Sutton-under-Whitestonecliffe

Look for bats around the cave at dusk.

54.245462, -1.222554

Hill Fort Windypit Tumulus, Boltby

Ruin of Iron Age hillfort over a grass-covered mound and ditch. The old fort was built into the limestone and sunken hollows known as 'Windypits Lake'.

54.263352, -1.225067

High Barn burial ground, Boltby, Hambleton

Burial ground at 300m, with views over Little Moor valley. Look for fungi among fallen branches and oak tree canopy.

54.273059, -1.223599

Hambleton Drove Rd, Hawnby

This prehistoric drove Rd is now a BW. Despite its ancient origins, Hambleton Drove Rd was busiest in the 18th and 19th centuries, when Scottish cattlemen drove their herds of sheep and cattle from the hills to market towns in England.

54.293939, -1.225994

Little Moor burial ground, Kepwick

Burial ground at 374m (1,225ft) above the heather of Little Moor. Look out for merlins.

54.306576, -1.247910

Whitestones, Kepwick

High peak of Whitestones Scar (372m (1,220ft)) for views over Kepwick Moor. Look for peregrines around the disused quarries. There are also old tramways to explore.

54.331642, -1.246509

186 NATIONAL TRAILS

CLEVELAND WAY 187

COTE GHYLL MILL YOUTH HOSTEL

 N York Moors hostel in a converted linen mill. Clean and good facilities. The hostel sleeps between 2 and 61. (Also features as part of the C2C path).

Cote Ghyll, Osmotherley, Northallerton, N Yorkshire, DL6 3AH

www.coteghyll.com/mill

01609 883425

Wainstones

St Peter's Church, Osmotherley
Find the original Viking hogback gravestone. Also 10th-century carved stones in the porch.

54.368275, -1.299764

Mount Grace Priory, House and Gardens, Staddlebridge
The largest Carthusian priory in Britain is a short detour from the path. (Also features as part of the C2C path).

54.379692, -1.310021

Arncliffe Wood, E Harlsey
Mixture of pine, beech and alder. C2C E path is close to the Cleveland Way here, which it follows for 64km (40 miles).

54.382717, -1.302851

Live Moor Cairn, Hambleton
Burial grounds span this stretch of five moors: Scarth Wood Moor, Live Moor, Cringle Moor, Cold Moor and Hasty Bank.

54.404859, -1.223149

Claybank

KILDALE CAMPING & BARN

 Working farm campsite for families and walkers. Toilets, showers and barbecues. Dogs, sheep, cows and the farm chickens.

Park Farm, Kildale, Whitby, N Yorkshire, YO21 2RN

www.kildalebarn.co.uk

01642 722847

 ### Lordstones, Carlton in Cleveland
Former mine centre for rare jet, found nowhere else in the UK. Views up here over Roseberry Topping and Captain Cook's Monument.

54.420893, -1.191483

 ### Clain Wood, Swainby
Pine woodland walk.

54.398699, -1.262911

 ### Top TEN Wainstones, Hambleton
Some of the best views over the N York Moors are from Hasty Bank.
▶ **Find** Clay Bank car park, TS9 7HX (54.424281, -1.1198496). Exit the car park W to find the Rd and then turn L and walk S 320m (1,050ft) to find the NT. Turn R onto the trail and follow it W for 3.2km (2 miles) to the site.

54.424417, -1.138531

COTE GHYLL CARAVAN & CAMPING PARK

 N York Moors camping and cottages on the edge of Osmotherley. On-site café. Toilets, showers and a stream for paddling. (Also features as part of the C2C path).

Cote Ghyll, Osmotherley, Northallerton, N Yorkshire, DL6 3AH

www.coteghyll.com
01609 883425

Greenhow Bank BW, Hambleton

Eagle owls hunt E of Wainstones. Giant female birds are taller than a golden retriever dog (75cm (2½ft)) and can even catch foxes and small deer. Look for the chalky-white faeces of eagle owls in the rock. The call of these birds is eerily human. They are most likely to be heard at dusk.

▶ **Find** Clay Bank car park (see left). Exit the car park W to find the Rd and then turn L and walk S 320m (1,050ft) to find the NT. Turn L onto the trail and follow it E for 6.4km (4 miles) to the site.

54.423717, -1.068591

Wainstones Boreen, Hambleton

A 16km (10 miles) BW and boreen from the Wainstones FP (54.422074, -1.118786 – BW is 1.6km (1 mile) from the stones) to Kildale (54.476355, -1.063922) to Combe Bank (54.541810, -1.003404).

54.426774, -1.070055

Round Hill, Urra Moor, Bilsdale Midcable

Views SW from Round Hill trig from the highest point in the N York Moors. The Bloworth crossing, just beyond Urra Moor, is an old railway crossing that brought ironstone out of Rosedale to the heavy industry plants of Teesside and Durham.

54.405696, -1.085942

Urra Moor

Ingleby Incline, Ingleby Greenhow
Scramble up one of the toughest climbs on the path.

54.417667, -1.068074

 ### Burton Howe Tumuli, Ingleby Greenhow
Bronze Age burials at a BW junction. Of the four large mounds, Burton Howe is the most southerly – it is 1.7m (5.5ft) high and 15m (50ft) in diameter.

54.420915, -1.065615

 ### The Park, Kildale
Grassy plateaux of rocks and springs. Area is fenced to keep farm animals in, so limited access.

54.469706, -1.063291

 ### Captain Cook's Monument, Easby Moor, Great Ayton
Captain Cook's Monument is an 18m obelisk erected in 1827 to one of England's most celebrated travellers. A landmark feature on the horizon, and surrounded in gorse and skylarks, it's good to see from a distance or up close.

54.482329, -1.090727

 ### Great Ayton Moor Enclosure, Great Ayton
First clear sight of Roseberry Well (see below) across the heather. Prehistoric settlements and farm site. Neolithic burial with Captain Cook's Monument to the rear.
▶**Find** Gribdale Gate, Capt Cook's car park, TS9 6HN (54.491393, -1.087248). Exit the car park N onto the NT and walk N for 1km (⅔ mile) to the site.

54.498348, -1.085451

 ### Roseberry Well, Guisborough, Redcar and Cleveland
Known as 'Yorkshire's Matterhorn'. But it's better than that. Look out for fossils in any rocks you pass as you climb. Views of Roseberry Well are better from below than those from the top. When Roseberry Topping comes into sight, it's quite remarkable and inspiring. This is the famous landmark on the N York Moors, as it sits isolated from the rest of the Cleveland Hills.

As good as it looks from the ground, the climb up the 320m (1,050ft) peak is necessary. Views of N York Moors and over Middlesbrough to the sea.

54.505460, -1.106874

CLEVELAND WAY 191

BROCKLEY HALL
AA 4-star hotel with a quirky bar. Restaurant and brasserie for breakfast, lunch, dinners.
Glenside, Saltburn-by-the-Sea, N Yorkshire, TS12 1JS
www.brockleyhallhotel.com
01287 622179

Roseberry Common, Guisborough
Look for roe deer around the common and bluebells in the woodland.
54.506264, -1.100781

Highcliff Nab, Guisborough
Climb through trees and past rock face to views over Guisborough, Roseberry Topping and the Captain Cook Monument. The rock formations are peppered in pink fireweed and lichen.
54.515941, -1.057216

Guisborough Wood Springs, Guisborough
The largest woodland on the Cleveland Way is pine and broadleaf trees over heather.
54.521019, -1.039548

Spa Wood, Guisborough
Hazel woodland mound and burial site. Good place for shelter.
54.532357, -1.014874

Airy Hill Ln, Cripple Hill, Skelton Green
BW walk, a 2.4km (1½ mile) unmade boreen from Skelton Green (54.554100, -0.986151) to Combe Bank (54.541810, -1.003404).
54.547183, -0.997014

Saltburn Railway Viaduct, Saltburn
The 55m (180ft)-high viaduct was designed for the rail line opening in 1872. Carriages carried rocks from the Skinningrove limestone mines for the Whitby, Redcar and Middlesbrough Union Railway.
54.572277, -0.979015

Ness Point, N Robin Hood Bay

Robin Hood Bay, Cleveland Way

THE FOX AND HOUND HOTEL
Single, twin, double and family rooms. Traditional English and Continental breakfasts. Discounts for single occupancy.

Slapewath, Guisborough, N Yorkshire, TS14 6PX

www.foxandhoundhotel.com/

01287 635280

Skelton Beck Waterfall, Saltburn
Minor detour past trees to a beautiful run of waterfalls. Relaxing place to rest.

54.572693, -0.975936

Signal Sculpture, Saltburn
Paddle at the beach via Skelton Beck path. It's a nicer walk than the main Rd of Saltburn Bank, but a minor detour from the trail.

54.583645, -0.969041

Saltburn Beach, Saltburn
Where Skelton Beck joins the sea. Find the highest cliffs along the E English coast a 800m (½ mile) walk E along the beach at low tide.

54.586091, -0.967482

Boulby mines, Boulby
Top TEN
One of the best places in UK to see bats. Ten species of bat live along the trail, several of them here. Look for the brown long-eared bat at night.

54.562405, -0.825423

Staithes Harbour, N Yorkshire
Cobbled streets, beaches and boats for mackerel fishing.
▶**Find** Bank Top car park in Staithes Ln, TS13 5AD. (54.533195, -0.751639104). Walk down 500m into the village and turn R for the harbour. Ammonites are found on the beach.

54.55992, -0.78462

NATIONAL TRAILS

YHA BOGGLE HOLE

 Budget accommodation in a great location beside the wooded mouth of a stream. Less than 200m from the waterside.

Mill Beck, Fylingthorpe, Whitby, N Yorkshire, YO22 4UQ

www.yha.org.uk/hostel/yha-boggle-hole

03453 719504

THE FISHERMAN'S WIFE

 Seafood restaurant with sea views over the bay from the Esk Estuary. Fresh fish from Whitby fish market, crab and lobsters caught daily from Whitby waters and locally supplied meats. Takeaways and beachfront seating.

Khyber Pass, Whitby, N Yorkshire YO21 3PZ

www.thefishermanswife.co.uk

01947 603500

Dunsely Dale, Runswick Bay
Broadleaf woodland over a sandy cove. Sea views close to toilets and parking.

▶**Find** the end of the Cleveland Way where it meets the sea at Runswick Bay, Saltburn-by-the-Sea TS13 5HU (54.532771, -0.750746). There are several car parks here. Continue around the bay, right along the wooded beach.

54.53056, -0.74807

Saltwick Bay, Hawsker-cum-Stainsacre
Sheltered sandy beach protected by rock on both sides. Best at low tide. Ammonites found along the foreshore or in nodules.

▶**Find** the fork where Hawsker Ln and Green Ln meet at Whitby, YO22 4EY. There is a car park here (54.485864, -0.603127). Turn L out of the car park and follow the Rd for 350m (1,150ft), past the ruined abbey, until it meets the Cleveland Way. Turn R onto the Way and walk another 1.6km (1 mile) through the caravan park to the top of the cliffs. There is a café in the park.

54.48456, -0.58897

The Coomb, Stainton Dale
Top TEN

Seals, sloes and broadleaf trees along a cliff platform looking over the sea.

▶**Find** St Hilda's Church, at the top of Raven Hall Rd, Ravenscar, Scarborough, YO13 0NA. Head down the Ln to the parking bays at the bottom, just before Station Rd. Facing Raven Hall Dr, take the FP to the L. Follow the FP for 300m (985ft) and then keep bearing R towards the cliffs and into and along the top of The Coomb. There are other paths that lead further N towards the cliff edge.

54.404615, -0.489340

Whitby

Filey

Beast Cliff, Stainton Dale
Springs, waterfalls and sea views.
▶Find The Coomb (see p193). At Raven Hall, turn R and then L onto the FP for a 3.2km (2 miles) walk to the wooded cliffs.

54.380667, -0.459897

THE GOLDEN BALL
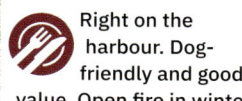 Right on the harbour. Dog-friendly and good value. Open fire in winter.
Scarborough Beach, N Yorkshire
01723 353899

Scarborough Castle, Scarborough
Fortified for thousands of years – more lately by the Romans, Saxons and Vikings – to control strategic crossings and approaches. Views across the N Sea, and walks around the castle grounds.
▶Find Scarborough harbour office, 18 W Pier, YO11 1PD (54.283699, -0.3917721). There's a public car park right next door. Facing the sea, walk L around the harbour and up towards the castle 800m (½ mile) away.

54.287000, -0.388000

Cornelian Bay, Osgodby,
Swim the 'inner lake' channel protected offshore by the High Scar rocks.
▶Find Holbeck car park, Sea Cliff Rd, YO11 3B (54.266677, -0.390372)J. At the end of Sea Cliff Rd, next to the car park and facing the sea, turn R onto the Cleveland Way FP. The rocky, wooded bay is 1.6km (1 mile) away.

54.258044, -0.371809

CLEVELAND WAY 195

 ### The Spittals, Filey Brigg
Wall of red rock jutting out into the N Sea. Sensational views over Filey Bay.
▶ **Find** Filey Brigg Country Park Camping & Caravan Site, YO14 9ET (54.216652, -0.282793). There is a large pay-and-display car park. Walk to the nearest cliff face and turn R towards the Brigg, 1,000m (3,280ft) away.

54.214914, -0.264042

 ### Filey Brigg Cliffs, Scarborough, N Yorkshire
The Cleveland Way starts/ends at a remarkable place: the start of another trail. The washing of feet at the beach of Filey Bay, again, to the sounds of people and water. The path finishes on a clifftop, a long, long way from a market town, and a very different landscape. Light inland-urban, to sea, across the largest upland heather moorland in England.
▶ **Find** Filey Brigg Country Park Camping & Caravan Site car park (see above), and walk N 800m (½ mile) to path start.

54.217793, -0.272566

WILD THINGS TO DO BEFORE YOU DIE

WATCH giant eagle owls hunt over Wainstones

CLIMB the highest point on the North York Moors

LOOK for cave bats at dusk

HIKE the Yorkshire Matterhorn

EXPLORE the largest woodland on the Cleveland Way

TOUCH mounds of an Iron Age hillfort

STAND at the foot of a giant limestone cliff

SCRAMBLE up the toughest trail climb

LOOK for seals from an overhead cliff

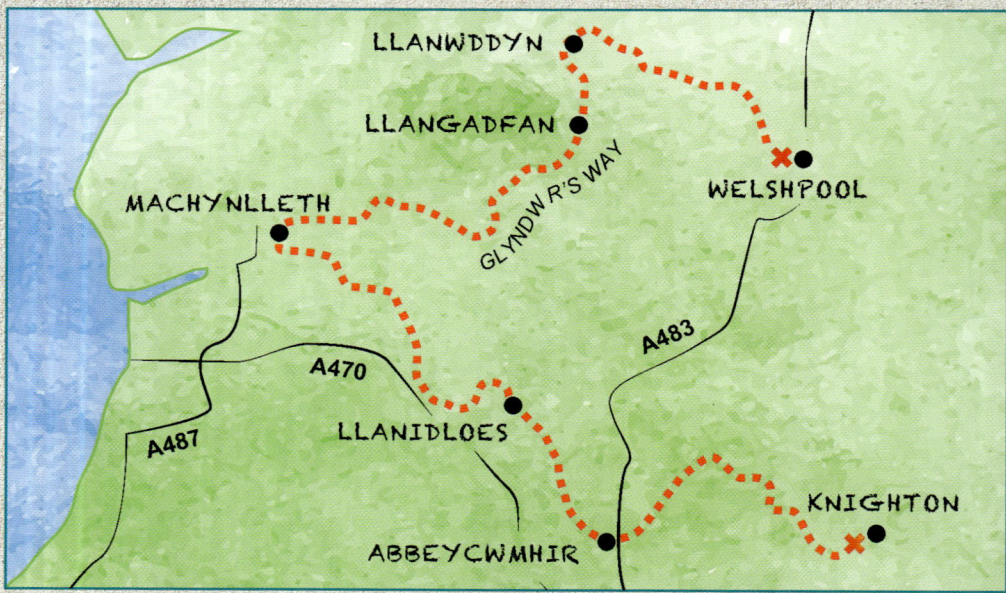

 Bachell Brook Woodland, Taste crowberries (mountain cranberries) from late summer on the plateau area.
52.345553, -3.346652

 Bachell Brook Mawn Pond, Explore ephemeral pools with views over Powys. Known as 'mawn' ponds.
52.349715, -3.339149

 Clywedog Rez N, Look for ospreys hunting along the waterside boreen.
52.489849, -3.642718

 **Bryntail Lead Mine Buildings**, Move along mine ruins at the base of a dam.
52.468662, -3.600583

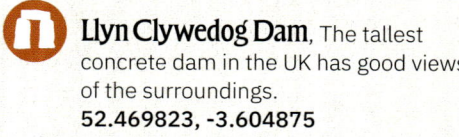 **Llyn Clywedog Dam**, The tallest concrete dam in the UK has good views of the surroundings.
52.469823, -3.604875

 Source of Severn, The source of the Severn predictably peppered in cairns and burials. Good place to rest and explore.
52.495301, -3.740661

 Glaslyn, Paddle the wild lake.
52.530603, -3.728093

 Lyn Glanmerin, Look for ospreys where pine forest trail ends. They occasionally breed 4.8km (3 miles) away at Cors Dyfi Nature Reserve.
52.578754, -3.840210

 River Banwy bridge, Listen for otters while packrafting. Find the sandbanks to rest around the river bend (52.687654, -3.466305).
52.686377, -3.464947

 Dyfnant Forest Boreen, Look for goshawks along this 3.2km (2 miles) forest boreen.
52.737755, -3.463838

GLYNDŴR'S WAY

BEST FOR: PINE AND YEW WOODLAND

Guerrilla track, mystical yew, roe deer

START: KNIGHTON   FINISH: WELSHPOOL

The tallest concrete dam in the UK is home to nesting ospreys. The wild interloping with human order.

Woodland in Wales is dominated by two problems: there are not enough trees; and what is there is too orderly. Row upon row of imported pine. Outside of the Wye Valley, most Welsh forest was planted by the Forestry Commission, which ran commercial operations from 1919 to 2013 like a debt manager with a gambling problem.

Things are changing. Non-native trees like spruce are gradually being replanted with native broadleaf such as oak, ash, birch and beech.

The Glyndŵr's Way is an opportunity to explore those non-native forests. For all their sterility, they are still places alive with the haunting spirit of malnourished nature: polecat, pine marten, brown hare, otter, turtle dove and goshawk. The Cambrian Mountains were the last refuge of the red kite in the British Isles – before the birds went down to a lone breeding female in the 1930s.

Radnor Forest is one of the darkest coniferous forests in the UK, with cypress, western red cedar, lodgepole pine, Douglas fir, Norway spruce and grand fir trees. Dyfnant Forest has some deciduous trees. The rivers along the trail are beds of rare wet woodlands of willow and alder.

The best way to see deer is to visit Glyndŵr's Way in thick snow. That's a rare event but, if it happens, you will see deer foraging on yew trees. The yews were not planted by humans, they were seeded by birds – a message in an aril to the commissioners of pine forest.

Cemmaes Road

THE LOFT

 Campsite and self-catering, with horse stabling, grazing, secure cycle storage.

Llugwy Farm, Llanbister Rd, Llandrindod Wells, Powys, LD1 5UT

www.llugwy-farm.co.uk

01547 550641

BRANDY HOUSE FARM

 Cottage and B&B accommodation, pod camping, glamping and wild camping.

Felindre, Knighton, Powys, LD7 1YL

www.brandyhousefarm.co.uk

01547 510282

TREVLAND

 B&B, campsite, self-catering and bunkhouse. Secure cycle storage.

Felindre, Knighton, Powys, LD7 1YL

01547 510211

LLANBADARN FYNYDD COMMUNITY SHOP

 A small selection of groceries, hot drinks and snacks, internet access.

Llanbadarn Fynydd, Powys, LD1 6YA

www.llanbadarnfynydd.org/llanbadarn-community-shop

01597 840448

Welshpool

🏰 The Clock Tower, Knighton

Glyndŵr's Way starts/ends at the top of Broad St, beside the busy town clock tower. The uphill walk out of Knighton soon becomes isolated. This is a walk defined by a mountain range that was the last refuge of a survivor. No, not Glyndŵr. In the 1930s, the Cambrian Mountains were home to Britain's last female red kite. This is a walk through a guerrilla landscape. A place to hide from enemies. A mythical range of mountain goats, yew trees, roe deer and raptors.

▶ **Find** the Knighton Clock Tower, Knighton, LD7 1BS.

52.344399, -3.049832

Garth Hill Boreen, Llanfair Waterdine

A 2.4km (1½ mile) metal boreen from Garth Hill (52.349578, -3.076262) to Downes's Dingle stream (52.345191, -3.103611) via the springs at Little Cwmgilla.

52.344261, -3.076374

Short Ditch, Beguildy

Ditch earthworks midway along 8km (5 mile) BW between Stanky Hill (52.382227, -3.232238) and River Lugg FB (52.341501, -3.157372).

52.366044, -3.190649

🔥 Beacon Hill, Beguildy

Feel the energy around a burial ground surrounded in heather moor at 547m (1,795ft).

52.383044, -3.211404

HOME FARM
 B&B and campsite. Abbeycwmhir, Powys, LD1 6PH
01597 851666

THE OAKS
 Budget B&B. Bike-washing, evening meals, laundry, packed lunches. One single and one twin room.
Abbeycwmhir, Llandrindod Wells, LD1 6PH
07967 298725

Bryn Mawr, Beguildy
A 3-mile boreen and BW from Felindre (52.423619, -3.224612) to Hope's Castle Farm (52.423383, -3.296681) via Rhuvid crossroads.

52.423288, -3.253942

Castell y Blaidd, Llanbister
Touch a castle ruin on a grassy mound. Horseshoe-shaped earthwork. No direct access to the hilltop but it sits impressively on the horizon. Mound is ringed in sheep and fence but lots of valley views.

52.409084, -3.288154

Fron Top Boreen, Llanbister
A 3.2km (2 miles) boreen from Coventry settlement (52.405076, -3.292682) to River Ithon (52.393843, -3.327246) via Fron Top.

52.400450, -3.309317

St Padarn's Church, Llanbadarn Fynydd
A medieval church rebuilt in the 19th century.

52.389665, -3.327767

Pont Llogel

GLYNDŴR'S WAY CAFE

 Snacks in the Community Centre on Glyndŵr's Way for cream teas and homemade cakes. The café is the only refreshment stop on a long stretch. Run by volunteers.

Community Centre, Bwlchysarnau, Nr Rhayader, Powys, LD6 5ND

www.bwlchysarnau.org.uk

WOODHOUSE FARM HOLIDAYS, BUNKHOUSE AND CAMPING

 Fully equipped bunkhouse sleeping up to 20 people. Meals available or self-catering. Also camping and caravanning and tipi rental during the spring and summer months. It's a 3.2km (2 miles) detour from the path. Bunkhouse and camping.

Woodhouse, St Harmon, Rhayader, Powys, LD6 5LY

www.woodhousefarmholidays.co.uk

07926 781394

PLASNEWYDD BUNKHOUSE

 Budget bunkhouse.

Gorn Rd, Llanidloes, Powys, SY18 6LA

www.plasnewyddbunkhouse.co.uk

01686 412431

Moel Dod round barrow, Llanbadarn Fynydd

Stargaze with views over Brecon Beacons. A 467m (1,532ft) peak, with a downhill walk into woodland.

▶**Find** A483 car park, Llandrindod Wells, LD1 6TS (52.361853, -3.332472). Exit car park to W onto A483. Walk N 275m (900ft) on Rd to L turn onto Ln. Walk 1km (⅔ mile) W to find NT. Follow the trail N for 3.2km (2 miles) to the site.

52.381055, -3.354200

Top TEN Bachell Brook Woodland, Llanbadarn Fynydd

Look for cowberries (mountain cranberries) from late summer on the plateau area. They are sweeter if found in early winter after frost around the Radnorshire Hills. Smell the pine on the wooded walk, dotted with springs.

▶**Find** A483 car park, Llandrindod Wells, LD1 6TS (52.361853, -3.332472). Exit car park to W onto A483. Walk N 275m (900ft) on Rd to L turn onto Ln. Walk 1km (⅔ mile) W to find NT. Follow the trail S for 2.8km (1¾ miles) to the site.

52.345553, -3.346652

Top TEN Bachell Brook Mawn Pond, Llanbadarn Fynydd

Explore ephemeral pools with views over Powys. Known as 'mawn' ponds, this one is next to the BW. These shallow pools were traditionally used by drovers for watering their stock.

52.349715, -3.339149

Dolwen

Glaslyn

DOL-LLYS FARM CARAVAN & CAMPING

Campsite with secure cycle storage on the banks of the River Severn. A working farm. Campers can feed the animals and watch the farm activities throughout the season.

Trefeglwys Rd, Llanidloes, Powys, SY18 6JA

www.dolllyscaravancampsite.co.uk

01686 412694

Abbey Cwmhir ruin, Abbeycwmhir
Walk a wooded trail that leads to Cwmhir Abbey in Abbeycwmhir. A ruined Cistercian monastery, the supposed burial place of Llewelyn ap Gruffudd, the last native Prince of Wales.

52.330441, -3.387887

Llandrindod Wells Church, Abbeycwmhir
Explore a church set in abbey grounds.

52.331539, -3.389739

Pistyll Wood, Llandinam, Abbeycwmhir
Look for yew tree and bracket fungi along a 2.4km (1½ mile) boreen through pine forest.

52.383337, -3.458496

Moelfre, Llandinam
Wild camp on an isolated peak (429m (1407ft)) a short BW diversion from the trail.

▶ **Find** Mount Ln car park, 41 High St, Llanidloes, SY18 6BZ (52.447939, -3.539259). Exit the car park N and find Great Oak St. Turn R onto the NT and follow the path E for 6.4km (4 miles) to the site.

52.435781, -3.479399

THE COACH AND HORSES

 B&B offering packed lunches. Bicycles can be securely stored. Clothes-drying service.

12 Smithfield St, Llanidloes, Powys, SY18 6EJ

www.coachandhorses bandb.co.uk

01686 413758

GARTH BARNS & COUNTRY HOUSE, POWYS

 Self-catering barns.

Garth Farm, Powys, SY18 6NN

www.garthbarns.com

07540 725398

TY CAPEL B&B

 B&B overlooking the Clywedog Rez and Cambrian Mountains. Evening meals available.

Deildre, Llanidloes, Powys, SY18 6NX

07484 143877

St Idloes Church, Llanidloes

Explore the church's 15th-century roof beams. Sit under a yew tree outside with views over the Severn valley.

52.449960, -3.540875

Bryntail Lead Mine Buildings, Llanidloes Without
Top TEN

Look for ospreys around the mine ruins at the base of the Clywedog dam (see below).

▶ **Find** Bryntail Lead Mine car park, Llanidloes, SY18 6NU (52.468137, -3.600587). Exit the car park N and walk 90m (295ft) to site.

52.468662, -3.600583

Llyn Clywedog Dam, Nr Llanidloes
Top TEN

The tallest concrete dam in UK has good views of the surroundings.

▶ **Find** Bryntail Lead Mine car park, Llanidloes, SY18 6NU (52.468137, -3.600587). Exit the car park N and walk 180m (590ft) to the site.

52.469823, -3.604875

Clywedog Rez S, Llanidloes Without
Top TEN

A waterside walk through trees. FP only but worth the trek from the dam. Find the FB before the short walk N along the shore with water and hills as a backdrop. Clywedog Sailing Club nearby.

▶ **Find** car park, Llanbrynmair, SY19 7DB. Exit car park to S onto Rd/boreen.

52.474244, -3.619417

Clywedog Rez N, Llanidloes Without

Look for ospreys fishing along the waterside boreen.

▶ **Find** car park, Llanbrynmair, SY19 7DB. Exit car park to S onto Rd/boreen. Walk E for 4km (2½ miles) to rejoin the NT (52.483648, -3.628253).

52.489849, -3.642718

Fign Aberbiga, Trefeglwys

Forage along the wooded walk from the Nant Felen river bridge (52.488901, -3.666442) into pine; FB and then boreen.

▶ **Find** car park, Llanbrynmair, SY19 7DB. Exit car park to S onto Rd/boreen. Walk S for 30m (100ft) on Rd to rejoin the NT. Turn R and walk N for 500m (⅓ mile) into pine woodland.

52.493778, -3.664427

Foal Fadian, near Glaslyn

Machynlleth to PenRhiw'rfelin BW, Cadfarch
Explore more than 26km (16 miles) of BW from Machynlleth (52.583418, -3.860942) to PenRhiw'rfelin (52.524626, -3.664478). The trail passes Glaslyn, Foel Fadian and km of forest track.

52.527717, -3.727996

Source of Severn, Blaenrheidol
The source of the Severn is predictably peppered in cairns and burials. Good place to rest and explore.

52.495301, -3.740661

Pumlumon Arwystli Burial Ground, Blaenrheidol
One of the most important sacred sites on the trail looms at 741m (2,430ft) above sea level.

52.475362, -3.745438

Source of Wye, Blaenrheidol, Llangurig, Ceredigion
Move along the start of the River Wye, just S of the path.

52.469053, -3.765069

HAFREN FOREST HIDEAWAY

B&B, bunkhouse for solo walkers or groups.

Staylittle, Llanbrynmair, Powys, SY19 7DB

www.hafrenforestbunkhouse.com

07871 740514

Clywedog Reservoir

TALBONTDRAIN GUEST HOUSE

 Family-run budget accommodation with a light breakfast included.

Forge, Machynlleth, Powys, SY20 8RR

07972 584915

MAENLLWYD GUEST HOUSE

 B&B providing single and double rooms.

Newtown Rd, Machynlleth, Powys SY20 8EY

www.maenllwyd.co.uk

01654 702928

Pen Pumlumon Fawr Burial Ground, Blaenrheidol, Ceredigion

Explore what was once the last refuge of the red kite in the British Isles – down to just a single breeding female in the 1930s. Today, they are more common than sparrows, but no less majestic.

52.467160, -3.782671

Top TEN Glaslyn, Cadfarch, Powys

Paddle the wild lake – white with cotton-grass in June, followed by purple heather. View of Foel Fadian sees the peaks rise gently from the E then fall to a steep drop into the next valley.

52.530603, -3.728093

Foel Fadian, Cadfarch

Forage for bilberries around the 564m (1,850ft) peak of heather moorland. Views over Glaslyn.

52.541910, -3.729915

Felindulas, Cadfarch

Listen to red grouse and skylarks around the river bridge over Afon Dulas. FB is towards the end of a 3.2km (2 miles) twisting boreen between Foel Fach river bridge (52.550253, -3.755442) and Cleiriau Isaf (52.555231, -3.778513).

52.559846, -3.776490

NATIONAL TRAILS

GLYNDŴR'S WAY

SUNNY LEA
Self-catered cabins with views right on Glyndŵr's Way.
Meifod, Powys, SY22 6YA, UK
www.sunnylea.co.uk
01938 500909

ARTISANS CAFE AND BIKE HIRE
Oswestry, Powys SY10 0NA
www.facebook.com/ArtisansLakeVyrnwy?locale=en_GB
01691 870317

ⓉⓄⓅ ⓉⒺⓃ Llyn Glanmerin, Cadfarc
Look for ospreys where pine forest trail ends over Llyn Glanmerin (52.574119, -3.838298). The birds occasionally breed 4.8km (3 miles) away at Cors Dyfi Nature Reserve.

52.578754, -3.840210

St Peter's Church, Machynlleth
This may have been the church Owain Glyndŵr worshipped in as Machynlleth was the capital of Wales in the medieval era. Explore the stained glass.

52.591690, -3.853491

Ffridd Cwm y Ffynnon, Llanbrynmair
Burial ground peak at 400m (1,310ft).

52.630670, -3.598987

Gwynion BW, Llanbrynmair
A 6.4km (4 miles) BW from the SE edge of Coedga Forest (52.609747, -3.608264) to the NE edge of Graig Lloyd pine forest (52.646844, -3.564896). The BW meets Gwynion pine forest halfway, bypassing Esgair Fraith peak.

52.633126, -3.593583

Afon Gam Boreen, Llanerfyl
A 4.8km (3 miles) riverside boreen that passes two FBs. (52.648404, -3.531503) and (52.656237, -3.516041), via Dolau-ceimion (52.641062, -3.537671) to Craig Wen (52.661583, -3.499259).

52.646202, -3.533306

ⓉⓄⓅ ⓉⒺⓃ River Banwy Bridge, Llanerfyl
Listen for otters while packrafting. Find the sandbanks to rest around the river bend (52.687654, -3.466305).

52.686377, -3.464947

Dyfnant Forest Boreen, Llanwddyn
Look for goshawk along this 3.2km (2 miles) forest boreen from the centre of the mystical Dyfnant Forest (52.728533, -3.476665) to River Conwy bridge (52.745313, -3.461598). Dyfnant is mainly cypress, red cedar, Douglas fir, Norway spruce, but there are also areas of oak and yew. Crossbills, owls and black grouse live here too.
▶**Find** the Pen y Ffordd car park, Dyfnant Forest, SY21 0QB (52.710189, -3.455745). Exit the car park to the E and then walk S through the woodland on R arching trail for 500m (⅓ mile) to NT.

52.737755, -3.463838

Llanidloes

LLWYDIARTH VILLAGE SHOP AND POST OFFICE

Small grocery shop and post office.

Llwydiarth, Welshpool, Powys, SY21 0QG

01938 820208

Llyn Vyrnwy Dam, Llanwddyn
Lake Vyrnwy views, woodland walks and packrafting. Check the sculpture trail.
➤**Find** Llyn Vyrnwy car park, Llanwddyn, SY10 0LZ (52.760507, -3.456088). Exit the car park on the W side and walk onto Rd. Turn R and walk N for 365m (1,200ft) to dam.

52.761902, -3.456695

Beddau'r Cewri burial ground, Llanfihangel
Sacred site, minor detour. Follow the FP through the trees and burials.

52.737991, -3.447410

River Vyrnwy Bridge, Llanfihangel
Waterfalls, white water, wildflowers. Bring a packraft and lots of mozzie repellent. The flies here are big.

52.727483, -3.434454

CAMP PLAS CAMPSITE

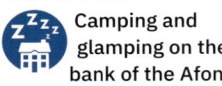 Camping and glamping on the bank of the Afon Vyrnwy. Warm showers, an open kitchen with a hob, microwave and kettle.

Plas Dolanog, Dolanog, Welshpool, SY21 0NA

www.camp-plas.com

07970 494851

 ### Dolanog Bridge, Llanfihangel
Find the stepping stones that predated the bridge.
➤ Find the car park, off the B4382, SY21 0LQ (52.705004, -3.383955). Exit the car park N and circle L onto the B4382 and meet the NT. Follow the trail S for 230m (750ft).

52.703331, -3.384690

 ### River Vyrnwy, Llangyniew
A 3.2km (2 miles) riverbank FP from Doladron (52.712195, -3.334484) to Dolanog bridge (52.702998, -3.383553) along white water.

52.710212, -3.362951

 ### St Tysilio and St Mary's Church, Meifod
Old churchyard full of yew and historic books. The first church was founded here in 550.

52.709770, -3.251690

 ### Broniarth Bridge, Meifod
Look for otters and kingfishers either side of the bridge, especially just after dawn.
➤ Find Meifod car park, SY22 6DF (52.711289, -3.255214). Exit the car park to the SW, onto main Rd and past the rugby club.

52.707235, -3.249994

Abbeycwmhir

SEVERN FARM
Pitches for camping, campervans and caravans.

Welshpool, SY21 7BB

www.welshpool.com/severn.html

01938 555999

ROYAL OAK HOTEL
Hotel with luggage transport service, packed lunches, pick-up service and secure cycle storage.

The Cross, Welshpool, Powys, SY21 7DG

www.royaloakwelshpool.co.uk

01858 438300

Golf Club, Welshpool
Café open to non-members. Call ahead of time.
www.welshpoolgolfclub.co.uk/visitor-information/bar-catering

52.6579149, -3.225251

Y Golfa, Castle Caereinion
Look for crowberries that grow around the castle peak (341m/1,120ft).

52.655316, -3.209743

Wern Wood, Welshpool
Springs, dells, ponds and gravel pits around the broadleaf and pine woodland. Minor detour.
▶**Find** the FP (52.658876, -3.184016) that links with the NT and walk 200m W into the wood.

52.659122, -3.187283

Y Lanfa/The Wharf: Powysland Museum and Welshpool Library
Explore the local history museum and library.

52.658474, -3.145452

Welshpool, Powys
Glyndŵr's Way starts/ends with a standing stone by the Montgomery Canal, less than 4.8km (3 miles) from where the canal joins with Offa's Dyke. The two trails meet properly at Knighton and then separate to make this partial reconciliation. Opposites attract. They are chalk and cheese. Glyndŵr's Way is all isolated in forest, ephemeral pools and ospreys; the Dyke the merging and warring together of England and in wild mountain and cultivated green valleys. Glyndŵr's Way epitomises a true rebel landscape. It is everything the Ridgeway aspires to, but can never be. An intimate alone-ness... with nature.

▶**Find** Welshpool Library and Museum, Canal Wharf, SY21 7AQ (52.658474, -3.145452). The commemorative stone and trail sign is 60m NE across Severn Rd on the little green known as 'Howell Park'.

52.658529, -3.144476

Ferley, Llangunllo

WILD THINGS TO DO BEFORE YOU DIE

LOOK for hunting ospreys

VISIT a prehistoric burial at the source of the Severn

TASTE mountain cranberries

EXPLORE ephemeral pools

SCALE the UK's tallest concrete dam

PADDLE a wild lake surrounded in heather

MOVE around mine ruins

LISTEN for otters, while packrafting

WATCH goshawks hunt a 3.2km (2 miles) forest boreen

Top TEN

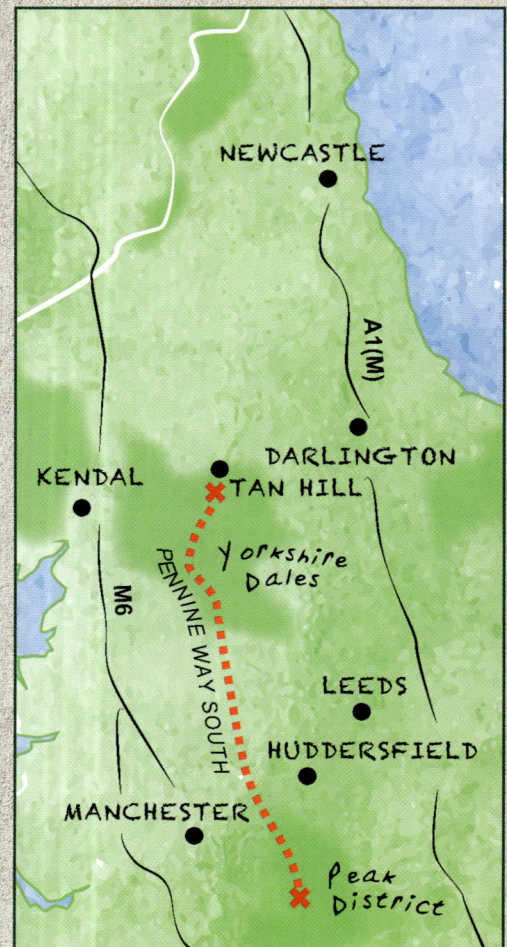

 ▶ **Kinder Scout**, Look for mountain hares among the boulders of Britain's most famous access protest platform.
53.384818, -1.873892

Stone Age Flint Factory, Explore a prehistoric flint factory.
53.409565, -1.907515

Ruins of Top Withens, Feel wuthering heights in Brontë Country. Best in autumn for views but also beautiful in heather and sunshine.
53.814688, -2.030167

 Malham Cove, Touch the curved arc of limestone before climbing up to the limestone pavement at the top.
54.070604, -2.158625

 Malham Tarn N, Inhale the air around one of only eight salt lakes in Europe.
54.098372, -2.157406

Foutains Fell, Explore the pockmarked and ruined relics of old collier pits.
54.140770, -2.208521

 Pen y Ghent, Look for the rare purple saxifrage – only found here and Ingleborough.
54.155904, -2.248867

 Hull Pot, The largest natural hole in England. Hull Pot Beck rises on the W side of Plover Hill.
54.166732, -2.270987

 Sell Gill Holes, Great for potholers, with vast underground caverns for those with the knowledge to hang, scramble and tread.
54.164414, -2.289380

 ○ **Kisdon Force**, Waterfalls surrounded by ash, wych elm and rowan wood.
54.404803, -2.157896

PENNINE WAY SOUTH

BEST FOR: SUNSETS AND HILLTOP VIEWS

Red squirrels, reservoirs, rivers

START: EDALE   FINISH: TAN HILL

The South Pennines is home to the world's best limestone pavement.

These rocky platforms were formed by ice sheets that scoured and sheared the tops off our mountains. The block-like stage is a surreal place to gaze out onto a sunset, sunrise or misty morning.

The pavement is splintered with deep cracks and grikes that provide growing spaces for ferns, rockrose and bloody crane's-bill.

Among the most famous views in England is Pen-y-ghent. The best platform is perhaps Malham Tarn – one of only eight upland salt lakes in Europe. It is the highest marl lake in Britain, and a place of rare beauty and salt air.

Where the S Pennine peaks erode and fall into the valleys, you'll find the most interesting landscapes. These highs are beacons – landmarks that have been used for thousands of years as markers, lookouts and safety points.

The most revered hilltop is Kinder Scout – the UK's access mecca: remote moorlands and pastures enclosed by drystone walls and politics. A view of the past, present and future.

Stoodley Pike Monument

Edale

UPPER BOOTH FARM CAMPSITE

 National Trust campsite for tents and campervans. Also a dog-friendly camping barn for up to eight people.

Edale, Hope Valley, Derbyshire, S33 7ZJ

www.nationaltrust.org.uk/holidays/upper-booth-farm-campsite

01433 670250

ⓝ Mary's Ln, Grindsbrook Booth, Edale

The Pennine Way S path starts/ends opposite the town pub. It's a pub-to-pub crawl along 183km (140 miles) of adventure, hard labour and purpose, with an ale house at either end. In between are pavements of limestone, dramatic waterfalls, dales, moor and a mecca of access. Kinder Scout is more important as a political and national statement than Magna Carta. Because it was an historic moment, it is of people rather than princes. Pennine Way S is dominated by heather moor and cotton-grass bog. The Dales and Peak districts are to the S what the N Pennines and Northumberland are to the N: a wonderful challenge.

▶**Find** Edale Station, Edale, Hope Valley, S33 7ZA (53.364801, -1.817281). Exit the station to the E onto Mary's Ln and walk N 800m (½ mile) to Edale.

53.370460, -1.816944

Jacob's Ladder, Edale

Tough rocky climb, up and down. Anticipate pain. Plenty of water needed in summer, so drink the night before, and on the morning, before setting out. Decent clothing needed, as severe weather comes in all its forms: hot, cold, dry and humid.

▶**Find** Barber Booth car park, Buxton Rd, Hope Valley, S33 7ZJ (53.359357, -1.839561). Exit the car park N onto the Rd and walk NW for 1.6km (1 mile) to Upper Booth. At Upper Booth, find the NT and follow it NW into the hills for 2km (1¼ miles) to the site.

53.373527, -1.870494

Kinder Low, Trig Point, Edale

Boggy, often wet air, but at 633m Kinder Low is almost as high as Kinder Scout. Many trails and Peak District views.

▶**Find** Jacob's Ladder (see above) and follow the NT W and then N for 2km (1¼ miles) to the site.

53.380314, -1.882725

Kinder Scout, Kinder Gates, Hayfield

Look for mountain hares among the boulders. Hidden bogs and featherbed mosses pose a risk, so stick to the paths, and don't take detours. This mountain marks the start of the Dark Peak, beyond the limestone of White Peak and the Derbyshire Dales.

53.384818, -1.873892

Explore a prehistoric flint factory.

▶**Find** parking at Snake Pass Summit, SK13 7PQ (53.432944, -1.869006). Exit the Rd S onto the NT and walk 4.8km (3 miles) to site.

53.409565, -1.907515

Torside Reservoir

Wain Stones, Torside Clough
Cliffs and large boulders, just W of the path, are viewing platforms all over the landscape. Two of the stones have Neanderthal profiles and appear to be about to kiss.
▶**Find** parking at Snake Pass Summit (see p213). Exit the Rd N onto the NT and walk 4km (2½ miles) to the site via Devil's Dyke.

53.459965, -1.862847

Torside Rez, Longdendale Trail, Charlesworth, Padfield
Where human engineering meets nature. These watery views are best at dawn. Serotonin-laced fumes of fantastic.
▶**Find** Torside car park, SK13 1JF (53.482648, -1.899402). Exit the car park SE following the path through woodland to the Longdendale Trail. Turn R onto the trail and walk W for 1.6km (1 mile) until it meets the Pennine Way at the Rez crossing.

53.481318, -1.917632

Laddow Rocks, Crowden
Stargaze from one of the best views in the Peak District. Immense scale of the rocks is impressive.

53.509479, -1.916122

Black Hill, Soldier's Lump, Tintwistle
Slopes clad with cotton-grass. Blanket bog is rare in the UK, but its preference for these peaks makes it dangerous. Care needed as people do get trapped. The climb up is tough. Mist can drift in as unexpectedly as a boggy foothold.

53.538381, -1.883551

Saddleworth Moor

PENNINE WAY SOUTH 215

HIGHGATE FARM

Camping… free to Pennine Way walkers. Aladdin's Cave shop. Mrs Stock has run the site for 50 years. Packed lunches available.

Colden, Hebden Bridge, HX7 7PF
01422 842897

Issue Edge, Holme Valley, Kirklees
More mountain hares here between white cotton-grass. Can be elusive as some keep their white winter coats into late spring.
▶**Find** the street parking on the A635, Pennine Way Holmfirth, HD9 4HW (53.561165, -1.887702). Follow the NT S for 2.4km (1½ miles) to the site.

53.545572, -1.879276

Wessenden Rez Waterfalls, Kirklees
Look for dippers around the waterfalls. The rocky gritstone falls are a short walk from the Rez.
▶**Find** the street parking on the A635 (see above). Follow the FP N for 3.2km (2 miles) to the site at the NW corner of the main Rez. (More falls at Blake Clough – 53.572877, -1.925388.)

53.574985, -1.917970

Black Moss Rez, Netherley
A waterside walk to the Rez edge to the W, or Swellands Rez to the E.

53.575715, -1.948589

Standedge Trig Point, Saddleworth
A relatively easy climb to the 448m (1,470ft) peak. Good views over the Harrop Dale.
▶**Find** Standedge Cutting parking, OL3 5LT (53.582152, -1.975162). Exit the car park N onto the NT and follow the path 1.6km (1 mile) to the site.

53.590298, -1.982807

Aiggin Stone, Rochdale
Touch the historic stone that once marked the crossroads of Blackstone Edge and the Old Packhorse Rd. The route was used and upgraded by the Roman armies.

53.650392, -2.042658

Warland Rez, Rain Stone, Ripponden
Waterside walk along more than 3.2km (2 miles) of Rez and stream. Good views S along the valley.
▶**Find** Parking View Point (53.657489, -2.050080) near Blackstone edge Rez, and follow the NT N for 4km (2½ miles) to the site.

53.675514, -2.058713

THE MILL AT PONDEN

 Fifteen pitches for tents and campervans on the River Worth, glamping and two B&B rooms.

Ponden Mill, Scar Top Rd, Oldfield, Keighley, W Yorkshire, BD22 0JR

www.themillatponden.co.uk

01535 643923

WINTERHOUSE BARN

 B&B and camping. Packed lunches and luggage transport service.

Colne Rd, Cowling, Keighley, W Yorkshire, BD22 0NN

01535 632234

 ### Stoodley Pike Monument, Todmorden

Touch the monument that marks the defeat of Napoleon. The original monument was completed shortly after the Battle of Waterloo in 1815, but collapsed. The replacement is 37m (121ft) tall. The rocky views are incredible.

53.714294, -2.042250

 ### Callis Wood path, Erringden

Listen to warblers singing around the birch and willow woodland. Lots of flowers in spring, including masses of buttercups and meadowsweet.

53.725283, -2.031192

 ### Colden Water, Hebble Hole, Colde

Find bilberries around the old packhorse bridge. Dippers feed along the stream.

53.750031, -2.049917

 ### Walshaw Dean Rez, Wadsworth, Calderdale

Listen to male woodcocks in spring and summer, mostly likely at dusk or dawn. They make a series of grunts and squeaks as part of a display known as 'roding'. The Rez is also a good place to see Canada geese.

▶**Find** Widdop Rez car park, HX7 7AZ (53.791915, -2.096089). Exit the car park to the SE and walk SE on Ridehalgh Ln for 1km (⅔ mile) until the R turn into the Pennine Way. Follow the NT for 800m (½ miles) E and then N to the edge of the waterside.

53.794597, -2.059726

 ### Ruins of Top Withins, Old Ln, Haworth and Stanbury

Feel wuthering heights in Brontë Country. Best in autumn for views but also beautiful in heather and sunshine.

▶**Find** Walshaw Dean Rez (see above) and climb to the ruin.

53.814688, -2.030167

 ### Ponden Wood, Ponden Rez Weir, Ponden Ln, Haworth and Stanbury

Feel the rough leaves of wych elm. These rare trees grow in this sheltered woodland of beech and sycamore. Also lots of wildflowers and bilberries.

▶**Find** Back Ln, Keighley, BD22 0HH (53.827345, -1.996086). Exit the Ln W and walk W for 500m (⅓ mile) until it forks at the NT. Take the R fork and follow the NT and BW another 500m (⅓ mile) to the waterside.

53.828820, -2.013864

PENNINE WAY SOUTH 217

THE VICTORIA INN
Single and double rooms.
Main St, Kirkby Malham, Skipton, N Yorkshire, BD23 4BS
www.victoriakirkbymalham.co.uk
01729 830499

RIVERSIDE CAMPSITE
A family-run farm campsite beside Malham Beck.
Cove Rd, Malham, N Yorkshire, BD23 4DJ
01729 830287

Cats Stone Hill, Cowling
Look for grouse and curlews. They feed around the blanket bog and wet flushes.
▶ **Find** the FP and Rd crossing at Pad Cote Ln, BD22 0NL (53.878106, -2.061503). Exit the Rd E on the FP and find the NT after 500m (⅓ mile). Turn R onto the path and walk SE, then S for 3.2km (2 miles) to the site.

53.858234, -2.043826

Damstones, Ickornshaw
Banks of bluebells and primroses in spring along a stream of watercress.

53.882249, -2.053462

Pinhaw Beacon, Carleton Ln, Elslack, Carleton-in-Craven
Look for red grouse that hide in the heath along this summit. Good views from up here over Pen-y-ghent on a clear day.
▶ **Find** Elslack Moor car park, BD23 3BB (53.921521, -2.094011). Exit the car park E and follow the NT for 800m (½ mile) to the site.

53.921083, -2.086372

Lumbutts Water Tower

River Calder Fish Jump, Charlestown

Ringstones Cairn, Clogger Ln, Elslack
Touch the ring of stones on Ringstone Edge Moor.
➤**Find** Elslack Moor car park (see p217). Exit the car park NW and follow the NT for 800m (½ mile), where it forks away from the Rd. Just after this, where the path splits into three, follow the centre FP for 550m (1,800ft) up to the site.

53.925310, -2.108819

Leeds & Liverpool Canal, Church Ln, E Marton
Packraft or cycle the canal and towpath.
➤**Find** Abbots Harbour, BD23 3LP (53.9562923, -2.139311). Exit the café and walk N on the Ln for 365m (1,200ft) until it crosses the river bridge and joins the NT. From here, turn R and follow the NT S for 1.2km (¾ mile) as it tracks along the canal to the site.

53.949683, -2.142575

THE ROWE HOUSE

Georgian Long House with 1 acre of grounds in the Yorkshire Dales, close to the Yorkshire Three Peaks of Pen-y-ghent, Ingleborough and Whernside. Luxury B&B, pitches for caravans and motorhomes plus a self-catering cottage. Produce from the walled garden.

Horton-in-Ribblesdale, Settle, N Yorkshire, BD24 0HT

www.therowehousehorton.co.uk

01729 860070

Mark House Ln, Gargrave
The boundary of the Yorkshire Dales National Park.

54.002308, -2.127503

River Aire, Eshto
Perhaps the best river walk on this section of path. Shaded by beech and willow trees. Wagtails and curlews flit about cowslips and primroses in spring.

54.013943, -2.138304

River Aire, old limestone quarry, Kirkby Malham
Walk the riverside path into Hanlith. The NT follows the water for almost 4.8km (3 miles).

54.037715, -2.152349

Malham Cove Entry, Malham
A green valley of water and plants that leads up to the famous cliff. Malham Beck was inhabited by farmers and settlers until the medieval period. The cliffs are at the end of the ash-lined beck.

54.070604, -2.158625

Malham Cove, Malham *(Top Ten)*
Stand beneath an arc of limestone. The limestone pavement at the top is as impressive as the view below.

➤ **Find** Malham car park, Chapel Gate, BD23 4DA (54.060302, -2.154606). Exit the car park E then walk N on the main Rd into Malham. Follow the Rd and the NT N for 1.6km (1 mile) to the site.

54.070604, -2.158625

Badger Lane

THE GREEN DRAGON INN
Pub B&B.
Bellow Hill, Hardraw, Hawes, N Yorkshire, DL8 3LZ
www.thegreendragonhardraw.co.uk
01969 667392

Tarn Foot, Water Sinks, Low Trenhouse
The S edge of Malham Tarn and its water sink stream.
➤**Find** Watersinks car park, BD23 4DJ (54.088038, -2.163211). Exit the car park N and keep walking N on the NT for 460m (1,500ft).

54.091335, -2.163156

 Malham Tarn N, Trough Gate, Malham
One of only eight salt lakes in Europe. The highest marl lake in Britain. Malham Tarn is a rare place of alchemical nature. Come here to inhale the air, salt and views. The tarn is surrounded by woodland on its N shore. The lake inspired Charles Kingsley's 1863 children's novel The Water-Babies, A Fairy Tale for a Land-Baby.

54.098372, -2.157406

Monk's Rd, Low Trenhouse
Explore an ancient path used by the monks of Fountains Abbey. They used the trail to manage the grazing of their sheep. The monks were also salmon farmers.
➤**Find** Tarn Foot (see above) and follow the NT for 1.6km (1 mile) N.

54.100112, -2.157044

Malham

Malham Tarn Wood, Trough Gate, Malham
Walk the famous woodland on the N shore of Malham Tarn.

54.100573, -2.160645

Fountains Fell, Halton Gill
Explore the pockmarked and ruined relics of old collier pits. The pits on the abandoned fell are predated by ancient burials, which make it a good place to explore. The peak gets its name from Fountains Abbey. Fountains Fell Tarn is 500m (⅓ mile) SE along the NT.

54.140770, -2.208521

Churn Milk Hole, Halton Gill
Shake holes, sinkholes and honeycombed by surface caves.

54.142237, -2.253276

Pen-y-Ghent, Long Ln, Studfold, Horton-in-Ribblesdal
Look for the flowers of rare purple saxifrage from late winter to spring. It can only be found here and Ingleborough. It has small triangular green leaves. The lowest of Yorkshire's famous 'Three Peaks' is a plateau of limestone pavement.
▶**Find** the boreen by the cattle grid, Pennine Way, BD24 9PX (54.146523, -2.226673). Exit the grid SW and walk the boreen for 1.6km (1 mile) until the NT leaves to the NWW (54.138576, -2.242358) via a GW. Follow the NT as it tracks W and then N for 2.7km (1⅔ miles) to the site.

54.155904, -2.248867

Hunt Pot, Horton in Ribblesdale
Waterfall that cascades into an extensive cave system, which rises at Brants Gill Head. Find where Hunt Pot Beck drops into Hunt Pot (below).

54.161915, -2.267504

Hull Pot, Horton in Ribblesdale
The largest natural hole in England. Hull Pot Beck rises on the W side of Plover Hill (54.17237, -2.23281) and flows into the pot, 2.75km (1.7 miles) SWW as the crow flies.

54.166732, -2.270987

Sell Gill Holes, Brackenbottom
Great for potholers, with vast underground caverns for those with the knowledge to hang, scramble and tread.

54.164414, -2.289380

CHAPEL GALLERY BUNKHOUSE

 Budget bunkrooms with kitchen, fridge-freezer, dishwasher and microwave. Lounge area. Drying room with heater, dehumidifier and boot sink.

Chapel Gallery, Burtersett Rd, Hawes, N Yorkshire, DL8 3NP

https://chapelgalleryhawes.com/stay-with-us/

01969 667584

 ### Jackdaw Hole Cave, Jackdaw Hole, Horton-in-Ribblesdale

Cave entrance to Jackdaw Hole. A large ash tree hangs over the abyss. Full of character and dark charm. Much care needed.

▶**Find** Yorkshire Dales National Park car park, BD24 0HG (54.149321, -2.295872). Exit the car park to W onto main Rd and walk N for 140m (460ft). Take the BW turning to R and follow NT for 2km (1¼ miles). Where the NT forks R, take the L fork to follow the Ribble Way for a 1km (⅔ mile) detour to the site is 1km (⅔ mile) S of the Pennine BW boreen (54.179342, -2.304900), which is accessed from Horton-in-Ribblesdale).

54.171360, -2.295441

 ### Ling Gill, Cam Rd, Horton-in-Ribblesdale

Limestone gorge full of rare alpine plants. Also good for rowan, birch and hazel foraging.

54.205604, -2.303517

 ### Dodd Fell, Gaudy Ln, Gayle, Hawes

A lonely peak for views and solitude. It can get very wet, so good boots and compass essential.

▶**Find** where the Pennine Way and BW meet Cam High Rd, Hawes (54.245850, -2.262743). Exit the point N and follow the NT 2km (1¼ miles) to the site.

54.279316, -2.240121

 ### Floshes Hill, Hardraw, High Abbotside, Appersett

Walk through butterflies and wildflowers around the hay meadows out of Hawes. Best in May and June.

▶**Find** Hawes National Park Visitor Centre, DL8 3NT (54.304543, -2.192483). Exit the car park E onto Brunt Acres Rd and find the NT. Follow the path N and W for 1.6km (1 mile) via the river to the site.

54.312977, -2.195773

 ### Hardraw Force Waterfall, High Abbotside

Famous waterfall with a 30m (100ft) drop. Claims to be the second tallest waterfall after Malham Cove (70m/230ft), albeit the latter only runs occasionally. Paid turnstile behind the Green Dragon Inn (see p220). JMW Turner and William Wordsworth both stayed at the Green Dragon Inn while visiting the fall.

54.318956, -2.204576

 ### St Mary and St John's Church, High Abbotside

Cross a bridge under the shade of cherry trees. There is a tearoom too.

54.316320, -2.205573

Malham Tarn

USHA GAP FARM AND CAMPSITE

Campsite for tents, touring caravans, campervans and motorhomes. Toilet and shower block. Also a two-bedroom self-catering cottage.

Long Close House, Usha Gap, Muker, Richmond, N Yorkshire, DL11 6DW
www.ushagap.co.uk
01748 886110

Piles of Stones, Fossdale, High Abbotside
Listen to thousands of dunlin that visit this 546m (1,790ft) high bog moor in summer.

54.340100, -2.240941

Great Shunner Fell, Fossdale, High Abbotside
Shelter in the stone wind hut that provides some protection from the elements. Great views from one of the wildest places on the trail.

54.370703, -2.234735

Thwaite Beck, Moor Close, Muker
Look for trout in the peat-stained waters.

54.378895, -2.172618

Top TEN Kisdon Force, Keld Ln, Keld, Muker
Several falls surrounded by ash, wych elm and rowan woodlands. Outstanding for wildflowers in spring. Primroses are the most common.
▶ **Find** Rukin's Park Lodge (see left). Exit the campsite E and follow the BW SE for 800m (½ mile) to the site.

54.404803, -2.157896

RUKIN'S PARK LODGE CAMPSITE

Budget camping and Caravan Club listed campsite. Toilets with hand basins, two hot showers and washing-up facilities.

Keld, Richmond, N Yorkshire, DL11 6LJ

www.rukins-keld.co.uk

01748 886274

FRITH LODGE

Upmarket B&B. Evenings meals and packed lunches available.

Keld, Richmond, N Yorkshire, DL11 6EB

www.frithlodgekeld.co.uk

01748 886489

C2C and Pennine Way, Keld Ln, Keld, Muker

Woodland meets the C2C Path at the famous Swale river crossing.

54.405519, -2.161557

Stonesdale Moor, Muker

An old packhorse trail across the wild moor.
▶ **Find** the boreen that meets the BW (54.433928, -2.179316) just N of Stonesdale Beck. Exit the boreen NE onto the BW and follow for 460m (1,500ft) until it meets the site and Lad Gill.

54.435999, -2.174758

Tan Hill Inn, Reeth, N Yorkshire

The Pennine Way S path starts/ends at the wonderful and isolated Tan Hill Inn. It's a place brimming with stories, energy and expectation. This was the meeting place for pack horse trails, and now of backpackers' tales. Beyond and behind the banter and chatter, everything moves S. A trope to trouble: the Dales, Dark Peak and White Peak. Wonderful.

www.tanhillinn.com.

54.455288, -2.159819

WILD THINGS TO DO BEFORE YOU DIE

FEEL the wuthering heights of Brontë Country

TOUCH the curved arc of a limestone cliff

EXPLORE a prehistoric flint factory

INHALE the air around a salt lake at altitude

PEER into the largest natural hole in England

SCRAMBLE around the edge of an underground cavern

STAND on the crevices of a limestone pavement

EXPLORE the pockmarked relics of collier pits

LOOK for rare purple saxifrage

PADDLE waterfalls in an elm woodland

LOOK for mountain hares among the boulders of an old protest platform

Kisdon Force, Keld Lane, Keld, Muker

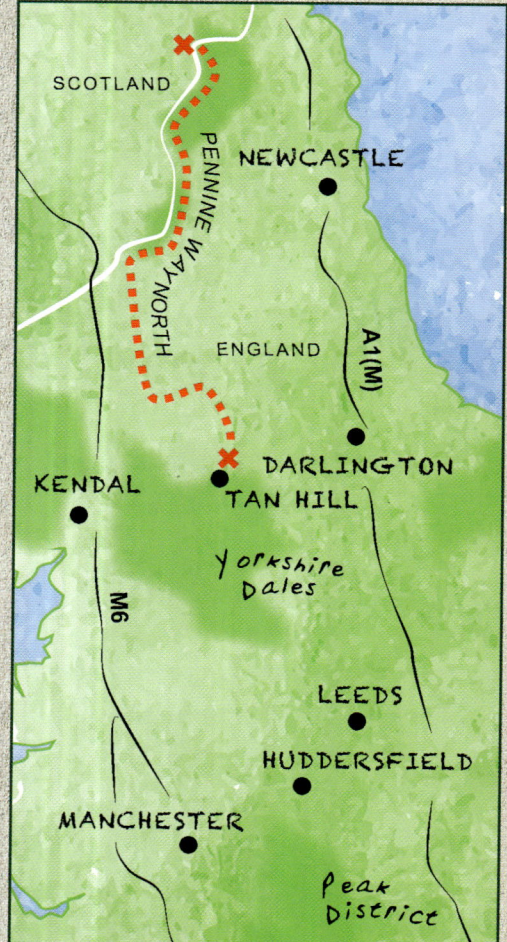

Top TEN

Shepherdshield Forest Entrance, Touch the standing stone called 'Comyn's Cross' at the entry to the forest. Legend has it that sons of King Arthur gave a gold cup to a local chieftain here.
55.056795 -2.3206842

Keedholm Scar, Explore the largest juniper wood in the N of England.
54.650651, -2.178598

High Force, The best of three waterfall crowns on the N path. Walk through meadows to see water cascade 21m (69ft) into a plunge pool.
54.649941, -2.187046

Cronkley Bridge, One of the best river walks in the Pennines.
54.659130, -2.215053

Cauldron Snout (Waterfall), Listen to explosive torrent of white spray from the Tees. It's a steep climb to the snout, a narrow crack in the Whin Sill.
54.652994, -2.289071

Maiden Way, Feel the coldest temperature and strongest winds in England. Dangerous place. Crossville is the highest point of the Pennines.
54703029, -2.486711

Broomlee Lough, A rare thing: a natural eutrophic lake, full of unique aquatic vegetation.
55.020463, -2.324134

Chew Green Roman Camp, Tramp along one of the UK's best-preserved marching camps.
55.370212, -2.334347

Red Cribs Shelter, Rest in a breathtaking mountain refuge.
55.475350, -2.195614

The Schil, One of the best views on the Cheviot range is this.
55.495021, -2.208471

PENNINE WAY NORTH

BEST FOR: BACKPACKING, WILD CAMPING, SCRAMBLING ON SCREE

Juniper forests, volcanic tors, remote camps

START: TAN HILL   FINISH: KIRK YETHOLM

The best trail in England and Wales is an adventure from top to dale.

Walk with mewing wild goats and eagles. Wild camp around mountain huts to escape treacherous bogs and the lonely boredom of bad weather.

The Cheviot granite mass intrudes into the volcanic rock like an inhospitable desert of grass and lava, and is home to peregrines, little owls, merlins and bats.

Everything here is trying to survive, including you. Red deer browse around the largest juniper wood in England. Red squirrels evade their grey cousins under darkest skies and high peaks.

The Yorkshire Dales, Northumberland and the Cheviot Hills are the most dramatic landscape from Land's End to the Scottish Highlands. Mighty waterfalls, the UK's largest forestation, the best-preserved Roman marching camps, and the largest continuous tract of blanket bog and fen across northern England.

For all its wilderness, human attempts to settle are both inspiring and unnerving. Castles, mining, quarrying, Neolithic and Bronze Age burials and Iron Age hillforts have come and gone. Even the Romans left eventually.

To leave and arrive at either end of this trail is to write and rewrite a book of errors and near disasters that you must shape and triumph over, whether it takes ten days or ten weeks. Timing, preparation, and – most importantly – luck will determine whether you win or lose.

Keedholm Scar

High Force, River Tees

Tan Hill Inn, Reeth
The Pennine Way N path starts/ends as the last one did: with a toast at the wonderful and isolated Tan Hill Inn. The trail N features remote camps of blanket bog, fen, juniper forest and military ruins of outstanding beauty. Hadrian's Wall is the greatest act of vandalism ever committed in these islands. Nature's remedy is an act of beautification beyond belief. The wall sets up a trail into Scotland that is beyond words. Not a wall... but, a guide line that is difficult to lose with its 160km (100 miles) of compass, map, mire and mist.
▶Find Tan Hill Inn, Reeth, Richmond, Swaledale, N Yorkshire, DL11 6ED. www.tanhillinn.com

54.455288, -2.159819

Ravock Castle, Bowes Moor, Bowes
Touch the ruins of a stone hut called 'Ravock Castle'. Lies in the middle of vast boggy moor and cairns.

54.522043, -2.075612

Burner Sike, Cotherstone Moor, Lartington
Inhale the perfume of flowering heather. The moor is awash with purple colour in August and September. The air is full of the sound of golden plover and curlews in May and June.
▶Find the cark park just before Clove Lodge, DL12 9UP (54.553986, -2.101047). Exit the car park on the boreen S and follow the NT for 800m (½ mile) to the springs known as 'Burner Sike'.

54.547499, -2.094819

BELVEDERE HOUSE B&B

 Budget B&B.

54 Market Place, Middleton-in-Teesdale, County Durham, DL12 0QH

www.belvederehouse.co.uk

01833 641277

Goldsborough Carr, W Briscoe

Look closely for rocks that bear cup and ring marks. These complex patterns were carved during the Bronze Age. An important area of copper and stone moor.

▶**Find** where the NT meets the boreen (54.556021, -2.083305). Exit the junction S and follow the NT for 800m (½ mile) along its BW, to the site.

54.554680, -2.072646

Grassholme Rez, Grassholme Ln, Lunedale, Mickleton

Walk along the impressive dam wall to see huge colonies of black-headed gulls.

▶**Find** Grassholme Rez car park, DL12 0PR (54.598949, -2.0811897). Exit the car park SW and walk onto the bridge and NT.

54.589139, -2.110854

Kirkcarrion, Bowbank

A Bronze Age burial site of some significance and energy. Planted with thick pine groves, it is a strange place that people avoid. A 1.6km (1 mile) round trip detour, but can be seen from the B6276 (54.606995, -2.093843).

54.609376, -2.096602

Low Force Waterfall, Sheep, Wynch Bridge, Holwick

Spectacular falls that are only bettered by the nearby neighbour, High Force.

▶**Find** High Force Waterfall car park, D12 0XH (54.652695, -2.179403). Exit the car park S and find the riverside FP. Follow SEE for 500m (⅓ mile) to the river bridge. Cross the bridge to find the NT. Turn L and walk E, following the woodland for 1.6km (1 mile) to the site.

54.646805, -2.151550

Keedholm Scar, Forest and Frith

The largest juniper wood in the N of England. Look for juniper bushes that cloak the slopes. The berries were harvested to flavour London gin. They are also devoured by birds. Walk the avenue of trees until you hear the rumbling crash of High Force.

54.650631, -2.178598

YHA LANGDON BECK

 Self-catering hostel with secure cycle storage. Packed lunches and evening meals.

Forest-in-Teesdale, Barnard Castle, Co Durham, DL12 0XN

www.yha.org.uk/hostel/langdon-beck

0845 371 9027

BROW FARM B&B,

 Self-catering cottage available. Minimum stay three nights.

Dufton, Appleby-in-Westmoreland, Cumbria, CA16 6DF

www.browfarm.com

01768 352865

 ### High Force, Forcegarth

There are three waterfall crowns on the N path, and this is the best. Walk through meadows of buttercups and meadowsweets to see water cascade 21m (69ft) into a plunge pool.

➤**Find** High Force Waterfall car park, D12 0XH (54.652695, -2.179403). Exit the car park S and find the riverside FP. Follow SEE for 500m (⅓ mile) to the river bridge. Cross the bridge to find the NT. Turn R and walk W, following the woodland for 1km (⅔ mile) to the site.

54.649941, -2.187046

 ### Dine Holm Scar, W Moor Riggs

Listen to sandpipers over the tops of heather and juniper.

54.648495, -2.206022

 ### Brackenrigg, Calf Holm

Explore some of the oldest junipers in the woodland range.

54.647800, -2.211764

 ### Cronkley Bridge, Forest and Frith

One of the best river walks in the Pennines.

54.659093, -2.215220

 ### Falcon Clints, Lingy Holm, Forest and Frith

Look for ring ouzels, which feed along this path.

54.648212, -2.274108

Cauldron Snout (waterfall), Old Mine Tramway

Listen to the explosive torrent of white spray from the Tees. It's a steep climb to the snout, a narrow crack in the Whin Sill.

54.652994, -2.289071

Old Peat Moor, near Newbiggin

NATIONAL TRAILS

Winshield Crags, Hadrian's Wall

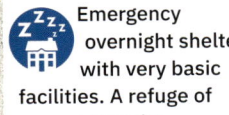

GREG'S HUT BOTHY, MAIDEN WAY
Emergency overnight shelter with very basic facilities. A refuge of some necessity.
www.gregshut.org.uk
54.713002, -2.480126

High Cup Nick, Narrowgate Path, Dufton
The best view on the Pennine Way is a hike up an old miners' route. The wild is peppered on the way up in streams, waterfalls and danger. Peregrines hunt up here in what is both a brutal and beautiful landscape.
▶**Find** Dufton public car park, CA16 6DB (54.619059, -2.482123). Exit the car park E and then walk N on the main Rd. Follow the main Rd E out of town, picking up the NT as it tracks E. Follow the BW from the edge of town for 6.4km (4 miles) to the site, via Dodd Fell Hill and Peeping Hill.
54.630089, -2.396134

Dufton Back Ln, The Ride, Dufton
Lanes lined with ash. The trees were used a stock fodder, for wood tools and fuel.
54.620570, -2.479592

Dufton Ghyll Wood, Dufton
Pignuts grow here in spring between bluebells and wild garlic. Large sweet chestnut trees drop their fruit in autumn.
54.648437, -2.488498

Knock Pike, Long Marton
Listen for curlews over conical hills that are reminiscent of the Lake District.
54.648437, -2.488498

LOWBYER MANOR COUNTRY HOUSE

 B&B with secure cycle storage. 11 en-suite rooms plus self-contained cottage.

Hexham Rd, Alston, Cumbria, CA9 3JX

www.lowbyer.com
01434 381230

KELLAH FARM B&B

 B&B and self-catering cottages with secure cycle storage and bike pick-up service.

Kellah Farm, Haltwhistle, Northumberland, NE49 0JL

www.kellah.co.uk
01434 320816

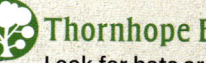

Maiden Way, Ousby

Cross Fell is the highest point of the Pennines. The coldest temperature and strongest winds in England were once recorded here. Dangerous place.

54.703029, -2.486711

Epiacum Roman Fort (Whitley Castle), Knarsdale with Kirkhaugh

Grassy ramparts grazed by sheep. Plenty of information boards.
www.epiacumheritage.org

54.832098, -2.476078

Thornhope Burn, Slaggyford, Northumberland

Look for bats around the five-arch viaduct and trees.

54.855079, -2.489346

S Tyne, Kirkhaugh

Walk along the bank of the pebbly Tyne.

54.858629, -2.491900

Simsholm Well, Merry Knowe, Knarsdale

Walk a disused railway line over Knar Burn. Wooded area across the burn is door shelter from sun and bad weather.
➤ **Find** car park by Slaggyford Railway Station, CA8 7NH (54.864960, -2.506087). Exit the car park NW and follow the trail 500m (⅓ mile) to the river and woodland.

54.869790, -2.511462

Remains of Thirlwall Castle, Greenhead

A romantic ruin on a grassy motte. Good place for photos.
➤ **Find** Thirwall View car park, CA8 7HL (54.986287-2.536569), and walk over the railway line on the NT, then 365m (1,200ft) N along the river to the castle. Alternatively, cross the Rd and follow the Pennine Way S towards the Roman Camp (54.982599, -2.545822).

54.988558, -2.534201

Walltown Crags, Greenhead

The first real sight of Bowness-on-Solway comes with 300m views along the lough valley. Look for the natural rocks that tell us why humans worked with it to such good effect.
➤ **Find** Walltown Visitor Centre car park, CA8 7HF (54.986892, -2.519461). Exit the car by the quarry gate E and walk along the NT E 1.6km (1 mile).

54.992513, -2.507376

Sewingshields, Hadrian's Wall

HOLMHEAD GUEST HOUSE

Self-catering cottage, bunk barn and campsite next to the Tipalt Burn and beneath the ruins of Thirlwall Castle. Holmhead is built over the foundations of Hadrian's Wall and is directly on the Pennine Way and Hadrian's Wall NTs.

Hadrian's Wall, Greenhead, Northumberland, CA8 7HY

www.bandb-hadrianswall.co.uk

01697 747402

Chesters Roman Fort, Chollerford
Roman fort without much signage.

54.994998 -2.4628620

Cawfield Quarry Hole Gap, Milecastle 42
Two gateways where the Pennine Way and Hadrian's Wall meet.
➤ Find the Cawfield Quarry car park, NE49 9PJ (54.993055, -2.450226). Walk E on path 45m (150ft) to the waterside.

54.993706, -2.447881

Winshield Crags E, Milecastle 40 (Winshields)
See across the Pennines to the Solway Firth and N over the Cheviots. The YHA hostel has a National Park visitor centre to the E and the Twice Brewed Inn to the W.

55.002314, -2.400267

Steel Rigg, Henshaw
The best views on the Pennine Way and Hadrian's Wall paths.
➤ Find Steel Rigg car park, NE47 7AN (55.003033, -2.390808), and walk onto the NT a few metres away for views along the trail path and cliff.

55.002232, -2.388954

Milecastle 39 (Castle Nick), Military Way
Wheatears nest in the stonework. The name 'wheatear' is a description of white 'arse' the birds show when in flight.

55.003533, -2.375893

The Cheviot

HADRIAN'S WALL CAMPSITE, MELKRIDGE

 Camping, glamping and a bunk barn 400m (¼ mile) from the Wall.

The Tilery, Melkridge, Haltwhistle NE49 9PG

www.hadrianswallcampsite.co.uk

01434 320495

SHITLINGTON CRAG BUNK HOUSE

 Budget bunks and pitches. Packed lunch available, and evening meal (by prior arrangement only).

Nr Wark, Hexham, Northumberland, NE48 3QB

01434 23033

 ### Sycamore Gap, Henshaw
The tree will return.

55.003349, -2.374314

 ### Crag Lough, Bardon Mill/Henshaw
Explore the lough as part of a N detour. It's the combination of these waters, the carnivorous plants (see Broomlee Lough, below) and the volcanic rock that make the trail truly unique and special. (Greenlee Lough is a 4.8km (3 miles) detour, but worth exploring, too 55.023450, -2.362697).

55.005727, -2.359877

 ### Broomlee Lough, Haydon
A rare thing: a natural eutrophic lake, full of unique aquatic vegetation. Carnivorous common butterwort around flushes and springs of the lough. Like a plant-controlled desert of calm.

55.020463, -2.324134

 ### Crag Lough, Military Way, Henshaw
Look for mute swans on the water.

55.005073, -2.365974

 ### Rapishaw Gap, Bardon Mill
Where the trail leaves Hadrian's Wall. This is a natural cleft in the Whin Sill between Hotbank Crags and Cuddy's Crags.

55.011817, -2.343633

 ### Hawk Side, Haughton Common, Simonburn
Woodland path. Moor is edged by spruce forest that is wild and still.

▶**Find** where the NT meets the boreen Pennine Way, NE48 3EF (55.070596, -2.317277). Follow the NT on the S side of the Rd for 2.4km (1½ miles) to the site.

55.052632, -2.329950

PENNINE WAY NORTH 235

BELLINGHAM CAMPING AND CARAVANNING CLUB SITE

 Grass pitches and hardstanding, camping pods, toilets and showers.

Brownrigg, Bellingham, Hexham NE48 2JY

www.campingandcaravanningclub.co.uk/campsites/uk/northumberland/hexham/bellingham-camping-and-caravanning-club-site

01434 220175

 ### Shepherdshield Forest Entrance, Simonburn
Top TEN

Touch a standing stone called 'Comyn's Cross' at the entry to the forest. Legend has it that sons of King Arthur gave a gold cup to a local chieftain here.

▶**Find** where the NT meets the boreen Pennine Way, NE48 3EF (55.070596, -2.317277). Follow the NT on the S side of the Rd for 1.6km (1 mile) to the site.

55.056795 -2.3206842

 ### Bellingham Bridge, Bellingham

Look for otters and sea trout. Sand martins nest here.

▶**Find** Hareshaw Linn car park and picnic area, NE48 2BZ (55.145550, -2.252051). Exit the car park S and walk 190m (590ft) on the FP to find the Rd and NT. Follow the NT down to the riverbank but take the N turning to follow the path NE along the River Tyne Trail. This is a 1.6km (1 mile) detour from the NT but it's a lovely walk to the site.

55.134802, -2.236687

 ### Parish Church of Saint Cuthbert, Hexham

A 13th-century church with an unusual stone slab roof.

55.143299, -2.256241

 ### The Shaws, Bellingham

Rest in a wooded valley of ancient wych elm and oak.

55.148696, -2.268674

Hareshaw Linn Waterfall, Bellingham

Smell wild garlic and bluebells in spring around the waterfall.

▶**Find** Hareshaw Linn car park and picnic area, NE48 2BZ (55.145550, -2.252051). Exit the car park N and walk the FP for 2.4km (1½ miles) N through the woodland and springs to the site.

55.163585 -2.2507525

RAF memorial, Black Hag Ridge

BORDER FOREST HOLIDAY PARK

 Pitches for tourers and motorhomes with electric hook-up, self-catered cottages.

Cottonshopeburnfoot,
Nr Otterburn,
Northumberland, NE19 1TF

www.borderforest.com

01830 520259

 ### Millstone Edge, Deer Play,
Best place to see red deer on the NT.
➤**Find** where the NT crosses the boreen at Hexham, NE48 1RP (55.219348, -2.277658). Follow the NT to the S for 2.4km (1½ miles).

55.208949, -2.255204

 ### Padon Hill, Rochester
A bell-shaped tumulus built in the 1920s by the Bell family.
➤**Find** where the NT crosses the boreen at Hexham, NE48 1RP (55.219348, -2.277658). Follow the NT to the N for 1.6km (1 mile).

55.229369, -2.284675

 ### Gunstone, Padon Hill, Otterburn
Look for carved cup and ring marks on sandstone boulders. Messages from the Bronze Age.

55.220651, -2.280382

 ### Brownrigg Head S, Padon Hill, Otterburn
Masses of purple heather moor in September. Very boggy.

55.234644, -2.292682

 ### Rooken Edge, Rooken, Rochester
Listen for sparrowhawks and goshawks that hunt here. Forest tracks are relief from the bogs.
➤**Find** Blakehopeburnhaugh car park, NE19 1SW (55.295532, -2.340594). Exit the car park S and pick up the NT. Follow the path 6.4km (4 miles) S through the pine woodland.

55.253535, -2.317341

 ### Kielder Forest N, Byrness
Smell the scent of conifer woodland after rain. Look for red deer around the edges.

55.310723, -2.363534

 ### Houx Hill, Windy Crag
Walk the ridge above the dark Kielder Forest – the UK's largest woodland.

55.337043, -2.357743

Halterburn Low Path

BORDER HOTEL

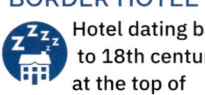 Hotel dating back to 18th century at the top of the village; steeped in histories and stories.

The Green, Kirk Yetholm, Kelso TD5 8PQ

www.borderhotel.co.uk

01573 420237

KIRK YETHOLM FRIENDS OF NATURE HOUSE

 Budget hostel. Waukford, Kirk Yetholm, Kelso, Roxburghshire, TD5 8PG

www.friendsofnature.org.uk/houses/kirk-yetholm

01573 420639

 ### Ravens Knowe, Rochester

The most isolated hill in Northumberland. Ravens are rare now.
▶ **Find** the Chew Green car park, NE65 7BX (55.370538, -2.326031) next to Chew Sike. Exit the car park to the SW and then walk S of the Roman Camp to meet the NT. Keep walking W and then S for 4km (2½ miles) on the trail to the site. The trail leads past the head of the River Coquet.

55.349695, -2.349665

 ### Chew Green Roman Camp, Alwinton
Top TEN

One of the UK's best-preserved marching camps.
▶ **Find** the Chew Green car park, NE65 7BX (55.370538, -2.326031) next to Chew Sike. Exit the car park to the SW and walk 365m (1,200ft) W to the site.

55.370212, -2.334347

 ### Black Hills, Alwinton

Wild goats survive here, but this is as far from human life as it gets. But then you will see the fence that marks the border between England and Scotland – it's a reassuring presence.
▶ **Find** Chew Green Roman Camp (see above). Follow the NT and GW to the N for 2.4km (1½ miles) to the site.

55.389053, -2.334966

 ### Yearning Saddle Refuge Hut, Buckham's Bridge

Wonderful place for rest and refuge, whether necessary or not.

55.410131, -2.311383

 ### Yearning Law, Buckham's Bridge, Alwinton

Look for white-tailed and golden eagles. They occasionally cross from the border. Much work is ongoing to reintroduce the birds in England.

55.400158, -2.289694

 ### Russell's Cairn, Scottish Borders, Scotland

Touch the Bronze Age mound of stones.

55.430634, -2.230119

Windy Gyle Cairns, Russell's Cairn, Scottish Borders

The atmospheric highlight of the Pennine Way – arguably the most isolated and dangerous place on the trail is this climb to Cheviot's summit. It's buried under snow for much of winter.

55.433353, -2.220903

Green Humbleton Fort

MOUNTHOOLY BUNKHOUSE
 Bunkhouse on a BW 3.2km (2 miles) N of the NT, and 8km (5 miles) from The Cheviot. Sleeps 24. Dog-friendly.

Mt Hooley, College Valley, Wooler, Northumberland, NE71 6TU

www.college-valley.co.uk/accommodation/bunkhouse

01668 216210

Clennell St, Cocklawfoot
The crossing point of an ancient trackway. Border fence of post over moss and heather.

55.438006, -2.205011

Bellyside Crag, The Cheviots
Look for snow buntings on this exposed and wild place. They are about the only thing that live up here all year, another than peregrines.
➤**Find** parking at Harthope Burn, NE71 6RG (55.496342, -2.074485). Move along the boreen W and follow the burn for 6.4km (4 miles) to Scotsman's Knowe. Turn NW for 500m (⅓ mile) to climb Cairn Hill where it joins the NT. Take the N fork and walk 1.6km (1 mile) to the summit.

55.478066, -2.146502

Hen Hole, Kirknewton
A hanging valley of great beauty formed by melting ice – a dangerous place of deep bogs.

55.475961, -2.182133

Red Cribs Shelter, Kirknewton, Scottish Borders, Scotland
A mountain refuge of breathtaking views.

55.475350, -2.195614

The Schil, Kirknewton, Scottish Borders, Scotland
One of the best views on the Cheviot range.

55.495021, -2.208471

Green Humbleton Fort, Northumberland
Wild goats have roamed these slopes since before the Bible was written. The descent towards the trail end is an incredible experience that can only be appreciated at its best in good weather and after completing the entire trail.

55.542101, -2.246057

PENNINE WAY NORTH 239

MILL HOUSE B&B

 B&B and self-catering, horsebox parking, pick-up bike service, secure cycle storage.

Kelso, Scottish Borders, TD5 8PE

www.millhouseyetholm.co.uk

01573 420604

THE PLOUGH HOTEL

 Family- and dog-friendly country hotel. Home-cooked food in the dining room and home-baked treats in the coffee shop.

Main St, Town Yetholm, Scottish Borders, TD5 8RL

www.theploughhotelyetholm.co.uk

01573 420215

Kirk Yetholm, High St, Scottish Borders, Scotland

The Pennine Way N path starts/ends beside a standing stone on a village green. Beyond the row of orderly houses and hotels is a chaos of mountain and moor. The Cheviot surrounds itself in weather that's as unpredictable and inhospitable as the volcanic lavas that shaped it. Like the maypole to life around which Morris Men dance, the Cheviot is totem of respect around which backpackers tramp in and out of Kirk Yetholm. The N Pennines are the spine of England. To successfully walk them requires something more than a backbone.

▶ **Find** the Border Hotel (see p237)... and sleep.

55.547457, -2.274729

Halterburn Ford

WILD THINGS TO DO BEFORE YOU DIE

TOUCH a standing stone with an Arthurian legend

REST in a mountain refuge

EXPLORE the largest juniper wood in the north of England

STAND beside the grandest waterfall in the NE path

FEEL the coldest temperature and strongest winds in England

TRAMP along one of the UK's best-preserved marching camps

MOVE along the best river walk in the Pennines

LISTEN to a torrent of Tees at Cauldron Snout

TOUCH a natural eutrophic lake

SAVOUR the best views on the Cheviot range

Top TEN

 ▶ **St Martha's Church**, Visit a churchyard with best S Downs views.
51.224605, -0.529268

 River Mole, Balance over stepping stones across the river beneath a giant horse chestnut.
51.248834, -0.321877

 Box Hill, Visit the best place in the UK to see common box trees.
51.247342, -0.311147

Coldrum Long Barrow, Touch Coldrum Longbarrow – a burial chamber at least 3,000 years old.
51.321507, 0.372827

White Horse Stone, Stand beside a giant standing stone – close to the parish boundary.
51.315100, 0.514777

No Man's Orchard, Scrumping doesn't get better than this. A communal free orchard full of birdsong and wild love. Come in July when the apples are red and ripe.
51.275734, 1.021107

 St Martin's Church, Explore the UK's oldest church that is still used for worship.
51.278026, 1.093738

 St Edmund's Chapel, Walk around the smallest church still in use in England.
51.127350, 1.309474

Dover Castle, Touch the castle and chalk cliffs – as iconic as Canterbury Cathedral.
51.121384, 1.303843

 ◉ **Western Heights**, Stand on the hills above Dover to see the French coast. It's both strangely ominous and exhilarating.
51.122635, 1.307528

NORTH DOWNS WAY

BEST FOR: SACRED AND HOLY

Peregrines, pilgrims, yews

START: FARNHAM   FINISH: DOVER

From Stonehenge to Canterbury, this Pilgrim's Path is defined by chalk, water and walking.

Today, the cathedral is home to the Archbishop of Canterbury — and is one of the oldest Christian structures in England.

If Canterbury is the classic end to a pilgrim's progress, Dover is no less important. Dover was a Celtic capital, and the word derives from the Celtic word 'dwfr', which means 'Water Holes' or 'Dove Holes'. A pilgrimage across waterholes, to celebrate water. From Stonehenge to Dover, via Canterbury, and on across the English Channel to the Holy Land, with Crusaders for company.

Humans still struggle with the meaning of life, but they have consistently marked death and the journey into the next world with the symbols of travel, navigation and life: standing stones rest as markers alongside tomb sites that date back as far as the last Ice Age.

Always set up in places of geographic importance, there's minimal difference between stones that mark prehistoric graves and those that stand in the churchyard close to your home. Limestone is a fossil reminder of the past. We leave those same stones about our towns and cities as reminders to something we have long forgotten.

Beech, yew, ash and hornbeam woods cover the dry chalk valleys along the N Downs. Rare plants and seabirds meet at the chalk White Cliffs of Dover, which are home to breeding seabird colonies and nesting hawks.

Neolithic monuments. Ancient churches. Beech hangers, cliffs, and nature cathedrals. Henges, standing stones, churches and cairns tell us how important our species considers both life and death. This trail embodies all of that better than the rest.

Box Hill Stepping Stones

PUTTENHAM CAMPING BARN

An eco-friendly bunkhouse and secure cycle storage. Advance booking essential.

The Street, Puttenham, Guildford, Surrey, GU3 1AR

www.puttenhambarn.uk

01483 811001

Start of N Downs, Carved Post, Farnham

The N Downs Trail starts/ends on the busy A31, Farnham Bypass. This is, for better or worse, the most connected trail in Britain. If you can shut out, or ignore, the bad, it's arguably the perfect trail. A bridge between chaos and order as it threads the traveller's body and mind along more than 240km (150 miles) of bypass, M25, M20 and M2 on its way to Rochester, Canterbury and Dover via chalk stream, beech wood, church, cathedral, cliff and yew. A path that marks this as the definitive Pilgrims' Way.

▶**Find** Farnham station, GU9 8AD at the traffic lights (51.21265, 8-0.793745). Walk 500ft (140m) NW to find the trail start. An information board and path design marks the spot.

51.212841, -0.793747

Snailslynch, River Wey, Farnham

NORTH DOWNS WAY 243

 ### River Wey, Farnham, Surrey
Walk across the River Wey. There are good views N, 500m (⅓ mile) E of the river, just after leaving the woodland.

51.211967, -0.769608

 ### The Tarn, Puttenham Common, Farnham
Listen for nightingales in spring beside the lake. Open water at the bottom of pine and broadleaf woodland, 1.6km (1 mile) S of the NT on BWs. The wood is riddled with water, trails and roe deer.
▶Find Suffield Ln car park, GU3 1BQ (51.204316, -0.695631). Exit the car park to the W and walk 180m (590ft) to the waterside.

51.204068, -0.696304

 ### Runfold Wood, Farnham
Listen out for roe deer barking in rutting season. Blackcaps sing in spring, almost as good as nightingales.

51.215331, -0.757365

 ### Hurt Hills, Compton
Taste hazelnuts in autumn while snaking along the narrow oak wood path. Just N of Hurt Hills is where the trees get thickest along this 1.6km (1 mile) stretch of BW. Stumperies for fungi and masses of blackberries.

51.220978, -0.639506

 ### E Warren, Artington
Look for deer after leaving W Warren woodland. This part of the trail skirts the N edge of E Warren wood with good views over the valley N.
▶Find Puttenham Common car park, GU3 1BG (51.206509, -0.683494). Exit car park N and walk N.

51.222546, -0.606226

 ### River Wey Navigation, Artington
Packraft across the river. It's no time saver but this is a beautiful place to rest for lunch... full of flowers in spring.
▶Find the Chantries car park, GU4 8AW (51.226386, -0.564106). Exit the car park W and follow the NT for 1.2km (¾ mile) to the site.

51.225056, -0.577145

 ### The Chantries, Whinny Hill
Thick woodland, best at night for the call of tawny owls.
▶Find Halfpenny Ln car park, GU4 8PZ (51.225951, -0.538567). Exit the car park S and find the NT 275m (900ft) S. Turn R and head W for 460m (1,500ft), crossing the Rd about halfway.

51.225704, -0.543157

Exploring the Stepping Stones at Box Hill

CHANTRY WOOD CAMPSITE

 Campsite 3.2km (2 miles) from Guildford.

Chantry Wood, Guildford GU4 8PZ

www.guildford.gov.uk/chantrywoodcampsite

01483 444718

Top TEN St Martha's Church, Guildford

Churchyard with the best views in Surrey over the S Downs. Also known as 'St Martha-on-the-Hill'. A Grade II listed building. Look out for rabbits and yew trees. Tea bar is sometimes open on Sundays. Take a detour S in spring to explore the bluebell woods.

51.224605, -0.529268

 ### Netley Heath, W Horsley

Smell the scent of pine and bracken on the gravel-lined BW. This track represents more than 24km (15 miles) of almost unbroken BW from Reigate to Guildford, a relative rarity in the 21st century. The trail follows the chalk ridge between Guildford and Dorking.

▶**Find** Combe Ln car park, KT24 6ES (51.235912, -0.458379). Exit the car park S and follow the GW and BW trail E for 1.6km (1 mile) to the site.

51.232897, -0.443872

 ### River Wey, Wotton

Listen for the bark-tapping of lesser spotted woodpeckers around Dunley Wood. The birds favour the rotten birch trees just E of White Down Ln, around the old quarry areas. Good place to collect birch bark too.

51.227282, -0.405826

NORTH DOWNS WAY 245

YHA TANNERS HATCH

 Budget campsite and hostel. Secure cycle storage.

off Ranmore Common Rd, Dorking, Surrey, RH5 6BE

www.yha.org.uk/hostel/tanners-hatch

03453 719542

THE BAKERY

Restaurant with seven soundproofed en-suite bedrooms. Egyptian cotton sheets on the beds.

Westmoor Green, Tatsfield, Nr Westerham, Kent, TN16 2AG

www.thebakeryrestaurant.com

01959 577605

Pickets Hole, Wotton

Tangle of beech, yew, birch and hazelnut woodland. Views S towards Westcott. Cool place to shelter from heat in summer.

51.232841, -0.395694

River Mole, Brockham

Stepping stones across the river beneath a giant horse chestnut. Time it in spring, when the tree flowers are alive with insects and scent. A stunning place to rest.

51.248634, -0.321877

Box Hill, Salomons, Brockham

The best place in the UK to see and smell common box trees. The trees flower in April and May. The view from this ancient woodland inspired 500 lines of John Keats poetry. One of the best places to touch nature and inhale clean air, 4.8km (3 miles) inside the perimeter of the M25. The ancient path Stane St connects Box Hill to Epsom, 9.6km (6 miles) N.

▶ Find Box Hill car park, KT20 7LB (51.248962, -0.312179). Exit the car park S and cross the Rd to the viewpoint. The NT is just S of the point.

51.247342, -0.311147

Brockham Hills, Brockham

Feel the shifting of time around the wooded cliff faces. Old quarries are magical places. The disused lime works at Brockham Hills are worthy of a detour.

51.247993, -0.281361

Hillydeal Wood

UP THE DOWNS B&B

B&B in cul-de-sac. Full English breakfast, packed sandwiches, clothes-drying facilities.

Kemsing, Sevenoaks, Kent, TN15 6SD

www.upthedowns.com

01959 526869

BADGELLS WOOD CAMPSITE

Off-grid campsite in ancient woodland with bluebells, butterflies and badgers. Badgells Wood was also once part of a Second World War training camp. Remains of concrete tracks and hut bases can still be seen between the trees. There is also 1km of trench remaining from the First World War, which children like to explore.

Whitehorse Rd, Meopham, Kent, DA13 0UF

www.badgellswoodcamping.co.uk

07528 609324

Reigate Fort, Reigate

Good S views and the fort is free to explore.

▶**Find** Reigate Hill and Gatton Park car park, RH2 0HX (51.256106, -0.191475). Exit the car park S and walk straight onto the NT. Turn R and follow the trail W for 800m (½ mile) to the site.

51.253974, -0.200770

The Millennium Stones, Gatton

Sit among oxeye daisies next to modern-day standing stones, over an ornamental lake with an ancient view.

▶**Find** Reigate Hill and Gatton Park car park, RH2 0HX (51.256106, -0.191475). Exit the car park S and walk straight on to the NT. Turn L and follow the trail E for 2.4km (1½ miles) to the site.

51.259949, -0.179229

St Katharine's Church, Merstham

St Katharine's Church, Merstham. Full of yews and wildlife.

51.268836, -0.151856

Ockley Hill, Compton, Bletchingley

BW crossing over the M25 and M23 into Ockley Wood and Hill. Follow BW and 'lost lanes' for 6.4km (4 miles) to Pilgrim Fort.

51.270678, -0.133161

Pilgrim Fort, Caterham

A surround sound of stars at night or orchids by day. Pilgrim Fort is built on chalk meadow with oaks, yews and views.

51.262653, -0.075379

Gangers Hill, Woldingham

Smell the garlic scent of ransom woodland just N of the path along this vast chalk ridge. Walk in bluebells in Great Church Wood, along the N BW.

▶**Find** Gangers Hill car park, CR3 7AD (51.269794, -0.032448). Exit the car park E and walk into the woodland centre. Walk S to find the NT across the Rd when leaving.

51.267670, -0.038520

Beech Plantation, Limpsfield

Look for hen harriers. The beech plantation itself is long gone, making this a good place to rest and watch from the top of the chalk meadow. It's full of flowers and butterflies in spring.

51.271378, -0.012630

St George's Church, Wrotham

COLDBLOW FARM, COTTAGES, CAMPING & BUNKHOUSE BARNS

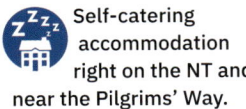 Self-catering accommodation right on the NT and near the Pilgrims' Way.

Cold Blow Ln, Thurnham, Maidstone, Kent, ME14 3LR

www.coldblowfarm.co.uk
01622 730439

Pitchfont Ln, Limpsfield
Steep-banked, 800m (½ mile) green Ln. Beech trees line either side of Pitchfork Ln, which takes you back 50 years. Stunning views halfway up, in-between occasional yew trees.

51.275519, 0.003183

Betsom's Hill, Westerham
Lost Ln on Betsom's Hill, edged in hazel and elder. Charles Darwin lived 4.8km (3 miles) N of here. He would walk and look at the trees and plants on these downs as part of his studies, after coming home from the Galápagos Islands.

51.285211, 0.049617

Hogtrough Hill, Westerham
Chalk ridge of flowers, edged by woodland to find shelter with views S.

51.290546, 0.073302

Kemsing Down, Childsbridge
Orchids and butterflies. Man, pyramidal and common spotted orchids. Brown argus, common blue, dingy and grizzled skipper butterflies between woodlands, glades and chalk grassland.

51.313680, 0.223777

Thurnham Castle

TOP TEN Coldrum Long Barrow, Trottiscliffe

Touch Coldrum Long Barrow – a burial chamber at least 3,000 years old. A group of Morris Men gather at the stones at dawn (before 5am) on 1st May each year to 'sing up the sun'. The site is a 500m (⅓ mile) detour S of the way, on the Wealdway. Rare musk orchid grows on the chalk grasslands along the trail at Trosley before this short detour.
➤**Find** Coldrum Long Barrow parking, ME19 5EG (51.321904, 0.366687). Exit the car park S onto the BW and walk E for 410m, where it meets the Wealdway. Turn R and walk 180m S to the site.

51.321507, 0.372827

Medway Bridge, Cuxton

Medway Bridge river view – one of the best views on the trail.
➤**Find** Plantlife's Ranscombe Farm Nature Reserve car park, ME2 1LD (51.379703, 0.466318). Exit the car park to the NE and follow the line of Sundridge Hill over the bridge and down.

51.376701, 0.475557

Nashenden Down Wood, Wouldham

Prehistoric burial ground on tree-lined BW. Westerly views right along the Medway Valley. Good for butterflies and wildflowers in spring. There's a path down into Nine Acre Wood and Monk Wood – both good for weather shelter.
➤**Find** Common Rd car park, ME5 9RG (51.332075, 0.500729). Exit the car park N onto Common Rd, turn L and follow the NT 2.4km (1½ miles) NW to the site.

51.357836, 0.477864

NORTH DOWNS WAY 249

White Horse Stone, Aylesford and Boxley border
Giant standing stone close to the parish boundary. There were two until the 1800s, when the other was removed. One of several Neolithic stone structures in the Medway Valley. There are said to be other smaller stones, particularly in surrounding woods. Kit's Coty and Little Kit's Coty megalithic burial sites are less than 1.6km (1 mile) W and NW.
➤**Find** Common Rd car park, ME5 9RG (51.332075, 0.500729). Exit the car park N onto Common Rd, turn R and follow the NT 2.8km (1¾ miles) SE to the site, following the line of the A229.

51.315100, 0.51477

Thurnham Castle, Detling
Rest among views and rubble or take a 1.6km (1 mile) walk E into Civiley Wood (51.290977, 0.604047).

51.293786, 0.592917

All Saints Church, Hollingbourne
GW along 19km (12 miles) from Hollingbourne to Westwell Downs Wood. The church is full of yew tree topiary.

51.260522, 0.655170

Lenham War Memorial, Lenham
Hill-figure cross carved into chalky hillside in remembrance of war dead from both world wars and others.

51.242284, 0.729020

Ranscombe Farm Nature Reserve

ROLLES COURT
 B&B, bike pick-up service, secure cycle storage. Single, double and twin rooms.

Whitfield, Dover, Kent, CT16 3HY

www.rollescourt.co.uk

01304 827487

Westwell Downs, Westwell
Beech woodland with maze of paths and fox runs into the undergrowth for shelter.

51.199178, 0.831266

St Mary's Church, Eastwell
One of the few places to find ancient yew trees. The 15th-century church fell into ruin after the roof collapsed in 1951. Some believe the collapse occurred because of the artificial Eastwell Lake. The lake didn't harm the trees as they prefer high water levels.

51.190050, 0.874830

All Saints, Boughton Aluph
A 13th-century pilgrim church on the path to Canterbury. A rare pilgrims' porch with Tudor fireplace. Open to visitors at weekends in summer or on request.

51.196209, 0.908671

King's Wood, Godmersham
Bluebells, bracken and birch. Look for chestnuts in autumn. The exit from the wood used to be pilgrims' first sight of Canterbury Cathedral. The Pilgrims' Way became an event to commemorate the death of Thomas Becket. Much later – 212 years after Becket's death – it became the subject of Chaucer's satirical Canterbury Tales, and associated with leisure and sin rather than penance.

51.226620, 0.937347

Chilham Castle, Canterbury
The path passes one of the oldest homes in Great Britain, Chilham Castle. A medieval castle built on a prehistoric settlement site, and reconstructed as the Jacobean mansion we see today in 1616.

▶ **Find** Chilham car park, CT4 8BZ (51.244664, 0.959566). Exit the car park N and follow the Rd SE for 275m (900ft) to the site.

51.242882, 0.958900

St Mary's, Chilham
Famous as the last known resting place of St Augustine. St Thomas Becket is buried in the churchyard. St Mary's Church dates back to the 7th century. The tower is 21m (68ft) in height, and the towers of Canterbury Cathedral can be seen on a clear day.

www.friendsofstmaryschilham.org

51.244557, 0.962902

Folkestone

No Man's Orchard, Chartham
Scrumping doesn't get better than this. A free communal orchard full or birdsong and wild love. Come in late summer when the apples are red and ripe or spring for the blossom. Like the Garden of Eden. A national highlight.

51.275734, 1.021107

Bigbury Camp, Harbledown
Iron Age hillfort in Howfield Wood. More than 2,000 years old, and likely to have been raided by Julius Caesar in 55 BC during his invasion of Britain.

51.279041, 1.033111

Canterbury Cathedral, Canterbury
The oldest Christian structure in England dates back relatively recently... to AD 597. St Augustine arrived on these shores on the orders of Pope Gregory the Great. His mission was to establish a base in Canterbury to revoke the town's pagan heritage. Canterbury was one of the most sacred locations in prehistoric Britain with links to Stonehenge, Watford in Hertfordshire, and Waltham Abbey.

51.279755, 1.082239

St Martin's Church, Canterbury
The UK's oldest church that is still used for worship. It was here that St Augustine arrived from Rome in AD 597 to convert the English to Christianity. It was a 'church' when he arrved, albeit a pagan Celtic church.

51.278026, 1.093738

St Mary's Church, Patrixbourne
Rare, palatial entrance doorway arch and Swiss stained-glass panels, complimented by an avenue of yew trees. Pilgrims have been arriving here for hundreds of years. Walk through the carved S door to see the 12th-century wheel window and unique stained-glass panels.

51.255862, 1.018100

Barham Downs, Bekesbourne-with-Patrixbourne
Walk or cycle the BW over Barham Downs between streams of summer poppies and barley. Part of a 8km (5 miles) BW from Patrixbourne church to Womenswold church.

51.232322, 1.144748

Barham Downs Burial Ground, Kingston
Stargaze over ancient burial ground peppered in tumuli and earthworks. Detour NE off the path on BW into Ileden Wood for shelter (51.222866, 1.172756).

51.222572, 1.158260

Three Barrows Down, Womenswold
BW of hazel, beech and birch through a wooded burial ground. Tumuli are on the NE side of the path.

51.201723, 1.215299

Lydden Spout, Abbot's Cliff near Dover

NORTH DOWNS WAY 253

 ### St Pancras Church, Coldred
Tiny Saxon church on the site of ancient earthworks, with a wild meadow area in the graveyard.

51.182307, 1.252971

 ### St Edmund's Chapel, Dover
Top Ten
The smallest church in England still in use. Built in the 13th century, downgraded to a store and smithy for about 400 years, it was reconsecrated in the 1960s after it survived Second World War bombing raids.

51.127350, 1.309474

 ### Dover Castle, Dover
Top Ten
The castle and chalk cliffs are as iconic as Canterbury Cathedral. Dover Castle views are one of the highlights of the trail.

51.121384, 1.303843

 ### Path start/end, 'We are all Winners' Podium, Clarendon
Sculpture homage to pilgrimage. A winner's podium in the shape of a bench with the engraved words 'we are' in Latin, created as a modern reference to much of the communal sense of achievement and knowledge that comes from walking with a purpose to a destination.

51.122513, 1.315273

 ### Memorial Crown, Broad Downs, Wye with Hinxhill
Views and orchids. The crown chalk emblem known as the 'Wye Crown' is carved into the chalk hillside of Wye Down, E of the village of Wye, and is 180ft tall. It was created in 1902 to celebrate the coronation of King Edward VII.
▶**Find** Wye Nature Reserve car park, TN25 5HE (51.169790, 0.973103). Exit the car park W and cross the Rd to the NT. Turn R and follow the NT for 1.6km (1 mile) NE.

51.181304, 0.962453

 ### The Devil's Kneading Trough, Broad Downs
Wildflowers and wide views.
▶**Find** Wye Nature Reserve car park, TN25 5HE (51.169790, 0.973103). Exit the car park W, cross the Rd to the NT and walk 460m (1,500ft) to the site.

51.169046, 0.971425

Samphire Hoe

THE VALIANT SAILOR, FOLKESTONE

Pub for motorhome and campervan stopovers. Good location on the B2011 between the port of Dover and the Eurotunnel, next to the Battle of Britain Memorial. Car park can accommodate up to four motorhomes each night. No electric hookups. Toilets during opening hours.

No charge for overnight, but you must eat and drink at the pub in the evening.

New Dover Rd, Capel-le-Ferne, Folkestone, Kent CT18 7JJ

www.thevaliantsailor.co.uk/motorhomes

01303 250737

☾ Caesar's Camp (Folkestone Castle), Folkestone

Rest on the vast, grassy domed earthworks that is Caesar's Camp – a horseshoe ring of ramparts. An Iron Age fort, or even earlier. The earth banks and ditches tower above the Channel Tunnel terminus. The site was last developed by the Normans as a motte and ringwork castle built in 1140. The ringwork at Castle Hill is one of the UK's largest, and the best in the SE of England.

51.097695, 1.160761

🌳 Steady Hole, The Warren

Grassy meadows that fall down into wild thickets. Green blankets of long grass and elder make way for cliffs and sea views down to Folkestone.

51.098799, 1.208904

☾ Battle of Britain Memorial and Wing Visitor Centre, Capel-le-Ferne

A memorial to those who gave their lives in combat. Lots of good information, even if arriving after close. Great views.

51.098207, 1.205624

🌳 Abbot's Cliff Sound Mirror, Hougham Without

Historic walk along the chalk cliffs of the English Channel. Look down on Samphire Hoe nature reserve, which covers the entrance to the Channel Tunnel. Much information about wartime technology linked to mirrors, as well as the tunnels that surround the place. These mirrors were the forerunner of radar.

51.102040, 1.249571

Western Heights, Dover

Stand on the hills above Dover to see the French coast. It's both strangely ominous and exhilarating.

▶ **Find** car park off Military Rd, CT17 9DZ (51.125755, 1.309176). Exit the car park E and onto the Rd. Turn R and follow the Rd S as part of the NT around the S edge of the site.

51.122635, 1.307528

Path start/end, 'We are all Winners' Podium, Clarendon

The N Downs Way starts/ends by the waterside in a sort of triumph: a winner's podium in the shape of a bench to rest. The bench is engraved with the words 'we are' in Latin, a modern reference to the communal sense of achievement and knowledge that comes from walking with a purpose. For those arriving here from Farnham, the destination was Dover.

▶ **Find** N Downs Way start/finish CT16 1LA (51.122521, 1.315266), overlooking the harbour.

51.122513, 1.315273

WILD THINGS TO DO BEFORE YOU DIE

SCRUMP around a free communal orchard

EXPLORE the UK's oldest church

TOUCH a castle and chalk cliff

REST on the grassy domed earthworks that is Caesar's Camp

STAND on hills to see the French coast

WALK around the UK's smallest church

TASTE hazelnuts on a wood path

VISIT a churchyard with the best S Downs views

BALANCE over stepping stones across the river beneath a giant horse chestnut

SMELL the UK's best box tree woodland

TOUCH a 3,000-year-old burial chamber

STAND beside a giant standing stone on a parish boundary

FORAGE autumn chestnuts

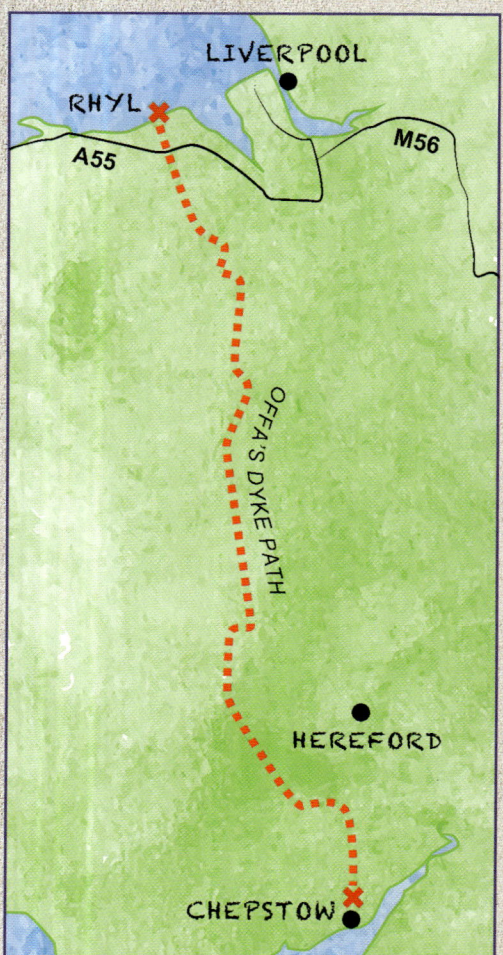

Top TEN

Chepstow Castle, Look out for dolphins, porpoises and seals around the 11th-century castle.
51.646652, -2.671982

 Devil's Pulpit, The UK's biggest population of lesser horseshoe bats roosts here.
51.692475, -2.662619

Monnow Bridge, Walk across the last medieval fortified river bridge in Britain.
51.808960, -2.720017

Llanfair Hill Shropshire, Find the best-preserved sections of Offa's Dyke where the Jack Mytton Way crosses the trail.
52.400031, -3.097543

 River Clun, Listen for otters whistling. They 'peep' to each other from the river crossing beside the timber farm of Bryndrinog.
52.434982, -3.095078

 Oak at the Gate of the Dead, Touch a 1,000-year-old oak tree.
52.931453, -3.095344

Sodom Covert, Tramp a 1.6km (1 mile) long wooded boreen along one of the most important historic sites in Britain. The earliest evidence of UK human settlement was found along this trail.
53.236292, -3.353700

 Plumweir Cliff, Look for herons that nest in the trees above the Wye.
51.687347, -2.665021

Gop Hill, Explore the limestone crevices where Palaeolithic remains have been found.
53.309976, -3.376475

 Graig Fawr, Big views over Prestatyn, Snowdonia and N Wales.
53.311931, -3.413021

World's End

OFFA'S DYKE

BEST FOR: WILD WOOD

Whistling otters, tidal woodland, Neanderthal finds

START: SEDBURY CLIFFS   FINISH: PRESTATYN

The rarest woodland in Britain runs beside the southern section of Offa's Dyke.

Meandering tidal waters, lined in yew, are what make the Wye Valley so special. The water cuts a deep slope on either side of the riverbank, creating a unique wet woodland of hazel, oak and whitebeam.

Tidal woodland is the richest habitat in England and Wales. This incised, meandering gorge is somewhere to go to look for seals or listen to whistling otters. Herons nest and roost along the lower parts of the Wye. Atlantic salmon feed here too. Salt air and trees provide coolness in summer and warmth in winter.

Taste, smell, hug and listen to immerse the senses in a primeval and nervous energy that puts our feelings on alert while our mind vibrates with nature.

The last Ice Age entirely wiped out all England's trees. When the climate thawed 10,000 years ago, pine and birch seeds blew in on the southerly winds, allowing the native trees here today to root: alder, elder, ash, aspen, bay willow, crab apple, hawthorn, hazel, holly, hornbeam, large-leaved lime, rowan, sessile oak, small-leaved lime, wild cherry, wild service tree, elm and yew. Start to identify them around the path one by one. Learn the names of trees, then give them a name of your own, and start to speak to them.

Wild wood blends with limestone caves, then transitions to Black Mountains moorland and shrub heath. Bog and blanket mire separates salt and fresh water that cascades as mist back into the rainforest, and then flows back out on the next tide like pollen seeding new life.

Sedbury Cliffs

BROADROCK ACCOMMODATION

 B&B close to the Wye Valley cliffs. En-suite rooms, pick-up service, boot room, drying room, wash-down area, cycle storage, bike-wash facility.

Woodcroft, Chepstow, Monmouthshire, NP16 7HY

www.broadrock.co.uk

07939 877293

Slimeroad Pill, River Severn, Tidenham

Offa's Dyke starts/ends with a view over the Severn and its bridge. What lies ahead is one of the most highly charged, boundaries in the world: the line between England and Wales. The dyke divides and separates like a folly... which in every sense is what the dyke is. Less monument, more mark in the sand. A mark carved by river, tide and time. These limestone caves, Black Mountains and Wye Valley woodlands hold clues to a history that predates our Stone Age ancestors. This is a good place to look for answers: at the water's edge.

▶**Find** the junction where Buttington Terrace meets Beachley Rd, Sedbury, Chepstow, NP16 7EX. (51.634178, -2.654776). With your back to the terrace, turn R along the main Rd and walk N for 55m (180ft) to the trail path. Turn R and follow the trail for 500m (⅓ mile) to the riverside, overlooking Slimeroad Pill and the Severn Rd Bridge.

51.632526, -2.648499

 ## Chepstow Castle, Chepstow

Look out for dolphins, porpoises and seals around the 11th-century castle on the Wye's steep muddy banks. Best seen from the Old Wye Bridge into Chepstow. It's an impressive castle, but dwarfed by the river's energy, soup-like waters and deceptively strong currents. This mystic river cuts a deep, meandering gorge all the way to Monmouth.

51.646652, -2.671982

 ## Woodcroft Cliff, Forest of Dean

Wild limestone caves and cliffs. Otters feed on young eels here. The elver swim between Llandogo and Bigsweir in April, 8km (5 miles) upriver as the crow flies.

51.660366, -2.665260

258 NATIONAL TRAILS

OFFA'S DYKE   259

BEECHES FARM CAMPSITE

 Camping for tents, campervans and small caravans. Laundry and toilet. Hook-up points for tents.

Miss Grace's Ln, Tidenham Chase, Chepstow, Monmouthshire, NP16 7JR

www.beechesfarmcampsite.co.uk

07791 540016

CAMP HILLCREST BUNKHOUSE

 Bunkhouse sleeps 16 across three rooms. Kitchen and communal lounge with a log burner. Two acres of grounds and views. Giant wood-fired hot tub, a high rope course, fire pit and pizza oven. Evening meals and laundry facilities. Wheelchair access.

Camp Hillcrest, The Common, St Briavels, Gloucestershire, GL15 6SH

www.independenthostels.co.uk/members/camphillcrest

01594 531220

Plumweir Cliff, Forest of Dean (Top Ten)

Herons nest in the trees along this section of river. Perfect views across the Wye from Shorn Cliff Rock, with a look at Tintern Abbey from the largest and longest river gorge in Wales.

51.687347, -2.665021

Devil's Pulpit, Tidenham (Top Ten)

Look out for bats that roost in limestone caves. The UK's biggest population of lesser horseshoe bats roosts here. Infamous site of limestone outcrop, from where monks were allegedly corrupted, no doubt by the views of such a remarkable gorge that falls to depths of up to 200m. This steep Wye Valley is home to Britain's rarest and most important woodland. Yews, hazel and whitebeam shore up the steep slopes, between a combination of upland oak and wet valley woodland.

51.692475, -2.662619

Tintern Abbey, Chepstow

On the wrong side of the river for the trail, but on the right side of spectacular. Too good to miss. There is a FP here (51.699787, -2.680937), which is a short but lovely detour. The abbey ruin sits on one of the most impressive U-bends on the Wye's winding journey. Good for fishing and canoes. Atlantic salmon travel up in early summer, when they return to spawn in the Wye's higher reaches.

51.697148, -2.676979

Tintern Abbey

MAYHILL HOTEL

 Affordable hotel with secure storage for bikes and kayaks.

Mayhill Close, Monmouth, Monmouthshire, NP25 3LX

www.themayhillhotel.com

01600 712280

GREEN DRAGON, MONMOUTH

 Pub for breakfasts, evening meals and bar snacks.

St Thomas Square, Monmouth, Monmouthshire, NP25 5ES

www.facebook.com/inMonmouth

01600 712561

OLD RECTORY GUEST HOUSE

 B&B with secure cycle storage, laundry facilities, luggage transport service and packed lunches provided.

Llangattock Lingoed, Abergavenny, Monmouthshire, NP7 8RR

www.visitmonmouthshire.com/accommodation/the-old-rectory-p1500121

01873 821326

Bigsweir Bridge, St Briavels

Peaceful place for fishing or paddling. The bridge is impressive in itself as a work of art against the landscape.

51.742592, -2.669269

The Kymin, The Round House

A hill with views across the valley and England/Wales border. The hill is most famous for the naval memorial temple built in 1800. The site was visited by Nelson, who is named on one of the plaques.

▶**Find** the Kymin car park, NP25 3SF (51.807783, -2.686201). Exit the car park E and find the NT, then turn R. Follow the path for 365m (1,200ft) to the site.

51.808511, -2.686328

Lady Park Wood, Monmouth

Lady Park is a unique experiment in neglect. It has been completely neglected, on purpose, since 1945. A 3.2km (2 miles) wooded detour from Beaulieu Wood (see below).

51.831658, -2.658897

Little Doward Woods, Monmouth

These woods stretch between Whitchurch and Wyastone Leys. The Wye Valley Walk leads through the woods. This site is important for its flora and fauna, geology, archaeology and industrial history. A large Bronze Age hillfort at the top of the hill offers spectacular views across the Wye Valley, while caves provide archaeological interest and roosting sites for greater and lesser horseshoe bats. They are across the river from Lady Park Wood, so a packraft is needed.

51.840790, -2.670651

Beaulieu Wood, Monmouth

Ancient woodland of beech, oak, birch and rowan, mixed with pine. Paths are accessible from The Kymin and Offa's Dyke NT, which runs along the SW margin of the wood.

51.812237, -2.686189

Monmouth Castle and Regimental Museum, Monmouth

Memorial gardens, many historic exhibits and birthplace of King Henry V.

▶**Find** Monmouth Rowing Club car park, NP25 3DP (51.813117, -2.708567). Exit the car park E and find the FP on the riverbank. Turn L and follow the FP SW to the bridge to meet the NT. Walk W into the town and castle.

51.812265, -2.716806

Bigsweir Bridge, River Wye

THE HUNTERS MOON

 Traditional pub trading since the 13th century. B&B, real ales, coffee and baguette or meal.

Llangattock Lingoed, Abergavenny, Monmouthshire, NP7 8RR

www.hunters-moon-inn.co.uk

01873 821499

RISING SUN

 Pub B&B and campsite. Caravan pitches and evening meals

Abergavenny, Monmouthshire, NP7 8DL

01878 890254

Monnow Bridge, Overmonnow
Top TEN

The last medieval fortified river bridge in Britain with the gate tower still in place. Henry V was born in the tower above the gatehouse.

51.808960, -2.720017

White Castle, Whitecastle

A moated 12th-century Norman castle. Remote ruin.

51.845719, -2.902141

St Cadoc's Church, Abergavenny

Beautiful white church with 13th-century features. Surrounded by wildflower meadow.

51.875712, -2.928924

Pentwyn Fort, Crucorney

The start of the wild moorland known as 'Hatterrall Ridge'. A dangerous place when mist rolls in, and easy to get lost along the higher parts. Very exposed, no shelter, no escape.

51.901603, -2.988939

THE GRANGE

 B&B (April to October), camping and glamping all year round.

The Grange, Capel-y-ffin, Abergavenny, Gwent, NP7 7NP

www.grangetrekking-wales.co.uk

01873 890215

LANCASTER GUEST HOUSE

 B&B with bike storage, luggage transport service and packed lunches.

Old Hereford Rd, Pandy, Abergavenny, Monmouthshire, NP7 8DW

01873 890699

Hatterrall Ridge, Black Darren, Herefordshire border Crucorney

Look for peregrine falcons along the 17.7km (11 miles) heather FP over the Black Mountains, Brecon Beacons. The path runs from River Monnow FB (51.890656, -2.972953) to Tack Wood (52.049760, -3.112373). The highest point is 700m (2,300ft). A pile of stones marks the 9.65km (6 miles) post N (see below).
▶**Find** the car park, Hereford, HR2 0NG (51.963444, -3.023607). Exit the car park NW and turn SE along the Rd. Follow the Rd for 685m (2,250ft) until the FP on the R. Take the FP SW and follow it for 1.6km (1 mile) onto the ridge, where it meets the NT. Turn R and follow the NT 1km (⅔ mile) NNW to the site.

51.957573, -3.026386

Pile of Stones, Craswall, Herefordshire / Crucorney, Monmouthshire

Rare whitebeams grow on these slopes. The fruit is good to eat if left on the tree until after frost... and a little rotten. Ash, hazel and yew also grow along these Black Mountain slopes.

51.980804, -3.06422

Buttington Cross, River Severn

OFFA'S DYKE 263

HAYBLUFF HOLIDAYS

 Self-catering cottage and lodges.

The Birches, Cusop, Hay-on-Wye, Herefordshire, HR3 5RN

www.haybluff.co.uk

07817 824937

BORDER BEAN

 Café and art gallery in the centre of Kington, serving great coffee and cake.

22–24 High St, Kington, Herefordshire, HR5 3AX

01544 231625

MELLINGTON HALL COUNTRY HOUSE HOTEL

 Hotel, holiday home park and caravan pitches with shower facilities in 270 acres of parkland. Path runs through the grounds, with woodland walks, pools and streams. Breakfast, afternoon tea, evening meal.

Mellington, Church Stoke, Powys, SY15 6HX

www.mellingtonhall.co.uk

01588 620056

HEATH COTTAGE FARM B&B

 Budget B&B and camp pitches, with secure cycle storage.

Forden, Welshpool, SY21 8LX

01938 580453

 ### Hay Bluff, Craswall, Herefordshire / Bwlch yr Efengyl, Llanigon

A 677m view over Hay-on-Wye, and the many ridge points along the S tracks.

▶ **Find** Hay Bluff car park, HR3 5RJ (52.028795, -3.110180), just S of the stone circle. To find Hay Bluff peak (and so divert from the NT), find the FP SW of the car park and follow the trail 1km (⅔ mile) up the hill. For the NT only, exit the car park N and follow the boreen N for 500m (⅓ mile) to meet the NT.

52.022846, -3.102731

 ### Hay-on-Wye Bridge, Clyro

Famous river crossing between two Norman castles, bookshops and cafés.

52.076446, -3.127717

 ### St Mary's Church, Kington

Wild church close to the River Arrow. Tea and biscuits in return for a donation to the honesty box. Beautiful stone wall and several yew trees.

52.149321, -3.147003

 ### Whetstone, Kington Rural, Herefordshire

Touch an impressive landmark stone of unknown origin. May have been used as an alignment beacon or a stone for sharpening knives. No one is quite sure, but the views are good.

52.204048, -3.084620

 ### Hergest Ridge, Monkey Puzzle Trees, Kington Racecourse, Kington Rural

Two puzzles in one: why would anyone park monkey puzzle trees and a racecourse on a raised moor. Trees or racecourse, this is one of the highlights of the entire walk.

52.203776, -3.083172

 ### Dolly Old Bridge, Presteigne

Bridge over the River Lugg for kingfishers, dippers and packrafting.

52.281078, -3.059896

Panpunton Hill, Llanfair Waterdine/Stowe,

Stargaze over the Teme Valley and back towards Knighton.

▶ **Find** Kinsley Wood car park (52.354776, -3.048188). Exit the car park W on the BW and travel 365m (1,200ft) to the NT. Turn R and head NE for 800m (½ mile) to the site.

52.358741, -3.057027

Montgomery Castle

THE POWIS ARMS
A 16th-century pub between the River Severn and the Montgomery Canal path.

Pool Quay, Welshpool, Powys, SY21 9JS

www.facebook.com/ profile.php?id=61556278960829

01938 739048

MAES OFFA STAYS
Campsite and self-catering in a touring caravan.

Maes Offa, Parson's Ln, Llandysilio, Llanymynech, Powys, Wales, SY22 6RA

www.maesoffastays.square.site

07944 178033

Llanfair Hill, Llanfair Waterdine
Best-preserved sections of Offa's Dyke, where the Jack Mytton Way crosses the trail.

52.400031, -3.097543

River Clun, Newcastle on Clun, Shropshire
Visit after dark to listen for otters whistling. They 'peep' to each other from the river crossing beside the timber-framed Bryndrinog farmhouse. This is one of the cleanest rivers in Wales, and is home to the rare freshwater pearl mussel – one of the last populations in England and Wales. Also Atlantic salmon and white-clawed freshwater crayfish.

52.434982, -3.095078

St John the Baptist Church, Mainstone
Church full of bats, yew tree and history. The stone from which the village got its name is next to the pulpit. Churchtown Wood is opposite.

52.478990, -3.084276

Montgomery Castle, Montgomery
Historic castle for stories and views. The walled town was sacked and burned by Owain Glyndŵr's army in 1402. The castle survived but the town remained a ruin until the 17th century. The site is a 1.6km (1 mile) detour from the path.

52.563240, -3.149785

River Camlad crossing, Devil's Hole
River crossing at the Wales/England border.

52.585687, -3.135944

LLYN RHYS CAMPSITE

 Campsite. Packed lunches provided.

Llandegla, Wrexham, LL11 3AF

www.llynrhyscampsite.co.uk

07555 660465

Green Wood, Forden with Leighton and Trelystan
Western views through the trees towards the Severn Valley from pine and broadleaf wood.

52.624992, -3.110740

Beacon Ring Fort, Forden with Leighton and Trelystan
A full circle of views over Welshpool and the Severn Estuary. Fort is 408m (1,340ft) at its highest point. Planted with pine trees, a 200m (655ft) wide saucer of foliage.

52.644774, -3.088782

Montgomery Canal, Pool Quay
Large fish sunbathe in the shallows. Look for them from the stone bridge over the canal, where the dyke joins the Severn Way.

52.697068, -3.102158

Pool Quay, Welshpool
Quay marks the start/end of a 6.4km (4 mile) walk along the River Severn. Views of Breidden Hill to the E, and the iconic Rodney's Pillar on the summit.

52.697068, -3.102158

Llanymynech, Carreghofa
The Welsh/English border runs down the main street of Llanymynech.

52.781851, -3.089078

Upper Pentire

PLAS DOLBEN FARM

Campsite and small caravans on a working farm a 20-minute walk from the path. Farm produce available to buy. Basic site, so no toilets, showers or electrical connections. Cold water tap close to the pitches. Horsebox parking, horse stabling, grazing.

Llangynhafal, Denbigh, LL16 4LN

www.pitchup.com/campsites/Wales/North-Wales/Denbighshire/Denbigh/plas_dolben

07984 521413

 ### Asterley Rocks, Carreghofa

Views W to Berwyn Mountains before crossing near to a golf club and following the Welsh border through oak woodland.

52.788780, -3.097381

 ### Oswestry Racecourse, Oswestry, Shropshire

Masses of wildflowers, including rare orchids.

▶ **Find** Oswestry Old Racecourse Common car park, SY10 7HW (52.866470, -3.102081). Exit the car park to the W and walk through the woodland 275m (900ft) to the site.

52.866329, -3.102196

Top Ten — Oak at the Gate of the Dead, Chirk Castle, Chirk

Oak tree more than 1,000 years old, thought to mark the site of the 1165 Battle of Crogen and named for a supposed burial site of battle dead nearby. The oak may have been standing at the time of the battle. The event marks when Owain Gwynedd is said to have defeated the English and forced King Henry II to retreat. According to legend, the dead were buried in the dyke. The oak is 300m (985ft) from the Rd on a permissive path open in summer.

52.931453, -3.095344

Sodom Covert

OFFA'S DYKE 267

THE OLD MILL
Family-run B&B on the path at the S end of Candy Woods. Evening meals and packed lunches. Small campsite with water and a loo. Hot drinks, and use the electricity and Wi-Fi in the Kettle House run on an honesty payment system. Bacon/egg rolls for breakfast from the house.

Candy, Oswestry, Shropshire, SY10 9AZ

www.oldmillcandy.co.uk
01691 900537

Vale of Llangollen, Llangollen Canal, Llangollen
Packraft on the canal for 4.8km (3 miles) from Pontcysyllte Aqueduct (52.971867, -3.091640) to Llandyn Hall (52.974955, -3.146331) as an alternative to walking the path.

52.965034, -3.112032

Pontcysyllte Aqueduct, Pontcysyllte
Outstanding feat of engineering. Incredible views from the top.
www.pontcysyllte-aqueduct.co.uk

52.970518, -3.087736

World's End, Llantysilio, Denbighshire
Big views from the riverside after a walk across the spectacular Eglwyseg Crags. These limestone crags tower 450m over Llangollen for 8km (5 miles).

53.021794, -3.145269

Llandegla Forest, Llandegla, Denbighshire
Pine and broadleaf boreen and BW from World's End. The forest and surrounding moors are home to the largest population of black grouse in Wales.

53.048239, -3.165652

Foel Fenlli Hillfort, Llanbedr Dyffryn Clwyd
Prehistoric settlement – a hoard of 1,500 Roman coins were found in 1816 after an accidental heather fire.
▶**Find** where the NT leaves the Rd at Ruthin, LL15 2YG (53.078842, -3.238879). Follow the NT N for 9.6km (6 miles) to the site, via) Moel y Plas, then Moel Llanfair, and Moel Gyw. For a short walk, find Bwlch Penbarras car park, Bwlch Penbarras, Mold, CH7 5SH. Exit the car park SE and walk 500m (⅓ mile) to the site.

53.131160, -3.255065

Moel Famau, Denbighshire
The lookout point from the Jubilee Tower is the best view towards Snowdonia and E over the English border. A smooth, rounded hill, covered in heather.

53.154500, -3.255900

Moel Arthur Hillfort, Denbighshire
Big views, dark skies, heather-covered ridges over hillforts. Stone tools dating back more than 9,000 years have been found here in excavations.
▶**Find** Moel Arthur car park, CH7 5NZ (53.182105, -3.278143). Exit the car park W and follow the NT 500m (⅓ mile) uphill to the site.

53.184492, -3.280591

Prestatyn

 ### Moel-y-Gaer Fort, Llanbedr
This hillfort is along the downhill trek into Prestatyn. Rare bilberry moor and limestone grasslands. The Clwydian Range is famous for Iron Age hillforts that line the summit crest of Moel y Gaer, Moel Arthur and Penycloddiau. This W-facing ridge line hangs over the Vale of Clwyd.

53.225638, -3.354903

 ### Sodom Covert, Sodom
A 1.6km (1 mile) long wooded boreen along one of the most important historic sites in Britain. The earliest evidence of UK human settlement was found along this trail at Ffynnon Beuno Cave, Tremeirchion ((53.240953, -3.371897). Stone tools have been dated to more than 40,000 years ago. Neanderthal remains dating to 230,000 years ago were found 8km (5 miles) W of the Clwydian Range trail, in Pontnewydd Cave, at Cefn Meiriadog near St Asaph (53.226944, -3.476111). Teeth from at least five Neanderthal individuals were recovered, along with hand axes. Later finds have shown possible encounters of Neanderthals and/or humans in the cave system.

53.236292, -3.353700

 ### Gop Hill, Denbighshire
Look for lesser horseshoe bats in the caves around the Clwydian hills. Palaeolithic remains are often found in these limestone crevices. Many have been found at the Gop Hill caves and cairns. Human bones and tools, as well as the bones of lions, spotted hyaenas, woolly rhinos and mammoths.

53.309976, -3.376475

NATIONAL TRAILS

 Graig Fawr, Prestatyn

Big views over Prestatyn, Snowdonia and the N Wales coast.
▶**Find** car park for Graig Fawr, Triangulation View Point, LL18 6BY (53.309257, -3.409426). Exit the car park to the N and follow the uphill path for 400m (¼ mile) to the site.

53.311931, -3.413021

Path end, Prestatyn

Offa's Dyke starts/ends in Prestatyn with a foot soaking in tide and sand. It's a contrast to mountain climbs and wilderness. Sand, sunsets and probably a bit overdeveloped as a lengthy tourist focus. Prestatyn is like a streetwise sherpa with benefits: a transit host into or out of the wild.
▶**Find** Beach Rd E car park, LL19 7EY (53.342935, -3.410706), looking over the sea.

53.342343, -3.412811

WILD THINGS TO DO BEFORE YOU DIE

TOUCH an oak tree more than 1,000 years old

TRAMP a 1.6km (1 mile) long wooded boreen

WAIT for dolphins around an 11th-century castle

WATCH the UK's biggest population of lesser horseshoe bats

WALK across the last medieval fortified river bridge in Britain

FIND the best-preserved sections of Offa's Dyke

LISTEN for whistling otters

EXPLORE the earliest UK human settlement

LOOK for herons that nest in trees

MOVE around the limestone crevices of palaeolithic remains

ENJOY views over Prestatyn, Snowdonia and N Wales

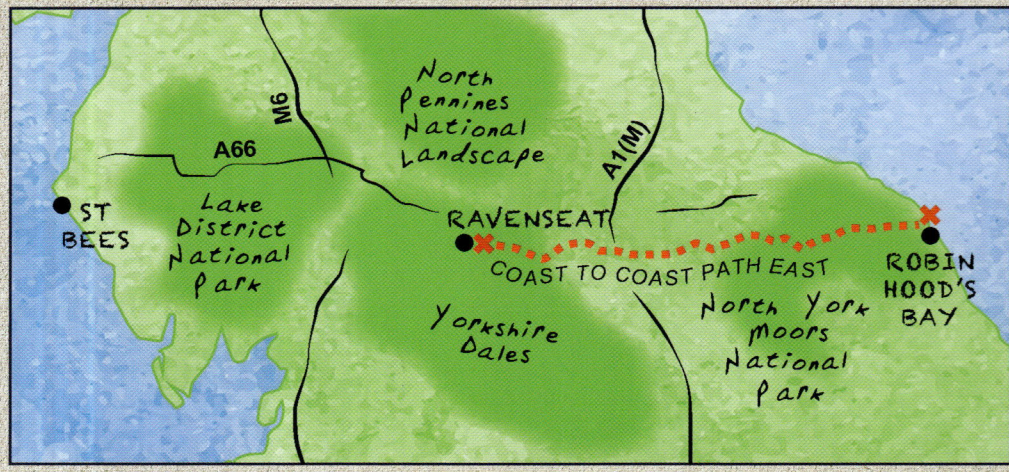

 Cut Rd Waterfalls, Look for the flashes of tiny nuthatches in the trees along the falls Ln at the end of a long BW.
54.405605, -0.898452

 Greenhow Plantation Pine Forest, Forage for mushrooms in the spruce and pine forest. Penny buns and chanterelles are common around spruce roots at the edge of the woodland.
54.421755, -1.112612

 Wainstones, Views as far as the North Sea and Middlesborough. Look out for rock climbers.
54.424417, -1.138531

 Mount Grace Priory, The largest Carthusian priory in Britain is a short detour from the path.
54.379692, -1.310021

 W Field Boreen, Find coal fungus to use as fire tinder. Look for the fungus, also known as 'King Alfred's Cakes', on ash trees.
54.408923, -1.755605

 Hudswell Woods Richmond Bridge, Feel the spooky air around 'Witch's Wood'.
54.400243, -1.740359

 Swinner Gill Falls, Feel plumes of water fall over a rocky summit. The waterfall at Swinner Gill, to High Whim (54.407201, -2.107076) is impressive.
54.406019, -2.136652

 Kisdon Force, Traditional wild swim spot but care needed.
54.404431, -2.157873

 Fort, Hurgill Rd, Touch Willance's Leap monument.
54.412700, -1.790319

 Richmond Falls, Listen to fish jumping around the series of falls.
54.400631, -1.734083

COAST TO COAST PATH EAST

BEST FOR: WATERFALLS, SPRINGS AND WELLS

Giant owls, Wainstones, waterfalls

START: ROBIN HOOD'S BAY   FINISH: RAVENSEAT

The sound and sight of water is one of the thrills of overland travel. A waterfall is an alchemical marriage between water and air: a merging and pulling apart of two elements gives birth to a misty haze that looks like pollen blowing from a birch.

The English and Welsh interior isn't flush with waterfalls, so this eastern section of the Coast to Coast is welcome, with falls sourced from rivers, wells and springs.

Waters are most dramatic and hazardous after heavy rain. The hard cliffs of this NT support maritime crevice and ledge vegetation that favours sloping rushes of water into the valleys.

It's remarkable how often you'll walk through the head of a fall on the trail without even noticing.

Arkle Beck, High Fremington

YHA BOGGLE HOLE

Hostel in an old smugglers' cove, with sea views and wooded grounds. Café and woodburning stove. It's 800m (½ mile) S of the path start, but a good place to stop over.

Mill Beck, Fylingthorpe, Whitby, N Yorkshire, YO22 4UQ

www.yha.org.uk/hostel/yha-boggle-hole
0345 371 9504

Brambles Bistro, The Dock, Robin Hood's Bay

The Coast to Coast E path starts/ends near a cobbled boat ramp down to Robin Hood's Bay. Most NT are carved from our landscape along raised fossil ridges or water to serve one of two purposes: military defence or travel. C2C is different. It was created for its beauty by Alfred Wainwright. This eastern section follows the best of the N York Moors and Yorkshire Dales: dramatic waterfalls, limestone pavement and upland heather. It's only one man's idea of what beauty is... which is why he wanted us all to leave 'his' path and find our own. To walk the C2C properly is to constantly look for the detours. That was the beauty in Wainwright's trail. It's not there to be remade or diverted by others. It's there to be diverted from, in your own time, on your own terms, by you and those that follow.

➤**Find** the end of New Rd, Robin Hood's Bay, Whitby, YO22 4SW, where it runs down to the sea.

54.430271, -0.532271

Graystone Hills Earthwork, Hawsker-cum-Stainsacre

Earthworks with heather, grass and sea breeze.

54.429063, -0.586778

Robin Hood Bay

THE OLD SCHOOL HOUSE

 Nine individual rooms sleeping 4–6 in each, 1.6km (1 mile) from Robin Hood's Bay. Shared bathrooms, showers and living spaces. All bedding is provided, but towels should be brought.

Fisherhead, Robin Hood's Bay, Whitby, N Yorkshire, YO22 4ST

www.oldschoolhouserhb.co.uk

01947 880723

N YORKSHIRE MOORS CARAVAN AND MOTORHOME CLUB CAMPSITE

 Tent and touring pitches. No toilets.

Sneaton, Whitby, N Yorkshire, YO22 5JE

www.ukcampsite.co.uk/sites/external_link.asp?site_id=5374

01947 810505

THE OLD MILL B&B

 B&B on the banks of the River Esk next to the famous stepping stones and the edge of the N York Moors. The moors are designated a Dark Skies Reserve.

Broom House Ln, Egton Bridge, Whitby, N Yorkshire, YO21 1UZ

www.theoldmillegtonbridge.com

Rocket Post Field

Falling Foss Waterfall, Eskdaleside cum Ugglebarnby

Listen for the sound of falling water. You'll hear it before you see it on the wooded path.
▶ **Find** Sneaton Forest car park, YO22 (54.420581, -C.631749). Exit the car park NW onto Foss Ln. Find FP opposite through the trees W and walk 365m (1,200ft) to the site.

54.420835, -0.634792

Little Beck Waterfall, Little Beck Wood, Eskdaleside cum Ugglebarnby

Look for deer around the falls. There is a ford (54.431950, -0.646262) close to the Littlebeck Methodist Church.

54.431272, -0.641619

E Arncliffe Wood River Walk, Egton

Smell the scent of wet plant life along the River Esk walk. Many traditional wildflowers, including buttercups and primroses, grow around the ancient woods.

54.437359, -0.792580

Beggars Bridge (by main bridge), Egton

Historic packhorse bridge over the Esk, known as 'Lovers' Bridge'. Stepping stones nearby at Egton Bridge, and bluebells woods.
▶ **Find** Beggars Bridge car park, YO21 2QL (54.43865, -0.792488).

54.438602, -0.792196

ARNCLIFFE ARMS B&B

A 19th-century coaching inn, for B&B and wild camping. Locally sourced meats, fresh fish and vegetarian options. Dog-friendly.

Arncliffe Terrace, Glaisdale, Whitby, N Yorkshire, YO21 2QL

www.arncliffearmsbb.co.uk

01947 897555

BANK HOUSE FARM HOLIDAY ACCOMMODATION

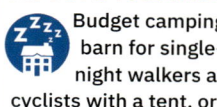

Budget camping barn for single-night walkers and cyclists with a tent, or B&B. DIY breakfast and the organic farm sells seasonal meats.

Glaisdale, Whitby, N Yorkshire, YO21 2QA

www.bankhousefarmhostel.co.uk

01947 897297

Cut Rd Waterfalls, Glaisdale Rigg

Look for tiny nuthatches in the trees along the falls Ln at the end of a long BW.

▶**Find** Knott Rd car park, YO21 2NL (54.401690, -0.927420). Exit the car park W and walk N along the Ln for 800m (½ mile) until finding BW on L. Follow the BW for 1.6km (1 mile) E to the site.

54.405605, -0.898452

Seavey Hill Rd, Danby

Forage along a wonderful 3.2km (2 miles) boreen and Rd, from the remains of Botton Cross (54.408534, -0.927179) to White Cross in W (54.409123, -0.949294).

▶**Find** Knott Rd car park, YO21 2NL (54.401690, -0.927420). Exit the car park W and walk N along the Ln for 800m (½ mile) until finding BW on L. Turn away from the BW and instead walk R and follow the track W for 460m (1,500ft) to the site.

54.404820, -0.926243

Gill Wath Waterfalls, Farndale Railway, Farndale E

Look for dippers around the bracken- and grass-laden waterfall. The water trickles beneath tree-lined skies 200m S of the path.

▶**Find** Blakey Ridge car park, YO62 7LQ (54.381554, -0.949342). Exit the car park W and cross the Rd to find NT. Follow the trail NW for 1.6km (1 mile) to the site.

54.388967, -0.966926

Carlton Moor, Cleveland

COAST TO COAST PATH EAST

THE LION INN

Rooms or camping at the highest point of the N York Moors. Big, iconic views over the valleys of Rosedale and Farndale from 1,325ft. Open fires burn in the ancient stone fireplaces.

Blakey Ridge, Kirkbymoorside, York, N Yorkshire, YO62 7LQ

www.lionblakey.co.uk
01751 417320

LORDSTONES COUNTRY PARK

Camping pods, yurts and tent pitches. Water, farm shop, café, and restaurant. Jumbo glamping pods open all year. Camping is seasonal from spring. (Also features as part of the Cleveland Way).

Carlton Bank, Chop Gate, N Yorkshire, TS9 7JH

www.lordstones.com
01642 778482

COTE GHYLL CARAVAN PARK & CAMPSITE

Pitches for walkers and cyclists on a large touring park. There's a café. (Also features as part of the Cleveland Way).

Cote Ghyll, Osmotherley, Northallerton, N Yorkshire, DL6 3AH

www.coteghyll.com
01609 883425

Cross Remains, Ingleby Greenhow

Look for stone markers along this moorland path, some with carved hands, others with faces. These stones marked a route between Stokesley and Kirkbymoorside. (Also features as part of the Cleveland Way).

54.412122, -1.058809

Round Hill/Cleveland, the Hand Stone, Ingleby Incline

Feel the energy around the burial ground of Urra Moor. Cairns at 454m on the BW.

54.406679, -1.086823

Greenhow Plantation Pine Forest, N York Moors National Park

Forage for mushrooms in the spruce and pine forest. Penny buns and chanterelles are common around spruce roots at the edge of the woodland, but also pine and bay boletes.

▶ Find the Clay Bank car park, TS9 7JA (54.424213, -1.119634) and walk S towards the southern edge, where the soil is warmer.

54.421755, -1.112612

The Wainstones, Bilsdale Midcable

Look out for rock climbers – everything from scrambles to pro climbs over the huge sandstone blocks that form the Wainstones. Some of the best views over the N York Moors are from Hasty Bank. (Also features as part of the Cleveland Way).

▶ Find Clay Bank car park, TS9 7JA (54.424213, -1.119634). Exit the car park W to find the Rd and then turn L and walk S 320m (1,050ft) to find the NT. Turn R onto the trail and follow it W for 3.2km (2 miles) to the site.

54.424417, -1.138531

Cringle Moor Throne, Bilsdale Midcable

Stone chair with views over Kirby Bank valley. Look out for jet and ironstone mining; aluminium as well in places.

54.422800, -1.177250

Lordstones, Carlton in Cleveland

Look for prehistoric stone carvings. The cup marks are cut into the kerbstones. These prehistoric stones define the perimeter of a Bronze Age burial mound. (Also features as part of the Cleveland Way).

54.420893, -1.191483

COTE GHYLL MILL YHA

 Budget hostel with drying room, lounge and communal kitchen. (Also features as part of the Cleveland Way).

Osmotherley, Northallerton, N Yorkshire, DL6 3AH

www.yha.org.uk/hostel/yha-osmotherley

01609 883425

THE WHITE SWAN

Award-winning village inn on the trail. B&B and five real ales during the walking season.

Danby Ln, Danby Wiske, Northallerton, N Yorkshire, DL7 0NQ

www.thewhiteswandanbywiske.co.uk

01609 775131

Beggars Bridge

 ### Scarth Nick Tumuli, Whorlton
Bracken-laden burial grounds with views over Scarth Wood.

54.394512, -1.278828

 ### Arncliffe Wood, Siddle Farm, E Harlsey
Look for kingfishers and herons around the wooded dells, pond and river walk. C2C is close to the Cleveland Way here and follows it for 64km (40 miles).

54.382717, -1.302851

 ### Mount Grace Priory, House and Gardens, Staddlebridge
Top TEN
The largest Carthusian priory in Britain is a short detour from the path. (Also features as part of the Cleveland Way).

54.379692, -1.310021

 ### Danby Wiske Church, Danby Wiske, Northallerton
Church for a rest, at the end of a yew-tree avenue.

54.379421, -1.481004

 ### Bolton Beck, S Ellerton
Waterside FP, lined with ash trees and wildflowers.
▶ **Find** Bolton-on-Swale Lake car park, DL10 6AP (54.383708, -1.618472). Exit the car park SE and walk onto the track. Turn L and follow the path SE 500m (⅓ mile) to Bolton Cross. Keep walking SE for 140m (460ft) and find a FP on the L. Follow the path NEE for 550m (1,800ft) to the site.

54.383336, -1.604168

COAST TO COAST PATH EAST

BROMPTON-ON-SWALE BUNKBARN

 Budget bunk barn with overnight parking for bikes. Village shop opposite. Kitchen, shower and toilet. Sheet sleeping sacks and towels for hire. Pub nearby.

24 Richmond Rd, Richmond, N Yorkshire, DL10 7HE

www.facebook.com/Bromptononswalebunkbarn

01748 818326

St Mary's Church, Bolton-on-Swale

Explore the churchyard. There is a story that a Henry Jenkins, a man associated with the church, died at 169 years of age. Accessible toilets nearby and hot drinks and light snacks available in the church.

54.387575, -1.613041

Howe Hill, Brompton-on-Swale

Find shelter in maple and willow on the River Swale.

54.391630, -1.642205

Crow Hole, Brompton-on-Swale

Paddle or packraft a few metres N or 300m N for the stone and pebble banks. Waterside FP on River Swale. Good place to shelter from weather.

54.389239, -1.670435

St Agatha's Church, Easby

Explore the church's medieval wall murals. The paintings were 'whitewashed' during the Reformation to protect them and remained hidden until Victorian times. The church's 9th-century cross base is in the V&A Museum.

54.396960, -1.719443

Easby Abbey, Easby

Abbey surrounded by a green. It has something of Tintern Abbey about it – Tintern is on the Wye, Easby Abbey on the banks of the Swale. Listen to the Echo Stone on entry.

54.396950, -1.719443

 Richmond Falls, Richmond

Watch fish jump around the series of falls.

▶ **Find** the Fosse car park, DL10 4JR (54.401399, -1.734419). Exit the car park SE and walk to the riverside and falls.

54.400631, -1.734083

Claybank, near Wainstones

THE KING'S HEAD HOTEL

Award-winning hotel and coaching inn. Fires in winter, a decked outdoor area and seasonal menus.

10 Market Pl, Richmond, N Yorkshire, DL10 4HS

www.kingsheadrichmond.co.uk

01748 850220

 ### Hudswell Woods, Richmond

Feel the spooky air around a river bridge and woodland. Known locally as 'Witch's Wood', the site is said to be haunted.

▶**Find** Richmond Falls (see p277). Exit the site W and follow the riverbank FP for 500m (⅓ mile) to site.

54.400243, -1.740359

 ### W Field Boreen, Westfields

Find coal fungus to use as fire tinder. Look for the fungus, also known as 'King Alfred's Cakes', along BW walk from Richmond to Willance's Leap monument via Whitcliffe Wood. They grow on dead ash branches that line the path. The route includes a boreen along 1.2km (¾ mile) from (54.407783, -1.749895) to Whitcliffe Farm (54.408699, -1.767176).

54.408923, -1.755605

Fort, Belleisle, Richmond

Touch Willance's Leap monument. FP to ruin and views.

▶**Find** Reeth Rd parking, DL10 4TJ (54.403467, -1.760159). Exit the car park S and follow the river FP W to the A6108. Cross the Rd to find the BW. Follow the BW W and then N onto Green Ln for 1km (⅔ mile). Take the BW W and follow for 2.4km (1½ miles) through Whitcliffe Wood to the site.

54.412700, -1.790319

Wainstones

BROMPTON-ON-SWALE CARAVAN PARK

Campsite on the banks of the River Swale and the edge of the Yorkshire Dales. Touring and camping pitches, glamping and self-catering.

Brompton-on-Swale, Richmond, N Yorkshire, DL10 7EZ

www.brompton caravanpark.co.uk

01748 824629

St Stephen's over Robin Hood Bay

Marrick Ford, Marrick Priory
Walk over a small beach of boulders at the bend in the river. A must-do diversion. Two-minute walk to the crossing.

54.374583, -1.896880

Marrick Priory, Marrick
Ruin, church and activity centre by the River Swale.

54.375693, -1.898327

Abbey Boreen, Marrick Priory
Follow a 1.6km (1 mile) boreen walk from Ewelop Hill (54.383900, -1.919979) W to abbey and Steps Woods.

54.379482, -1.907869

Reeth Bridge, Fremington
River bridge over Arkle Beck. Bench, picnic table, and paddling over stones and under tree canopy.

54.388083, -1.937964

Old Gang Beck, Strands
A 6.4km (4 miles) BW along the waterside, from Gunnerside Beck waterfall in W (54.413834, -2.097533) to Surrender Bridge (54.395932, -2.016894) via Hard Level Force waterfall.

▶ **Find** High Ln parking, DL11 6PN (54.393970, -2.018265) by Old Gang Beck. Cross the RB and walk 365m (1,200ft) to find the BW.

54.402168, -2.049113

ORCHARD CARAVAN & CAMPING PARK

Family-run site for small tents, motorhomes and caravans. Camping pod also available.

Back Ln, Reeth, Richmond, N Yorkshire, DL11 6TT

www.orchardcaravanpark.com

01748 884475

KELD BUNK BARN

Budget bunk rooms or private doubles. Keld Bunk Barn specialises in looking after walkers on the C2C and Pennine Way. The team work with Sherpa Van and Packhorse bag deliveries. This is a special place for walkers with open-plan living, dining and kitchen. Private hot tub, on-site washing and drying facilities, and boot drying. Home-cooked meals.

Park House, Keld, N Yorkshire, DL11 6DZ

www.keldbunkbarn.com

01748 886549

Old Gang Smelting Mill, Strands

Former mines at Moor House. Explore the mill ruin and peat stores.

▶ **Find** High Ln parking, DL11 6PN (54.393970, -2.018265) by Old Gang Beck. Cross the bridge and take the path to follow Mill Gill Beck up to the Old Gang mines.

54.406917, -2.067415

Swinner Gill Falls, Muker Meadows (Top Ten)

Feel water spray fall over a rocky summit. The waterfall at Swinner Gill to High Whim (54.407201, -2.107076) is impressive.

54.406019, -2.136652

Kisdon Force, Keld (Top Ten)

Traditional wild swim spot but care needed. Also a steep ravine and narrow path. Not for younger children or if you dislike heights! Beauty spot waterfall by woodland.

54.404431, -2.157873

Wain Wath Force, Muker

River Swale waterfall by woodland.

▶ **Find** parking on the B6270, here (54.409015, -2.180250) and here (54.409665, -2.187459) to get photos of the river and fall.

54.409565, -2.180099

Jenny Whalley Force (Fall), Ravenseat

A waterfall on the River Swale, close to Ravenseat Farm. A mire of cobbles, stepping stones and fords to explore. Grassy verges awash in buttercups and wildflowers.

54.426875, -2.213328

Richmond Castle

Rukin's Campsite, Keld

Whitsun Dale Beck Ford, Ravenseat

The C2C E path starts/ends at a ford crossing. This eastern section of the Yorkshire Dales contrasts with the rugged beauty of the N York Moors, before falling into the sea at Robin Hood's Bay. The halfway point along the C2C is where E meets W. The Irish Sea and the Lake District lie to the W.

▶**Find** Wain Wath Force waterfall, 6DZ (54.409027, -2.179877). Facing the river, turn L and follow the Rd W for 3.2km (2 miles) to the stone barn on the L. Opposite the barn, turn R and follow the Rd 2.1km (1⅓ miles) to the beck to meet the path.

54.426875, -2.213328

WILD THINGS TO DO BEFORE YOU DIE

HUNT for penny buns in a spruce woodland

EXPLORE the largest Carthusian priory in Britain

FEEL the spooky air around a 'witchy wood'

READ prehistoric stone carvings

FIND coal fungus to use as tinder

TOUCH a waterfall from a rocky summit

FORAGE for berries along a boreen

TAKE the plunge at a wild swim spot

LOOK for nuthatches beside a tree-lined waterfall

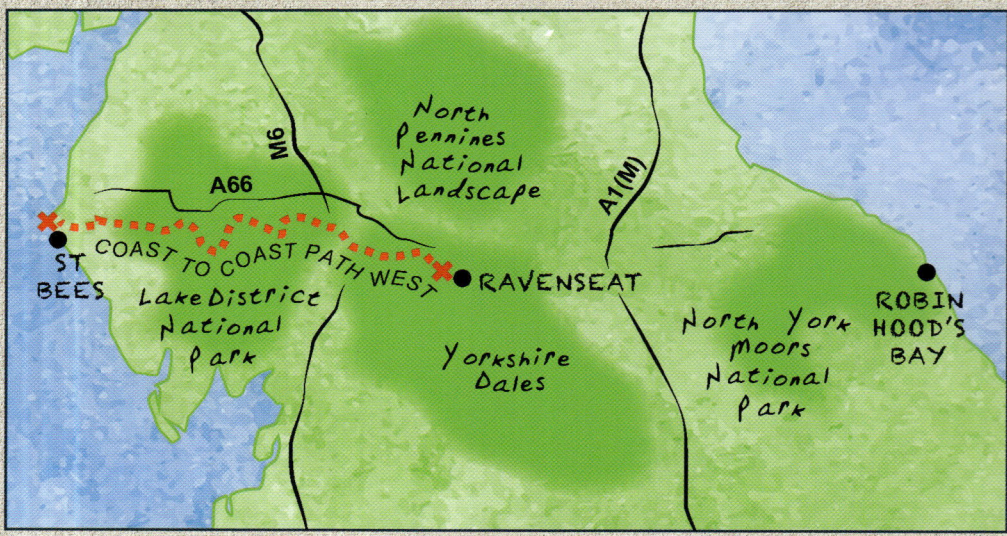

Top TEN

 ▶ **Nine Standards Rigg,** Touch stone cairns that look like wizard hats.
54.450098, -2.270743

 Gamelands Stone Circle, Feel the energy around a large and isolated stone circle site.
54.467726, -2.557070

 Oddendale Stone circle, Walk in and around a double stone circle.
54.509891, -2.631328

 M6 Yin and Yang, M6 meets 'out in the sticks'. A lonely pedestrian FB over the tide of crowded, crushing metal. Beautiful.
54.526699, -2.659001

 The (Haweswater) Forces (Falls), Keep eyes out for golden eagles. Last seen here in 2015, much work is underway to attract them back.
54.532087, -2.794817

 Grisedale Forest and Tarn, Look for red deer along the wild waterside walk, past Grisedale Forest.
54.500066, -3.003423

 Galleny Force Waterfall, Popular wild swim spot with many rocky dips locals call 'fairy pools'.
54.507810, -3.123769

 Hay Stacks, One of Wainwright's favourite peaks.
54.507900, -3.247420

 YHA Black Sail, The YHA's most remote youth hostel.
54.500311, -3.244795

 ▶ **Lining Crag,** Move over a sweeping basin of lunar rock carpeted in turf and sky.
54.490764, -3.107910

COAST TO COAST PATH WEST

BEST FOR: STONE

Golden eagles, lake views, stone circles

START: RAVENSEAT   FINISH: ST BEES

Walk through stone circles and scramble over shale.

Seabird colonies nest on the soft sandstone cliffs of St Bees, where the Coast to Coast W section ends/starts.

The most important bird breeding site in the NW has turned the red cliffs to white over time. Guano from fulmars, guillemots and razorbills shape the rocky head. Below are pebble beaches honeycombed in fossilised worm reefs.

Stone tells us what our ancestors understood about the meaning of life: reproduction.

Everything in the stories and symbols from the ancient and prehistoric world features themes on the survival of the species, not the individual.

The stone circle is the most obvious symbol of the eternal. Mostly sedimentary – these stones will still outlive yew trees. We plant yew trees in churchyards to preside over our stone graves. Headstones and stone circles don't grow branches that threaten our inability to celebrate change. Maybe that's why topiary is so annoyingly popular with churchwardens.

Apart from the likes of Stonehenge and Canterbury, sacred places are much less visited in the 21st century than the historic ruins and fossil beaches listed in books like this. That's why it's so nice when you stumble upon empty churches, isolated standing stones and ignored stone circles.

They are wonderful places to spend an hour or two, sitting in the shade of the past.

Ennerdale

Haweswater, Burnbanks

 ### Whitsun Dale Beck Ford, Ravenseat

The Coast to Coast W path starts/ends at a ford crossing. This W section of the Yorkshire Dales sets up an encounter with perhaps the most beautiful part of any trail in England and Wales: The Lakes. The Lakes are dominated by the most varied views in the world: U-shaped valleys that radiate surreal patterns of water, carved by ice 14,000 years ago. If time isn't a priority, move slowly to feel, hear and maybe see the unique wildlife: golden eagles, red squirrels and ospreys.

▶**Find** Wain Wath Force waterfall (54.409027, -2.179877). Facing the river, turn L and follow the Rd W for 3.2km (2 miles) to the stone barn on the L. Opposite the barn, turn R and follow the Rd 2.1km (1⅓ miles) to the beck to meet the path.

54.426875, -2.213328

 ### Nine Standards Rigg, Muker

Touch stone cairns that look like wizard hats. Impressively different. A 662m (2,172ft) peak via a BW, although the bogs can be troublesome for bikers. It's also a rough, bumpy path up. Lakes and Pennines views.

▶**Find** Birkett Ln car park, CA17 4JJ (54.472609, -2.3364360). Exit Ln SE onto BW and follow the path 4.8km (3 miles) SE and NE to the site.

54.450098, -2.270743

NATIONAL TRAILS

KIRKBY STEPHEN HOSTEL

 Former YHA hostel converted from a Methodist chapel. Still offers dormitory rooms with bunk beds, and most are en-suite. Lounge, kitchen with tea and coffee (donation appreciated), as well as bike storage and a drying room. Also a lounge/reading room.

Breakfast is available, but the hostel is surrounded by restaurants, cafés, pubs, takeaways.

Market St, Kirkby Stephen, Cumbria, CA17 4QQ

www.kirkbystephenhostel.co.uk

07812 558525

THE BLACK BULL

 Good-value food and rooms. Stacked burgers, pub classics, bar snacks and desserts.

38 Market St, Kirkby Stephen, CA17 4QW

www.blackbullkirkbystephen.co.uk

01768 372803

Hartley Fell, Hartley

Moorish walk on BW, a continuation of Birkett Ln. Good spot as it continues on up to Nine Standard Rigg.

➤ **Find** Birkett Ln car park, CA17 4JJ (54.472609, -2.3364360). Exit Ln SE onto BW and follow the path 1.6km (1 mile) to where the BW forks NE.

54.457223, -2.296421

Fell House Boreen, Hartley Castle, Hartley

A 2.4km (1½ mile)-long boreen along Birkett Ln, from Hartley to Birkett Hill via Hartley Quarry.

54.470706, -2.318450

Northern Viaduct Trust walk entrance, Hartley

Listen to the sound of chirping finches over an impressive piece of human engineering. Views down the Eden Valley. Lots of plant life along the old railway.

54.470581, -2.333614

Frank's Bridge, Hartley

Riverside walk to the bridge. The water is very clear here. There's a little stone bank under the bridge to explore. Good place for a barefoot paddle.

54.473419, -2.346444

Easedale Beck, River Rothay, Grasmere

NEW ING LODGE

B&B and space for campers between the Lake District and Yorkshire Dales. Grade II listed 18th-century farmhouse with ten bedrooms and holiday let. Camping field and facilities. Cooked breakfasts. Local beers on tap in the on-site bar, The Staggering Wanderer.

Main St, Shap, Penrith, Cumbria, CA10 3LX

www.newinglodge.co.uk

01931 716719

Croglam Castle, Kirkby Stephen
A ruin circled in trees. Spans an area of 200m in length.

54.464480, -2.358476

Smardale Gill Viaduct, Smardale Gill National Nature Reserve, Brownber
Look for red squirrels while exploring the viaduct. Good place for photos. Smell the scent of wildflowers.

54.456890, -2.422599

Begin Hill settlement and tarn, Ravenstonedale
Settlement ruin, and dew pond just N over the stone bridge.

54.453360, -2.434567

Bents Hill Burial, Great Ewe Fell, Brownber
A burial site at something of a hub of radiating spokes. An interesting navel of FPs and energy.

54.455302, -2.456999

Gamelands Stone Circle, Raisbeck
Top TEN

Feel the energy around a large and isolated stone circle site. Touch the stones and sit inside them. Best seen from above on the adjoining hill. Sadly, many of the fossilised stones have toppled over. Lots of orchids in the area.

➤ **Find** free hardstanding car park at the end of Knott Ln (54.465600, -2.558393). A brief walk along Knott Ln will bring you to the stone circle on your R through a gate.

54.467726, -2.557070

Little Gatesgarthdale

COAST TO COAST PATH WEST 287

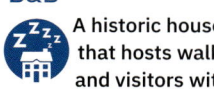

THE HERMITAGE B&B

A historic house that hosts walkers and visitors with a great deal of care. Special place with unique features including exposed beams, hand-carved wall panels and stained glass.

Main Rd, Shap, Penrith, Cumbria, CA10 3LX

01931 716671

 Crosby Ravensworth Fell Stone Circle, White Hag Stone Circle, Crosby Ravensworth
Touch the White Hag stone circle. Crosby Ravensworth Fell is also an important burial site.

54.497936, -2.607667

 Oddendale Stone Circle, Crosby Ravensworth — Top TEN
Walk in and around a double stone circle: the inner is about 5m (16ft) in diameter, the outer roughly 15m. The stones aren't huge. They were sunk into the ground thousands of years ago, perhaps to mark the site as a burial, perhaps to map the stars or time.

54.509891, -2.631328

 M6 Yin and Yang, Shap Rural, Shap — Top TEN
M6 meets 'out in the sticks'. A lonely pedestrian FB over the tide of crowded, crushing metal. Beautiful.

54.526699, -2.659001

 Shap Abbey remains, Shap
Secluded 14th-century ruin inside a hill basin. Impressive tower on the W side of River Lowther and wood. Stone-carved coffins inside the abbey. £2 to park, and just off M6.

54.530213, -2.700702

 Thornthwaite Force (Fall), Bampton
Beauty spot with lots of running water and birdsong.

54.537618, -2.755007

 Burnbank Wood, Bampton
Look for red squirrels in the broadleaf and pine woodland.
▸**Find** the dead-end Rd at Burnbanks, CA10 2RW (54.537884, -2.761806). Exit the Rd S onto the FP and follow down through the trees to the river.

54.537337, -2.760576

 Haweswater Waterside Walk, Naddle Bridge, Naddle Gate, Bampton
Listen for jumping trout, salmon and schelly. Schelly fish – like a salmon – are believed to have lived in Haweswater since before the last Ice Age.
▸**Find** the dead-end Rd at Burnbanks, CA10 2RW (54.537884, -2.761806). Exit the Rd W and follow the FP for 1.6km (1 mile) to the site.

54.536563, -2.778647

Hause Gill

🔟 The (Haweswater) Forces (Falls), Shap Rural

Keep eyes out for golden eagles. Last seen here in 2015, and much work is underway to attract them back to nest. Beauty spot, where Measand Beck meets Haweswater.
➤**Find** Haweswater Waterside Walk (see p287) and keep walking W along the FP for 1.6km (1 mile) to the falls.

54.532087, -2.794817

The Rigg, Shap Rural

A fat peninsula of pine and waterside views.
➤**Find** Mardale Head car park, CA10 2RP (54.489659, -2.820456). Exit car park W onto FP and follow the path NW and then NE around the waterside. Follow the path for 1.6km (1 mile) NE around the shoreline.

54.497207, -2.810426

Castle Crag Fort, Birks Crag Camp, Bampton

Rocky crag and ruin above Haweswater.
➤**Find** Mardale Head car park, CA10 2RP (54.489659, -2.820456). Exit car park W onto FP and follow the path NW and then NE around the waterside. Follow the path for 4.8km (3 miles) NE and then W to the site around the shoreline.

54.507346, -2.821188

GILLSIDE CAMPING AND CARAVAN PARK

 Bunkhouse sleeps up to 20 on the edge of Glenridding next to Ullswater and at the foot of Helvellyn. Open all year. Also 60 camping pitches (March to mid-November) and luxury holiday homes. The site is a 1.6km (1 mile) detour from the path, but worth it. The bunkhouse has a kitchen. Single bookings can be taken, but the Bunkhouse is aimed at groups. Breakfast Van open on Saturday and Sunday mornings.

Gillside Farm, Glenridding, Penrith, Cumbria, CA11 0QQ

www.gillsidecaravanand campingsite.co.uk

01768 482346

Angle Tarn, Heck Cove, Martindale

Perhaps the most famous wild swim and camp spot in Britain. Waterside FP. A beautiful symbol of what it is to be human. Remote and crowded... depending on your timing and luck. Don't feel down about litter louts. Just clear up after them.

54.522253, -2.901046

Bordelle Hause, Hause Gate, Rooking

Move over the grassy burial ground at 399m, between Place Fell and Angle Tarn. Views W to Patterdale and Helvellyn, St Sunday Crag and Fairfield. Views E by Red Crag and High Street. It's only 1km (⅔ mile) S to Angle Tarn.

54.533838, -2.916038

Saint Patrick's Church, Patterdale

Decipher and explore the stained-glass windows and paintings. Touch the wild grasses around the church grounds.

54.536755, -2.939762

Top TEN Grisedale Forest and Tarn, Brothers' Parting Stone

Look for red deer along the wild waterside walk, past Grisedale Forest.

▶ **Find** Dunmail Raise parking, LA22 9RS (54.4910497, -3.035836). Exit the car park N and follow the N bank of the A591 for 550m (1,800ft) and then follow the path E along Raise Beck. Find Grisedale Tarn FP after 1.6km (1 mile). Take the L fork and walk NE and then E for another 1.6km (1 mile) to the FB as it circles around the NE side of the water.

54.500066, -3.003423

Honister Pass, Seatoller Fell, Hause Gill fords

YHA GRASMERE BUTHARLYP HOWE

 Best budget accommodation in Grasmere is in this old mansion close to shops and restaurants. Private rooms, dorms and camping.

Easedale Rd, Grasmere, Cumbria, LA22 9QG

www.yha.org.uk/hostel/yha-grasmere-butharlyp-howe

0345 371 9319

 **Fairfield Peak, Nettle Cove**

Stone circles and giant raptors are the No.2 and No.3 highlights along this path, but the views are No.1. Much care is needed on this 873m (2,864ft) peak. Access from Hause Gap just S of Grisedale Tarn. Savour the views from a burial ground over Striding Edge, Helvellyn, Grasmere, Windermere, Coniston and the Scafell.

▶ **Find** Dunmail Raise parking, LA22 9RS (54.4910497, -3.035836). Exit the car park N and follow the N bank of the A591 for 550m (1,800ft) and then follow the path E along Raise Beck. Find Grisedale Tarn FP after 1.6km (1 mile). Take the R fork and walk SE and then E for another 1.6km (1 mile) to the site.

54.496574, -2.991549

 Seat Sandal, Gavel Crag

Scramble to this exposed peak at 736m (2,415ft). Steep, but slightly easier from the N.

54.494818, -3.014677

 Tonguefill Force (Fall), High Broadrayne

Wide slab path that feels like the road to Oz with a stone wall either side.

54.477794, -3.020729

 Helm Crag, Grasmere

A Wainwright peak at 405m (1,329ft) – steep at times, and like all these peaks, they are not places to visit in bad weather, especially snow and ice. Good views over Grasmere and Morecombe Bay.

54.474506, -3.040612

 Calf Crag, Carrs,

Touch rock pools and tundra around this wild peak at 537m (1,762ft).

54.484592, -3.079105

 Lining Crag, Greenup Edge, Borrowdale

Move over a sweeping basin of lunar rock carpeted in turf and sky. A wilderness peak at 545m (1,788ft).

54.490764, -3.107910

 Eagle Crag, Bleak How

More than a challenge. This rock rampart is well protected by steep sides. Incredible views down to the water valley from 500m (1,640ft) if you can find a way up, but not for the inexperienced.

54.498486, -3.119748

Buttermere

TRAVELLER'S REST INN

 A 16th-century coaching inn with oak beams, log fires and beer gardens. Real ales, affordable rooms, award-winning food and a range of malt whiskies.

Grasmere, Cumbria, LA22 9RR

www.lakedistrictinns.co.uk/travellers-rest

01539 435604

 Galleny Force Waterfall, Smithmire Island
Popular wild swim spot with many rocky dips the locals call 'fairy pools'. Sunbeams and silver fish flash on the surface in summer. Waterside walk and falls. Gowbarrow Fell is en route.
▶**Find** Rosthwaite National Trust car park, CA12 5XB (54.524154, -3.1483938). Exit the car park E and walk towards the B529, turn L and then first R across the stone bridge on Hazel Bank Dr. Once over the bridge, turn R onto the BW and follow the river path 3.2km (2 miles) to the falls.

54.507810, -3.123769

CHAPEL HOUSE FARM CAMPSITE

 Campsite at the foot of Bessyboot, in the Borrowdale Valley. No electric hook-up points. Hot showers, toilets and dish-washing.

Chapel House Farm, Stonethwaite, Borrowdale, Keswick, Cumbria, CA12 5XG

www.chapelhousefarm camp site.co.uk

01768 777256

YHA BORROW DALE

Budget hostel with drying room, communal kitchen, dorms, camping pods and tent camping.

Longthwaite, Keswick, Cumbria, CA12 5XE

www.yha.org.uk/hostel/yha-borrowdale

0345 371 9624

Ennerdale Forest

 ### Johnny Wood, River Derwent, Borrowdale
Balance over stepping stones that navigate rock pools. Broadleaf woodland by the waterside.
➤**Find** Rosthwaite National Trust car park, CA12 5XB (54.524154, -3.1483938). Exit the car park W and walk the Ln W for 550m (1,800ft) to the River Derwent ford. Cross the river, find the FP on the E side of the river and turn L. Follow the FP S for 1km (⅔ mile) along the riverside to the woodland.

54.516799, -3.153152

 ### Slate Mine, Honister Pass, Borrowdale, Keswick
Jumps, climbs, zip wire, mine tour and much more. Activity centre for those who need more than what nature alone can throw up. Look for the waterfall just S of the centre. Beauty spot and parking.

54.511152, -3.200099

COAST TO COAST PATH WEST   293

LOW GILLERTHWAITE FIELD CENTRE

 Field centre and hostel. Like an Eden in Ennerdale. Self-catering accommodation for up to 40 people and a perfect base for fell and lake activities. This was once one of the largest and most important sheep farms in England. Open all year, with the exception of Christmas. Kitchen, dining and two lounges with log fires. The small lounge has a closed wood-burning stove.

Ennerdale, Cleator, Cumbria, CA23 3AX

www.lowgillerthwaite.com

01946 861229

Top TEN YHA Black Sail

The YHA's most remote youth hostel. Only caters for 16... so book in advance. Self-catering kitchen, café and tranquillity.

Ennerdale Bridge, Cleator, Cumbria, CA23 3AX

www.yha.org.uk/hostel/yha-black-sail

54.500311, -3.244795

Top TEN Haystacks, Great Stack, Buttermere

One of Wainwright's favourite peaks. A 3.2km (2 miles) return detour to 597m (1,959ft) peak and cairn. Makes a stopover at Black Sail Hut (see above: 54.500311, -3.244795) worthwhile. Views of Buttermere, Crummock, and loads more. Much scrambling to be had and there are bothies about.

54.507900, -3.247420

Ennerdale Forest Island, River Liza, Ennerdale and Kinniside

Pine and waterside adventure. Explore the river, its rock pools and the surrounding islands of pine. Packrafting is good here.

54.513560, -3.307683

YHA ENNERDALE

 A special place to rest in a remote wooded valley surrounded by fells and peaks. Hostel in converted forestry cottages. The site is off-grid, with hydro-electric power supply and self-generating drinking water.

Cat Crag, Ennerdale Bridge, Cleator, Cumbria, CA23 3AX

www.yha.org.uk/hostel/yha-ennerdale

0345 371 9116

Angler's Crag, Ennerdale

SHEPHERDS ARMS

Hotel where the C2C turns R towards wild Ennerdale. Popular walkers' stop in the peaceful Ennerdale Valley. Eight rooms and a lively bar with walkers from New Zealand, Australia, Canada and the USA.

Kirkland Rd, Ennerdale Bridge, Cleator, Cumbria, CA23 3AR

www.shepherdsarms.com

01946 861249

ENNERDALE COUNTRY HOUSE HOTEL

Gardens, restored fireplaces and spectacular scenery from the bedrooms. Dog-friendly.

Main St, Cleator, Cumbria, CA23 3DT

www.bespokehotels.com/ennerdalehotel

01946 813907

Ennerdale Water S, Ennerdale and Kinnisid

Waterside-woodland walk. Much of the path is narrow and splintered by masses of streams. Go N for a wider ride on BW.

➤**Find** Ennerdale Water N (see below) and follow the FP E and then N and W around the water for 4.8km (3 miles) to the site.

54.514484, -3.365537

Ennerdale Water N, Ennerdale and Kinniside

BW waterside ride. The wooded shore on the N side is incredibly wild beneath Bowness. A good diversion.

➤**Find** Bowness Knott car park, CA23 3AU (54.525341, -3.376826). Exit the car park S and find BW. Turn L and follow path E for 500m (⅓ mile) to site.

54.522093, -3.370244

Angler's Crag, Ennerdale and Kinniside

Explore steep, rocky banks where they fall down into clear water.

➤**Find** Bleach Green car park, CA23 3AS (54.525328, -3.414727). Exit the car park S onto the weir FP and turn L. Follow the FP for 1.6km (1 mile) E towards the shore path and the site.

54.523565, -3.394006

Path between St Bees and The Lakes

COAST TO COAST PATH WEST

SEACOTE HOTEL & HOLIDAY PARKS

 Campervans, motorhomes, caravans and trailer tents. Tents have their own large grassed area.

Beach Rd, St Bees, Cumbria, CA27 0ES

www.seacote.com

01946 822777

FAIRLADIES BARN

 Good value B&B. Singles taken at discount. Rooms are in a 17th-century sandstone barn on the main street in the village.

St Bees, Cumbria, CA27 0AD

www.fairladiesbarn.co.uk

01946 822718

Blakeley Raise Stone Circle, Ennerdale and Kinniside

Stargaze from this rocky beauty spot at 228m (748ft). Easy access from the Rd. Also good for sunsets.

54.512824, -3.453348

Flat Fell Standing Stones, Lagget

Touch the stones set up on this 247m (810ft) raised ground.

54.503077, -3.459192

Path Start at St Bees Head, Fleswick Bay

The C2C W path starts/ends on a wild pebble beach and rocky stalls. The Lakes and the Yorkshire Dales are beyond and behind.

▶ Find St Bees Beachfront car park, CA27 0EY (54.491390, -3.605336), then walk down to RNLI St Bees Lifeboat Station.

54.490848, -3.606935

WILD THINGS TO DO BEFORE YOU DIE

KEEP looking for golden eagles

TOUCH 'wizard hat' stone cairns

SWIM in fairy pools

WALK Wainwright's favourite peak

STAY at YHA's most remote youth hostel

FEEL the energy around an isolated stone circle site

MOVE over a basin of lunar rock

FIND the White Hag stone

SEE where the M6 meets 'out in the sticks'

LOOK for red deer along the wild waterside walk

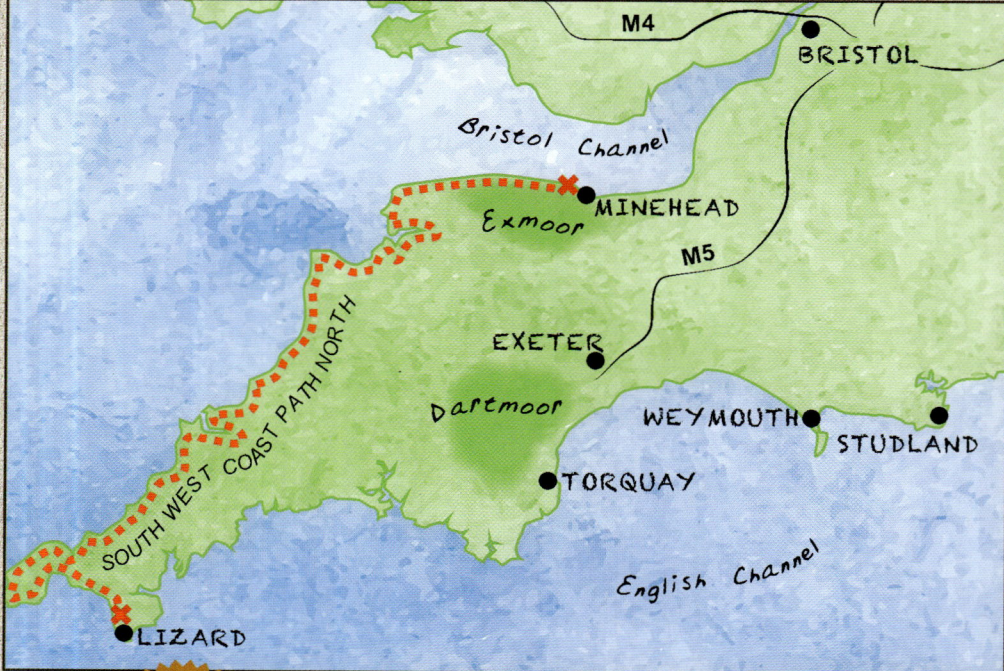

Top TEN

 Selworthy Sand, Fish for the first run of mackerel in early June and cook on a barbecue over stone or a Kelly Kettle. Best at low tide.
51.220736, -3.549308

 Woody Bay Pool, Victorian pool carved into rock for low-tide fun.
51.223881, -3.896672

 Rockham Beach, Find the shipwreck if you can make your way down the hazardous cliff.
51.193247, -4.209309

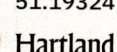 **Hartland Point**, Look for fin whales and the spectacular views over Lundy Island and S Wales.
51.022371, -4.525943

 Speke's Mill Mouth, Dramatic waterfall into a plunge pool; sandy bays either side of falls.
50.9848, -4.5297

 The Rumps Entrance, Inhale wild thyme, while listening to the roar of rocky headland and angry gulls.
50.592856, -4.920311

 Bedruthan Steps, Perhaps the wildest and best beach in Cornwall.
50.486319, -5.033223

 Droskyn Point, Touch the remains of the tin mine. Avoid exploring tunnels and gaps as invisible shafts can collapse.
50.346733, -5.162294

 Giant's Rock, Sit on the mysterious Giant's Rock at low tide.
50.081641, -5.321502

 Porth Ledden Pools Feel the tingle of cold water and history. A row of three man-made tidal pools blasted out by miners into the rock platforms.
50.129130, -5.708135

SOUTH WEST COAST PATH NORTH

BEST FOR: HIDDEN BEACHES
Shipwrecks, mackerel fishing, waterfalls

START: MINEHEAD   FINISH: LIZARD

The SW coast has the best variety of beaches in the world. Different states of the tide are uniquely controlled by the moon. The push and pull of water can, within a few hours, reveal a raging boulder quarry or a tropical sunken paradise on the same beach. Coves can change from golden sands to black rock, and back to sand, every few km. Both space and time play a role.

Finding hidden and quiet places means different things in different areas at different times. Your timing, luck and preparation needs to be impeccable. A hidden, isolated beach will sometimes be that way for a reason. It's hazardous. Either to get to, to swim, or to escape from. Sometimes, it won't be hazardous but you might need a 45-minute hike around a cliff edge. Other times it will mean skipping down from one of the busiest beach car parks at Padstow, in Cornwall, to a rocky corner of sand that is all yours.

Speak to local people. But also learn about the tides and the moon. This is the key to finding hidden places. Research spring tides and the lowest equinox tides. It doesn't take much. At the very least, search the web for tide times and extreme lows. Or even better, buy a tide watch and set it to your location.

Remember that tide times are subject to change, just like buses. Not because of human error, but because of weather, wind and moon pull. Try to arrange your coastal trips to coincide with the moons and the tides. That way, you get to see it all at both high and low.

Reaching a remote beach doesn't always require a canoe or kayak, and there's a huge sense of empowerment and freedom in being able to reach somewhere that you'll have to yourself.

BASIC SAFETY: Make a note of when low tide occurs, and make sure you're back long before the water starts to come in. It will always return quicker than it goes out — both psychologically speaking and in real terms. There are so many deaths around this coast each year from people who either didn't time it properly or who took on an old cliff path that was too eroded, worn or fragile to support one eager swimmer. Don't let that be you. None of the beaches below are safe. But they struck me at the time, maybe just before sunrise, maybe just after sunset, or perhaps after a long walk, as worthy of mention.

Bedruthen Steps

Valley of Rocks

PORLOCK WEIR HOTEL
 Hotel overlooking Porlock Weir harbour. Afternoon teas served in a picnic hamper. Bar and wood-fired pizza oven on the terrace with sea views. Dog-friendly.

Porlock Weir, Exmoor National Park, Somerset, TA24 8PB

www.porlockweirhotel.co.uk

01643 800400

THE RISING SUN
 Situated right on the edge of Exmoor National Park, by the river estuary. Specialises in lobster, sea bass and local mussels. Rooms with sea views.

Harbourside, Lynmouth, EX35 6EG

www.risingsunlynmouth.co.uk

01598 753223

MOTHER MELDRUMS TEA GARDENS AND RESTAURANT, LYNTON
 Café hidden in the Valley of Rocks for hot drinks, cakes and snacks.

Lee Rd, Lynton, Devon, EX35 6JL

01598 753667

Quay Street, Higher Town, Alcombe
The SWCP N starts/ends just S of Minehead Harbour. Lay both palms on the SW Coast Path 135m (442ft) bronze monument. Listen to herring gulls on the next beach. What lies ahead and behind is the best variety of beaches in the world: different colours, sizes, shapes and geology. From raging boulder quarry to tropical sunken paradise.

▶**Find** Minehead station, TA24 5BG (51.207172, -3.468434), and walk 90m (295ft) NW to the seafront at Jubilee Café for a cuppa on the terrace overlooking the sea. Facing the shore, turn L and walk 550m (1,800ft) along the sea wall to the monument.

51.211056, -3.473928

Selworthy Sand, Minehead Without
Top TEN

Fish for the first run of mackerel in early June and cook on a barbecue over stone or a Kelly Kettle. Best at low tide when the lighter sands and rock pools are exposed.

51.220736, -3.549308

Valley of Rocks, Wringcliff Bay
Listen for peregrines that hunt where Exmoor meets the sea. Climb down to the beach along the steep, snaking paths patrolled by nervous mountain goats and their kids.

51.231553, -3.857470

Woody Bay Pool, Slattenslade
Top TEN

Victorian pool carved into rock for low-tide fun swims.

51.223881, -3.896672

NATIONAL TRAILS

LITTLE MEADOW CAMPSITE

 Tents, caravans, huts and luxury cottages. Showers and toilets on the campsite. Just across the A399, about 135m (440ft) from the coast path.

Watermouth, Ilfracombe, Devon, EX34 9SJ

www.littlemeadow.co.uk

01271 866862

WATERMOUTH VALLEY CAMPING PARK

 Camping on the edge of Exmoor National Park, near sandy beaches and the SWCP. Great views over the bay. Showers and all facilities right next to the coast FP. Explore Watermouth Cove. Boat launching facilities at Watermouth Harbour into the Bristol Channel. Kayaks can be launched for a small fee at the nearby cove, or for free at Hele Beach.

Watermouth, Ilfracombe, EX34 9SJ

www.watermouthpark.co.uk

07564 214336

Woody Bay Wood Waterfall, Slattenslade
Feel the spray of fresh water under the waterfall.

51.223881, -3.896672

Highveer Point, Parracombe
The coolest place in Devon on a hot day. Locals call the ridge's W side 'the fridge'. Sit among campions and nibble a primrose while watching walkers below on Heddon's Mouth.

51.232047, -3.926031

Watermouth, Berrynarbor
Natural harbour and perfect boat café. Best at high tide..

51.215731, -4.073377

Tunnels Beach, Ilfracombe
Hand-carved tunnels next to shingle beach and tidal pools.

51.208523, -4.126966

Bull Point Lighthouse, Mortehoe
Look for giant sunfish in summer. The 19th-century lighthouse is best seen at night when the light is visible for 32km (20 miles).

51.200373, -4.201155

Top Ten — Rockham Beach, Mortehoe
Find the shipwreck if you can make your way down the hazardous cliff.

51.193247, -4.209309

Woody Bay

WATERSMEET HOTEL & RESTAURANT

 Hotel and restaurant with sea views over Woolacombe Bay and Combesgate Beach. Private steps down to the sandy beach. Three-night Ramblers' Package available in spring and autumn, including dinner, bed and breakfast and a cream tea.

The Esplanade, Woolacombe EX34 7EB

www.watersmeethotel.co.uk

AVONCOURT LODGE B&B

 B&B on a private Rd that is part of the SWCP, and a short walk from the cliff around Breakneck Point and the Torrs 1km (⅔ mile) W. Drying room for clothing, lounge library and a fully stocked 'honesty' bar. Dog-friendly.

6 Torrs Walk Av, Ilfracombe, EX34 8AU

www.avoncourtilfracombe.co.uk

01271 862453

WESTACOTT FARM CAMPING

 Dog-friendly campsite on a working farm. Middle Meadow is the non-electric area with the best views and open space. Go for a shepherd's hut if you don't like sleeping on hard ground.

Abbotsham Rd, Abbotsham, EX39 5BN

www.westacottfarm.co.uk

01237 472351

 Crow Point, River Taw, Braunton
Like a wild scene from a real-life Pirates of the Caribbean saga. Pay a toll fee to drive up the path to get next to the beach.

51.0667063, -4.1904747

 Westward Ho! Sea Pool, Torridge
Low-tide Victorian pool/lido.

51.040785, -4.243102

Peppercombe Beach, Alwington
Dark stones heat up so much the summer sun, the sand and beach shimmers into a mirage. Swim later afternoon as the cold water warms on the hot pebbles.

51.005138, -4.293957

 The Hobby Dr, Clovelly
Feel the long and winding road... woodland walk of substance out of, or into, Clovelly.

50.987352, -4.378008

 Hartland Point, Stoke
Look for fin whales and spectacular views over Lundy Island and S Wales.

51.022371, -4.525943

 Speke's Mill Mouth, Hartland Quay Wood
Dramatic waterfall into a plunge pool; sandy bays either side of falls.

50.9848, -4.5297

Heddon Waterfall

Ilfracombe

BIDEFORD BAY HOLIDAY PARK

 Caravans, luxury lodges or chalets in woodland close to path.

The Lodge, Buck's Cross, Bideford, EX39 5DU

www.parkdeanresorts.co.uk/location/devon/bideford-bay/

0344 381 9128

THE RED LION HOTEL, CLOVELLY

An 18th-century four star inn that stands on the quay alongside the ancient harbour. Check out the local museum to read up on the Clovelly estate, originally owned by William the Conqueror. Until the middle of the 19th century, Clovelly was largely unknown to the outside world. It was partly as a result of Charles Kingsley's novel *Westward Ho!*, set in and around the village, that visitors began to come. There is still a charge to enter Clovelly village, which is perched on a 135m (400ft) cliff, with no vehicular access.

48 The Quay, Clovelly, EX39 5TF

www.redlion-clovelly.co.uk

01237 431237

Marsland Mouth, Mead
Taste whelks foraged from the rock pools around the beach and cooked into broth.

50.929264, -4.544054

Duckpool, Coombe
Look for glow-worms in July at dusk.

50.874733, -4.560154

Bude cliffs, Bude Bay
It's rare, but the Bude cliffs are home to a 300-million-year-old, goldfish-sized sea creature — Cornuboniscus budensis. It has never been found anywhere else in the world.

50.830533, -4.549466

Lower Longbeak Tumulus, Marhamchurch
Sit in sea campion and pink thrift and look N to Hart and Point and S to Widemouth Bay.

50.800766, -4.559514

Crackington Haven, St Gennys
Smell coconut-scented gorse in spring when the hills are lit up in yellow. Flowers are most fragrant in April and May.

50.741340, -4.634358

Museum of Witchcraft and Magic, Boscastle
One of most interesting museums in England, and the largest of its kind in the world.

https://museumofwitchcraftandmagic.co.uk

50.690722, -4.6948937

The Sisters, Bossiney
Rocky reef around two islets where cormorants, razorbill and guillemots nest.

50.677317, -4.746141

Woolacombe

MILL HOUSE
 Mill house dating from around 1700, now owned by the Landmark Trust. The house is divided into two parts, one sleeping three and the other four. Both are dog-friendly.

Coombe, Cornwall, EX23 9JN

www.landmarktrust.org.uk/search-and-book/landmark-groups/mill-house-coombe

THE DOLPHIN
 Pub and restaurant opposite Combe Martin beach. Log fire in winter.

Seaside Hill, Combe Martin, Devon, EX34 0AW

www.dolphincombemartin.uk

01271 883424

THE WEIR BISTRO
 Coffee house, bistro and wildlife centre on Whalesborough Farm. Lakeside location, serving breakfast (daily 'til noon), lunch or supper. There are heaters on the terrace for those cold but bright days.

Whalesborough Farm, Marhamchurch, EX23 0JD

www.weir-restaurant-bude.co.uk

01288 362234

 ### Merlin's Cave, Tintagel Coast
A freshwater well inside a magical cavern under 3 million tonnes of rock. Only an open mind for myths and magic is needed.

50.668236, -4.759280

 ### Tintagel Castle, Tintagel,
Look for ancient pottery around one of the most important Celtic settlements in England.

www.english-heritage.org.uk/visit/places/tintagel-castle/history-and-legend/#

50.668144, -4.762593

 ### Doyden Castle, St. Minver Highlands
Folly built on Doyden Point, rented out by the National Trust.
➤**Find** the National Trust Port Quin car park, PL29 3SU (50.589484, -4.867041), and walk E 135m (440ft) on Rd and then N on SWCP 275m (900ft) to castle.

50.589292, -4.873405

 ### The Rumps Entrance, Pentireglaze
Burrow a nose into the gentle sway of wild thyme and dog violets, and inhale, while listening to the roar of rocky headland and angry gulls.

50.592856, -4.920311

 ### Little Petherick Creek and Saints' Way, Tregonna
Schools of bass feed on the surface of the creek on a calm day.

50.515744, -4.939682

 ### Stinking Cove Tumulus, Constantine Bay, St. Merryn
Ancient burial ground a few metres N of Dinas Head. Find and feel history in the hand: look for 6,000-year-old flint arrow heads around the coast between Booby's Bay and Trevose Head.

50.546942, -5.036831

TREVIGUE

Clifftop accommodation, a five-min walk above The Strangles beach, between Boscastle and Crackington Haven. The farm has steep valleys and hills, with the highest cliff in Cornwall. Choose between a cottage that sleeps six, or self-catering accommodation for two in a wing of the main house that's entered via a private courtyard. The Strangles beach is accessed via a winding FP next to the farmhouse, where the family lives.

Trevigue Farm, Crackington Haven, EX23 0LQ

www.trevigue.com
01840 230492

Pepper Cove Settlement, Porthcothan, St Eval
One of the UK's most unique and mysterious castle ruins spanning three separate headlands.

50.522736, -5.027279

Bedruthan Steps Beach, Newquay — Top TEN
Feel the rush of beauty and danger – irresistibly attractive to mortals. Perhaps the wildest and best beach in Cornwall, reclaimed by nature to create a human-free zone since it has eroded out all the steps. The beach is closed, but no less wonderful for that. Take care if attempting access from the N at low tide as each year people lose their lives here doing exactly that.

50.486319, -5.033223

Fistral Beach, Newquay
Surfers' paradise. Taste salty marsh samphire around the wet shady edges at the N and S edge of the beach.
▶ **Find** Towan Head (50.417432, -5.100043) and walk 275m (900ft) SW to beach.

50.415427, -5.100913

Droskyn Point Perranporth — Top TEN
Touch the remains of the tin mine, visible at various gaps and holes in the rocks at low tide. Avoid exploring tunnels and gaps as invisible shafts can collapse and lead to death or injury.

50.346733, -5.162294

Peppercombe

ROBBIE LOVE'S CAMPSITE

 Campsite in 4½ acres, surrounded by fields, NT farmland and sea views. Ten-min walk to Polzeath Beach and Baby Bay.

New Polzeath, PL27 6QX

www.robbielovescampsite.co.uk

01208 869091

BEDRUTHAN STEPS CAMPSITE

 Camping in a 14-acre clifftop field, with basic facilities. Tents and campervans. Tipis and a shepherd's hut. Pop-up food vans and parking in July and August.

B3276, Wadebridge PL27 7UP

www.bedruthansteps.com

07877 240015

MERRMOOR INN

 B&B serving pub food, situated between Newquay and Padstow, run by three generations of the same family. There are dramatic beach and cliff views over the River Menalhyl.

Mawgan Porth, TR8 4BA

www.merrymoorinn.com

01637 860258

 ## St Agnes Head, off Beacon Dr, St Agnes

Listen for nesting razorbills, guillemots and kittiwakes. Also look across to Bawden Rocks offshore for puffins.

50.318768, -5.234718

 ## Natural Arch Cave, Goonvrea

Fabulous for bats, thanks in part to the many mine shafts and natural caves along this stretch of coast.

50.303667, -5.235083

 ## Portreath Submerged Forest, Portreath

Submerged forest that gets exposed at low tide after winter storms. Surfing and bodyboarding on the N shore beside the pier.

50.262520, -5.292734

 ## Crane Island, Cornwall

Look for sunfish – sometimes seen here in summer. Basking sharks too.

50.248516, -5.318465

 ## Mutton Cove, Illogan

Look for the large colony of almost a hundred grey seals that breed and fish here.

50.240409, -5.388582

 ## The Three Brothers of Grugith, St Ives

Feel the energy of stone set over water – especially around a graveyard. The cemetery beside the water's edge continues to hold the sea at bay.

50.217335, -5.480534

Sloo Wood

NATIONAL TRAILS

Mulgram Hill

THE UNICORN ON THE BEACH

Pub by Porthtowan beach for seasonal dishes or crafted cocktails. Five beachside en-suite rooms.

W Beach Rd, Porthtowan, Truro TR4 8AD

www.theunicornonthebeach.com

01209 890381

MAGOR FARM CAMPSITE, CAMBORNE

Tree-lined field situated just below Magor Farm, a short walk from Godrevy and its famous lighthouse. No reception, just pitch and pay later… when the owners arrive.

Magor Farm, Magor Hill, Camborne, TR14 0JF

www.magorfarm.co.uk

01209 713367

22 SANDYACRES RD

Camping, glamping in beach pods, yoga, surf school. Café on the beach.

Sandy Acres, 22 Sandyacres Rd, Hayle, Cornwall TR27 5BA

www.sandy-acres.co.uk

07494 436635

Pendour Cove, Zennor
Legendary spot better known as 'Mermaid's Cove'. Visit at summer dusk to hear the singing man who fell in love with a mermaid and followed her out to sea.

50.194877, -5.581509

Botallack Mine, Botallack
Look for copper ingots that wash up here and to the S, remnants of cargo from the steamship Malta that ran aground in 1889.

50.140531, -5.693227

Porth Ledden Pools, Boswedden
Feel the tingle of cold water and history. A row of three man-made tidal pools blasted out by miners into the rock platforms. The central and largest is known as 'Pullandase Pool' and can be seen at mid and low tides.

50.129130, -5.708135

Maen Castle Fort, Sennen Cove
Look for pottery and arrow heads around this Neolithic and Iron Age site.

50.072758, -5.708507

Can Greeb, Land's End
Crouch down to smell sea campion, thrift and red fescue grass. Feel the still air that sits in the shallow cliff valley beneath the westerly winds.

50.069007, -5.717132

Lamorna Cove Quay, Lamorna and Paul
A natural rock quarry that has been borrowed by humans and more recently claimed back by nature.

50.061826, -5.563545

Porthowan Beach

THE MERMAID, ST IVES

A converted sail loft steeped in smuggler and pirate tales, the pub was once linked to the harbour by one of the many tunnels that criss-crossed the town. It's in the old fishing quarter, less than 90m (295ft) from the harbour and in the older part of St Ives, known as 'Down-A-Long'. Visit the narrow cobbled streets in the spring and summer months when they are ablaze with flowers.

21 Fish St, St Ives, TR26 1LT
www.mermaidstives.co.uk
01736 796816

YHA LAND'S END

The YHA's westernmost hostel offer tent pitches, bell tents, camping pods, private en-suite rooms, family rooms and dormitory style rooms.

Letcha Vean, Penzance TR19 7NT
www.yha.org.uk/hostel/yha-lands-end
0345 371 9643

11 Penzance

Blazoned with historic buildings and artefacts to touch and feel. The rail journey along the coast is fabulous. St Michael's Way is the visual highlight from almost every angle.

▶ Find Harbour Long Stay car park, TR18 2JX (50.120798, -5.532166).

50.123781, -5.530149

Top TEN Giant's Rock, Porthleven

Sit on the mysterious Giant's Rock at low tide, just near the entrance of Porthleven Harbour.

▶ Find Tregear Point (50.085310, -5.327214) and walk 460m (1,510ft) SE on SWCP.

50.081641, -5.321502

Mullion Cove, The Lizard

Cloud-watch around the stormiest, most hazardous stretch of coast in England. During a six-year period in the 19th century, nine ships were wrecked and 69 lives lost. Walk S from the edge of Polurrian Cove.

50.021984, -5.256152

THE RED LION INN

 Pub overlooking Newlyn Harbour for fish and chips, ale pie and more.

36 Fore St, Newlyn, Penzance, TR18 5JP

01736 362012

MULLION COVE HOTEL & SPA

 Awe-inspiring views. Stormy winters and sunny summers... watch the sun go down from the clifftop outdoor hot tub.

Mullion Cove, Lizard Peninsula, Cornwall, TR12 7EP

www.mullion-cove.co.uk/the-hotel

01326 240328

 ### Mullion Cliff, Porth Mellin

Wild and isolated. Deceptively high cliffs draped in a blanket of silver rock and gorse. Look out for dolphins off Mullion Island.

50.012379, -5.258315

 ### Kynance Cove Caves, The Lizard

Explore caves and rock stacks at low tide, or walk to the aptly named 'Asparagus Rock' to see... wild asparagus.

50.215723, -3.690348

 ### Bass Point, Landewednack

Rocky headland of wildflowers, sea views and gorse.

▶Find the National Trust Lizard Point car park, TR12 7NT (49.960959, -5.2042658), and walk 2.4km (1½ miles) E on SWCP.

49.963262, -5.185282

 ### The Lizard Lifeboat Station, Landewednack

The SWCP N starts/ends at a lifeboat station: a powerful totem of order surrounded by chaotic and unpredictable tides, and the magic of The Lizard. Nature always wins in the end, but above the Gulliver-like boat ramp is a good place to sit. What lies ahead and behind are some of the best beaches in the world, revealed, in part, not by guidebooks or photos on social media, but by the changing tides. A hidden, isolated beach will sometimes be that way for a reason. It's hazardous. Go N with much preparation, good timing and perhaps a little luck.

▶Find Bass Point (see above) and walk 1km (⅔ mile) N on SWCP.

49.969667, -5.186741

WILD THINGS TO DO BEFORE YOU DIE

FIND arrow heads around a Neolithic site

EXPLORE caves at low tide

SIT in sea campion and pink thrift

LOOK for glow worms

TASTE whelks foraged from the rock pools

VISIT the largest witchcraft museum in the world

DREAM in sleep beside a holy well

TASTE salty samphire on a surfers' beach

WATCH bats at dusk around derelict mines

LISTEN to the sounds of a mermaid's cave

Top TEN

 ▶ Gillan Harbour, Navigate a natural harbour by kayak or on foot.
50.086789, -5.103587

Helford Passage, Hear the silence at the green rump over Helford's estuary entrance.
50.100739, -5.103023

 Rosemullion Head, Snorkel safari over fluorescent seaweeds.
50.110276, -5.082399

 Saddle Cove, Look for basking sharks.
50.296790, -4.052901

 Bolberry Down, Hear the sound of male sika deer in rutting season.
50.231902, -3.845113

 Steeple Cove, Shrimp and fish for early evening beach barbecues.
50.216217, -3.816403

 Meadfoot Beach, Launch a kayak from the beach.
50.459295, -3.503121

 Middle Beach, Snorkel through carpets of edible seaweed.
50.987352, -4.378008

 **Mackerel Cove**, Catch mackerel on rod and line with feather.
50.511246, -3.510997

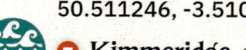 **◉ Kimmeridge**, Snorkel in the sunlight.
50.609742, -2.129967

SOUTH WEST COAST PATH SOUTH

BEST FOR: SECRET SWIMS
Line fishing, rocky reefs, foraging
START: LIZARD FINISH: STUDLAND

The coastal waters around Devon, Cornwall and Dorset are treacherous – even when taking a dip surrounded by literally hundreds of other swimmers.

So why bother with swims?

Swimming overwhelms the five senses in a passive-aggressive encounter with nature. The shock of cold water is a... shock. But the impact it has on the human hormone pool is profound. Dopamine is released in buckets. Its nirvana-like sensations can last longer than any drug. That's why people get addicted to cold water swimming. They are literally taking the plunge to experience an altered state of consciousness.

Floating on the surface or simply dipping bare feet into surf maximises the sensations by multiples impossible to quantify. It is a magic beyond eating, music and good company, because it overwhelms the senses of touch, hearing, taste and smell in an environment of intimacy with nature that can only be bettered by sleeping under the stars. If wild camping outdoors, or in your back garden, is not your thing, then swim. It's as close to being intimate with nature as it's possible to get while awake. Much like forming a healthy, intimate relationship with a partner, it stimulates, lightens and fixes the baggage we all pick up day to day.

BASIC SAFETY
- If in any doubt about safety, enjoy the view and stay back from the water's edge.
- Never swim alone.
- Take local advice wherever possible.
- Even when wearing a wet suit, be wary of cold water, which can cause limbs to seize up and panic inhalation of water.
- Beware of waves and currents that can sweep you out from the shore.
- Look out for motorcraft – wear a hat or a tag a boat behind you.
- Look out for dangerous obstacles below the surface of the water that can cause injury.

Middle Beach

Church Cove, Lizard

PARIS HOTEL

 This hotel is named after the SS *Paris* liner that ran aground on the headland on Whit Monday 1899. The pub serves local seafood, meats and vegetarian dishes, which are best eaten on the outdoor benches looking out to sea on a warm summer's day.

The Cove, Coverack, TR12 6SX

www.pariscoverack.com

01326 280258

The Lizard Lifeboat Station, Landewednack

The SWCP S starts/ends at a metaphorical ramp into and out of a swimmers' paradise. Beaches, coves and estuaries, individually peppered in pine, sea currents and seaweed-laden shellfish. This entire section of coast path is rarely anything other than treacherous to swim – even when surrounded by scores of other swimmers. But it is addictive, and momentarily life-changing, if you live to tell the tale.

▶**Find** Bass Point (see p307) and walk 1km (⅔ mile) N on SWCP.

49.969667, -5.186741

Chair, Landewednack

Sit back in the chair – a rocky platform that has been used for centuries as a lookout point by pilchard spotters, customs officials and birders.

49.974880, -5.187666

Kennack Sands, Poltesco, Kuggar

Swim, sunbathe and touch history. Stone tools have been found here that date back more than 10,000 years.

50.004539, -5.163645

Chynhalls Point Fort, St Keverne, Coverack

Touch and walk the cliff castle fort. There are several banks to explore, and a ditch still visible across the rocky headland that may have acted as defence.

50.015722, -5.092388

Porthallow Cove, Porthallow

Swim in the cove at high tide. Explore rock pools at low tide.

50.068906, -5.078792

310 NATIONAL TRAILS

THE HIDDEN HUT

This café in a hut on the SWCP near Porthcurnick Beach serves fresh food al fresco at lunchtime, and puts on open-air feast nights during the summer. Access is only possible by foot, over rugged ground. When the SWCP meets the granite steps leading down to the beach, carry on up the other set of steps over the brow of the hill to locate the hut.

SWCP, Porthcurnick Beach, TR2 5EW

www.hiddenhut.co.uk

Top TEN Gillan Harbour, Flushing
Natural harbour that can be navigated by kayak or walked by path. Sit awhile and listen to waders. A ferry is sometimes available.

50.086789, -5.103587

Top TEN Helford Passage, Trerose
Hear the silence at the green rump over Helford's estuary entrance at Toll Point. Incredible views.

50.100739, -5.103023

Top TEN Rosemullion Head, Mawnan
Snorkel safari over a jungle of multicoloured fluorescent seaweeds.

50.110276, -5.082399

Gyllyngvase Beach, Falmouth
Low-tide swims and rock-pooling. Smell flowers at Queen Mary Gardens.

50.144493, -5.067430

Great Molunan, Bohortha
Snorkel and swim over reef, rocks and seaweed. The two sheltered beaches are best at low tide.

50.145218, -5.015594

Porthbeor Beach, Bohortha
Swims and rock snorkelling along a large beach.

50.149393, -4.991797

Meadfoot Beach

COOMBE FARM B&B

 There are two double rooms here from which to watch the fishing boats returning to Fowey. This is a NT-owned working farm, above the valley of Coombe Hawne. Smuggling tales suggest that the last ever recorded 'run of spirits' in Fowey took place at Coombe on 9 August 1845. There is a cavity between the kitchen and dining room that's reputed to have been used as a smugglers' hole. It's also one of the few places in Fowey that offers a guaranteed parking space.

Lankelly Ln, Fowey, PL23 1HW

01726 833123

 ## Pendower Beach, Lower Mill
Walk barefoot over sand and shingle onto Gerrans Bay at the mouth of a freshwater stream that runs across the beach. Shallow sea for safer swims.

50.206324, -4.944019

 ## Portloe Point, Veryan
Basking sharks occasionally come to the surface in late spring.

50.217258, -4.891135

 ## Turbot Point, Mevagissey
Lookout point for watching dolphins and porpoises.

50.253738, -4.768446

 ## Pentewan Beach, Sconhoe
Views of undulating fields and the white stretch of Pentewan Beach beyond.

▶ **Find** Pentewan Sands car park, PL26 6BT (50.289775, -4.787194), and walk 365m (1,200ft) S to the beach.

50.289804, -4.777775

 ## Black Head, Ropehaven, Pentewan Valley
Cormorants and fulmars nest on tree-lined cliff ledges at Ropehaven.

50.299276, -4.754854

 ## Ropehaven Cliffs Nature Reserve, Pentewan Valley
Look for fossils, dating back more than 400 million years.

50.309643, -4.762147

 ## Lansallos Cove, Polperro
Touch tombstones that tell fascinating stories.

50.3319, -4.5785

 ## Chapel Pool, Crumplehorn, Polperro
Tidal bath pool cut into the rock. Warms up quickly in summer sunshine.

50.329778, -4.516068

 ## Sharrow Grotto, Antony
The man-made cave next to Sharrow Point was apparently dug out in the early 1780s by a seaman attempting to cure his gout.

50.347509, -4.260333

SOUTH WEST COAST PATH SOUTH

Bat's Head

 ### Kingsand Beach, Maker-with-Rame,
Explore and bathe in rock pools. Forage for seaweed in the shallows.

50.332995, -4.200702

 ### Wilderness Point, Cremyll
Watch and listen to the sound of a historic ferry running the Tamar between Cremyll and Stonehouse.

50.358436, -4.171308

 ### Fort Bovisand, Wembury
A 19th-century fort, converted to posh housing, beside Bovisand Harbour.

50.336520, -4.126618

 ### Wembury Bay, Heybrook Bay
Find shore crabs at low tide. Forage for dry seaweed in winter. Rock-pool rambles provided by Devon Wildlife Trust in summer.

50.316852, -4.101021

 ### Gara Point, Worswell Barton
Listen for peregrines and gulls that hunt here. Views from lookout hut E to Newton Ferrers and W from mouth of the Yealm to Rame Head and Wembury Point.

50.303261, -4.074146

THE JOURNEYS END INN

 This 13th-century pub is in an area known as the 'South Hams'. There are four fires to enjoy in the winter, as well as a conservatory and a large beer garden for warmer months.

Ringmore, TQ7 4HL
www.thejourneysendinn.co.uk
01548 810205

 ### Saddle Cove, Worswell Barton
Top TEN

Basking sharks have been seen along this stretch between Saddle and Netton Island 1.6km (1 mile) W. Small sandy cove, best explored at low tide, 365m (1,200ft) SW and then SE from National Trust's Warren car park.

50.296790, -4.052901

 ### Cockleridge, Bigbury

Summer ferry across the Avon to Bantham. Some try to wade at low tide but it's deep.

50.281432, -3.873489

 ### Loam Castle, Thurlestone

Rocky headland with a narrow, hazardous path.

50.268333, -3.873249

 ### Bolt Tail Fort, Bigbury Bay

Look for greater horseshoe bats around this wild and open naze.

50.24229, -3.86655

Bolberry Down, Malborough
Top TEN

Listen for the sound of male sika deer in rutting season. Clifftop views.

50.231902, -3.845113

Charmouth

SOUTH WEST COAST PATH SOUTH 315

QUAYSIDE HOTEL
Family-run hotel, award-winning restaurant and 29 bedrooms. Ask for a sea view.

49 King St, Brixham, Devon, TQ5 9TJ

www.quaysidehotel.co.uk

01803 467789

Steeple Cove, Furzeball
Top TEN

Shrimping and fishing for early evening beach barbecues. Large bass on small lures are best in July.

50.216217, -3.816403

Fort Charles (Salcombe Castle), Salcombe

Ruin of fort built by Henry VIII to defend the Kingsbridge estuary against pirates.

50.228513, -3.780295

Sunny Cove, E Portlemouth

Favourite with boaters. Best after dusk when the water is warm and clear.

50.230572, -3.767650

Prawle Point, Woodcombe

Touch and walk rows of standing stones known as 'orthostats', thought to be thousands of years old.

50.202116, -3.721382

Ravens Cove, Stokenham

Get blown off your feet, literally. SW gales have been known to knock people over. Part of the shipwreck coast that epitomises the treacherous nature of the lonely wild.

50.220227, -3.651698

Jenny Cole's Cove, Strete

Secluded S section of Blackpool Sands. Care needed as it's possible to get cut off by the tide.

▶**Find** Blackpool Freshwater Lake (50.318126, -3.613207) and walk 275m (900ft) W.

50.316358, -3.613217

Warren Point, Dartmouth

Point gets its name from rabbits that were once bred here in vast warrens for fur and meat. Southern views to Start Point Lighthouse on Start Bay. Watch guillemots and cormorants fish in the waters here.

50.324947, -3.576550

Dartmouth Castle

Look for dolphins in the bay. Coastal fort guards the Dart Estuary and the strategic port of Dartmouth.

▶**Find** Gomerock Remains (50.341764, -3.565777) and walk 275m (900ft) S on SWCP.

50.34203, -3.56829

Gad Cliff

KINGSWEAR COFFEE CO

 Coffee shop beside the ferry, steam train station, sailing club and post office. Somewhere to buy local produce, too: coffee from Exeter's Exe Coffee Roastery, bread from 5 Doors Up in Brixham, local jams and marmalade from Clare's Preserves based in Bovey Tracey, and ice cream tubs from Surfing Cow.

2A The Square, Kingswear, TQ6 0AA

www.kingswearcoffee.co.uk

07813 582273

🏰 Kingswear Castle, Brookhill,
Walk up and out of the castle through Monterey and Corsican pines with views across the Dart.
▶Find Gomerock Remains (50.343705, -3.561252) and walk 275m (900ft) S on SWCP.

50.341853, -3.559766

Man Sands, Woodhuish
Look for Cetti's warblers and reed warblers in the reed bed and pools just inland of the existing coastline. Unique area of brackish plain and farmland that has been allowed to flood into the sea with wall defences not replaced.
▶Find Woodhuish Beach NT car park, TQ6 0EF (50.360372, -3.531732), and walk 1km (⅔ mile) down the Ln to SWCP above Long Sands. Facing the sea, turn L and walk 1.6km (1 mile) N to sands.

50.370964, -3.514927

Shoalstone Point, Brixham
Look out for stunning fulmars gliding about the sandstone platforms.

50.401270, -3.495961

Broadsands Beach, Paignton
Sand beach for snorkelling. Easy for launching a packraft or kayak.

50.407366, -3.554147

NATIONAL TRAILS

SOUTH WEST COAST PATH SOUTH

THE HARBOUR INN

Pub with views over Paignton Harbour.

59 Roundham Rd, Paignton, TQ4 6DS

www.harbourinnpaignton.com

01803 552680

SEA SHANTY BEACH CAFE

Traditional food and drink, with an emphasis on seafood, beside the beach. Fresh crab is landed on the beach beside the café. Local ales come from the microbrewery nearby. Organic, free-range eggs are from Bulstone Springs farm. Salad and herbs are grown in the village. Try the homemade soup or sprats with bread and salad.

The Beach, Branscombe, EX12 3DP

www.facebook.com/seashantybranscombe

 Broadsands Railway Viaduct, Broadsands

Touch Brunel's legacy, especially when a steam train passes overhead. Limestone for the viaduct came from neighbouring Churston.

50.407784, -3.558760

 London Bridge, Torquay

Paddle through a natural arch in a limestone cliff S of Torquay Harbour. The neighbouring cave is popular too, with kayakers and bats.

50.454374, -3.519141

 Meadfoot Beach, Wellswood

Launch a kayak from the ramp over the beach. The beach is best at low tide; better launch at high tide.

50.459295, -3.503121

 Oddicombe Beach, Babbacombe

Cliff railway runs in summer overhead. Nosy seals come in to look about in summer.

50.481861, -3.515096

 Mackerel Cove, Maidencombe

Catch mackerel on rod and line with feather, and barbecue later on the beach. Wooded walk for shelter overhead.

50.511246, -3.510997

Durdle Door

MOONFLEET MANOR

A manor estate linked to a novel about smuggling and the ghost of Col 'Blackbeard' Mohune, who is said to still haunt the local churchyard. It's all fiction of course – ahem! – apart from the name of the original owners, the Mohune family. To explore this wonderful piece of coast and estate, choose either an afternoon tea or a luxury night or two in a colonial-feel room. Dog-friendly.

Fleet Rd, Weymouth, DT3 4ED

www.moonfleetmanor hotel.co.uk

02080 765555

 ### Labrador Bay, Shaldon
An isolated stretch of coast famous for Devon sandstone cliffs.

50.52956, -3.50199

 ### The Ness, Shaldon, Teignbridge
Look for ospreys in March and April on their migration N. Views to Shaldon.

50.537536, -3.497029

 ### St Clement's Church, Powderham
Touch the brick and stone church next to the River Exe.

50.650396, -3.4546013

 ### Estuary, Countess Wear, Topsham
Starling murmurations at dusk and dawn over the Exe Estuary. Best seen from the Topsham side of the River Exe or from the FP under the M5. Also look out for sand martins and avocets.

50.686774, -3.477832

 ### Orcombe Point, Littleham, Exmouth,
Walk the cliff around Orcombe Point. The rocks slant at a descending angle to Dorset, which means you can literally walk back through time over thousands of years as layer upon layer descends.

50.606274, -3.384990

Hobarrow Bay fossils

SOUTH WEST COAST PATH SOUTH

LULWORTH COVE INN

 This is an old mail stagecoach stop, almost 400 years old, on the Rd from Wareham. The pub was once popular with smugglers. Today, it provides food, drink and beds in 12 nautically themed rooms and a restaurant. Family and dog-friendly.

Main Rd, W Lulworth, BH20 5RQ

www.lulworth-coveinn.co.uk

01929 400333

 ### Salcombe Hill Cliff, Southdown, Sidmouth
Watch fulmars glide with a background of views of northern France, Channel Islands and Portland Bill.

50.680536, -3.226034

 ### Branscombe, Clovelly, Torridge
Stand aboard and touch the last relic here of the shipwrecked MSC Napoli, a 14-tonne anchor. The cargo ship was grounded and controversially plundered here in 2007.

50.987352, -4.378008

 ### Branscombe Mouth Beach, Devon
1.6km (1 mile) of shingle beach beside cliffs to swim, and paddle in pools of sea anemones.

50.687657, -3.122521

 ### Pinhay Bay, Branscombe
Forage for seaweed to eat raw or dry. Deep water and rocks along a sweeping cove and reef that is perfect to snorkel. Best accessed from Lyme Regis at low tide. Tree-lined cliffs at Ware or Pinhay. Find fish, ammonites and shell fossils on the beach, in rock and chalk.

50.71294, -2.96478

 ### Church Cliff Beach, Lyme Regis
Catch shrimps, in cupped hand, from rock pools at low tide. Listen as the River Lym flows over the beach into the bay 180m (590ft) W of the rocks.

50.725121, -2.929882

 ### Mouth Rocks, Charmouth
Listen cliff-side as the River Char trickles or gushes, depending on rain or season, into the sea at Charmouth.

50.733266, -2.899685

 ### Golden Cap, Golden Cap Estate, Morcombelake
Inhale the sea air on the highest cliff on the S coast.

50.726493, -2.842088

W Cliff, Eype, Bothenhampton
Taste fresh-caught mackerel cooked on a campfire or Kelly Kettle. Look for fossils and rock-pool wildlife while listening to buzzards mewing overhead.

50.712824, -2.773041

NATIONAL TRUST KNOLL BEACH CAFE, STUDLAND BAY

 Relax around one of the best beaches in Dorset. Warm drinks or local ciders, beers and fruit juices.

Ferry Rd, Studland, Swanage BH19 3AQ

www.nationaltrust.org.uk/visit/dorset/studland-bay

01929 450500

Cogden Beach, Bridport
Chew on sweet gorse and hawthorn flowers on your way down to the water, before foraging for sea kale on the deserted pebble beach.

50.691048, -2.708399

W Bexington Nature Reserve, W Bexington
Look for adders in spring around the beach edges. Fry dandelion flowers in oil over a Kelly Kettle.

50.678918, -2.672233

Chesil Beach, E of Abbotsbury
A mass of plants. Find sea holly and rare sea pea on the shingle. Blue holly flowers bloom from July to September. Find mats of white flowering sea campion.

50.660314, -2.628459

W Cliff, W Bay, Portland
Look for porpoises from the top of West Cliff back along Chesil Beach and the Fleet Lagoon. Taste mallow flowers when they bloom from June to October. The leaves can be boiled.

50.552507, -2.448642

Blow Hole, Portland
Famous. Listen... it blows hard at high tide.

50.518188, -2.459863

Kimmeridge Bay

Cave Hole, Portland
Hikers carrying mattresses are in fact... climbers. They only need to climb 3m (10ft) at most to gain fitness, skill and to repair injuries. They can be seen all around the island.
▶**Find** Portland Bill Obelisk and walk 1.6km (1 mile) NE on SWCP to cave hole.

50.520188, -2.443606

 ### Sand Holes, Portland
Look out for lizards bathing in the midday sunshine on the altar-like rock from April between Sand Holes and Cave Hole. They're usually quick, but get sluggish when the sun goes in.

50.523927, -2.440796

 ### Rufus Castle (remains), Wakeham,
The remains of 15th-century Rufus Castle. Look for the broadleaf plantain that's common around the ruin.

50.539553, -2.426961

 ### The Alley, Portland
The views to Portland Harbour and the cliffs of Purbeck: Portland Harbour is very sheltered and therefore an ideal home for the National Sailing Centre. It was a natural choice as the venue for the sailing in the Olympics of 2012.

50.562959, -2.440988

 ### Lodmoor Nature Reserve, Lodmoor
Listen for bearded tits and Cetti's warblers in the reed beds. One of the largest common tern colonies is here.

50.628221, -2.441075

 ### Osmington Mills, Osmington
Look for fossilised burrows of creatures that lived in the sea here 155 million years ago. Look for the changes in the cliff rock from Osmington around to Ringstead.

50.632778, -2.371239

 ### White Nothe, Chaldon Herring
White Nothe is one of the highest cliffs along the Dorset Coast. Feel chalk cliffs beneath your feet, with superb views over Weymouth Bay and Portland.

50.625300, -2.324012

 ### Lulworth Cove, W Lulworth
Cold, lazy swims around the healthy scent of fish and warm September sea air. Arrive and leave early... even out of season.

50.618750, -2.249280

Shell Bay

Kimmeridge Bay, Dorset
Snorkel in the sunlight to see beds of pink coral weed and fields of snakelocks (sea anemones). Plunge into freezing water to explore the 400-metre (1,310-foot) snorkel trail around the bay. Wear a wet suit. Even in summer. It's cold.

50.609742, -2.129967

Seacombe Cliff View, Worth Matravers
Listen for the long squeaky-door sound of sika stags in autumn. Look for rare Chalk Hill blue and Adonis blue butterflies in June and July.

50.589160, -2.021567

Spyway, Langton Matravers
Touch the Limousin Cow sculpture in the stone wall.

50.594441, -2.002898

Old Harry Rocks, Handfast Point, Studland
Listen for peregrines that hunt close to one of the most famous pirate haunts around the S coast.

50.642496, -1.923121

SOUTH WEST COAST PATH SOUTH

The Foreland, Purbeck Way, Studland
Walk barefoot through meadows of buttercups in spring, on the sea side of the path, down towards Warren Wood.

50.641026, -1.937510

Middle Beach, Studland
Top TEN
Snorkel through carpets of edible seaweed to see… sea horses. Two species live here.

50.987352, -4.378008

Studland Dunes, Studland
Look for sika deer in the marshes and woodland.

50.668583, -1.946046

Shell Bay Beach, Studland
The SWCP S ends/starts at the very N end of Shell Bay Beach. Touch the blue metal sculpture beside the ferry that thousands of people before you have felt. What lies ahead and behind is a swimmers' paradise. For all the lifeguards, warning notices and rip tides, the coastal waters around Dorset, Devon and Cornwall are perhaps the best way to overwhelm the five senses in a passive-aggressive encounter with nature. The shock of cold water is a… shock, as are some of the hazards associated with wild swimming. The impact is profound. Take care!
▶ **Find** Shell Bay Beach, BH19 3BA (50.678404, -1.949130), and walk to the end of the Rd where people queue for the ferry. The start is just to the R of the Rd.

50.679478, -1.950177

WILD THINGS TO DO BEFORE YOU DIE

LISTEN for sika stags in autumn

SNORKEL a coral reef

WALK barefoot through meadows of buttercups

LOOK for fossils 155 million years old

CHEW on sweet gorse and hawthorn flowers

INHALE the sea air on the highest cliff on the south coast

WATCH starling murmurations at dusk

STAND aboard a shipwrecked relic

Top TEN

 ▶ **Red Rocks Marsh,** See the rarest birds in England: bee eaters, shrikes and wintering snow buntings.
53.383246, -3.195233

 Flamborough Cliffs, One of the most important seabird colonies in Europe. Tens of thousands of breeding auks, gannets, gulls and puffins.
54.10431, -0.14204

Formby Footprints, Prehistoric footprints from humans who walked these shores thousands of years ago.
53.548210, -3.106243

Holme-next-the-Sea, The original home of Seahenge I and II.
52.977704, 0.548412

 The Barrows, The only sea-cliffs in Lancashire. Woodland, open grassland over sand beach and rock pools.
54.044674, -2.9049503

Dog Holes, Series of caves, chambers and passages in the limestone rock.
54.150479, -2.792595

 Humphrey Head, Breathtaking woodland ramp where peregrines nest and bluebells flower.
54.158106, -2.932695

Sunbrick Stone Circle, 12 stones inside 20 more. Thought to date from early Bronze Age, about 4,000 years ago.
54.156555, -3.085196

Dunstanburgh Castle Among the largest forts in England. The ruins and their rock defences span almost 3.2km (2 miles) of headland that have been occupied for thousands of years.
55.4911, -1.5932

○ **Sugar Sands** The oldest Stone Age settlement in England dating to 7,800 BC was found here in 2002. More than 18,000 pieces of flint were recovered, as well as charred animal bone, hazelnut shells and red ochre.
55.442599, -1.592949

ENGLAND COAST PATH NORTH & EAST

BEST FOR: FORAGING AND FREE FOOD

Golden eagles, lake views, stone circles

START: CHESHIRE FINISH: SUFFOLK

The northern and eastern coasts of England are a free-food larder. Mackerel, spider and brown crabs, razor shells, shrimps, oysters, samphire and purslane.

Samphire, sea beet and purslane are easier to find and prepare than seaweed. They eat off the stem and are tasty raw or cooked. They're also easy to identify. Sea kale, sea cabbage and almost all seaweed – from kelp to dulse, you will find bucket-loads of the stuff everywhere. This isn't a guide to foraging, so do a little research. Seaweed and sea beet is an easier place to begin than mushrooms. Use scissors. A knife is OK, but a bit clumsy. Pulling just destroys roots, and gets messy, so avoid.

Shrimps netted out of a rock pool are tastier than almost any meat available from a supermarket.

Foraging is an important part of connecting and interacting with nature and the outdoors. Whether you are cooking a crab on a fire or eating nettle tips on the move, it's an important psychological cure to say thank you to either the creature or plant for the food, and – if food is plentiful – ask for permission. This showing of respect might be laughed at by your friends, but it is just another powerful link between us to the natural world that helps bridge the gap between magic and science.

BASIC SAFETY
- Check with the beach owner before removing shellfish, plants or seaweed.
- Don't eat anything you haven't positively identified as safe.
- Check the status of waters to ensure they're not polluted by outfalls or recent sewage.
- Ensure all foods – including, especially, oysters and some seaweeds – are thoroughly soaked, washed and cleaned before cooking in line with expert advice.

Happisburgh

Formby

THE DERBY POOL

Terraced views over the grassy banks that fall down to the beach. Great value food and rooms in a wonderful setting.

Bay View Dr, Wallasey, Merseyside, CH45 3QS

www.harvester.co.uk/restaurants/northwest/thederbypoolwallasey#/

01516 305370

Grosvenor Car Park, River Dee, Newtown
The ECP N path starts/ends with feeding squirrels while exploring church ruins, overlooking a former Roman fort and castle across the water. This start/end is not currently official. Just like the ECP S path, it's something of a minor path extension, entirely in keeping with the spirit of the ECP's 2012 Olympic legacy: pushing the boundaries. What lies ahead and behind is the best free-food larder in England: samphire, seaweed and shellfish.

▶ Find the Grosvenor car park, CH1 1DE (53.189706, -2.888978), a 2-minute walk from the Chester Roman Amphitheatre. Walk through the theatre grounds, into the church, then into the park.

53.189602, -2.880691

RSPB Burton Mere Wetlands, Burton
Raptors, hides and walks. The entrance to the Dee Estuary.

53.254163, -3.029925

Thurstaston Beach, Merseyside
Peaceful sands and tree-lined cliffs, with views over N Wales. Good for horses. Visitor centre and boat launch.

53.336967, -3.141661

Top Ten — Red Rocks Marsh, Hoylake
See the rarest birds in England: bee eaters, shrikes and wintering snow buntings. Views out towards Hilbre Island.

53.383246, -3.195233

ENGLAND COAST PATH NORTH & EAST

PREMIER INN

Budget rooms surrounded by docks and river traffic.

E Britannia Building, Albert Dock, Liverpool, L3 4AD

www.premierinn.com/gb/en/hotels/england/merseyside/liverpool/liverpool-city-centre-albert-dock.html

0333 321 1232

Hilbre Island, Wirral
Wallow in the shallows at low tide. Chance to see sea lions and seals here, across the Dee Estuary sandbanks or near the old lighthouse end of the island.

53.378696, -3.216336

Leasowe Lighthouse, Merseyside
The UK's oldest brick lighthouse, built from 660,000 handmade bricks in 1763.

53.413084, -3.126039

Fort Perch Rock, Marine Promenade, Wirral
Napoleonic fort built at the mouth of Liverpool Bay to defend the port. The Mess café is open seven days a week.

53.442479, -3.041056

Eastham Country Park, Eastham
Woodland along a 800m (½ mile) stretch of Eastham Channel, known as 'The Warrens'.

53.327470, -2.957749

National Waterways Museum Ellesmere Port, Ellesmere Port
History and showcase of England's great canals. Listen to recordings of people of old who lived on the water and boats.

53.287893, -2.891971

Hoylake

HOLE IN THE WALL CAFE

 Café with outside seating, open spring until autumn.

420 Promenade, Blackpool, Lancashire, FY1 2LB

01253 521611

 ### Warburton's Wood, Kingsley
More than 50 species of wildflowers bloom here, including wood anemone, yellow archangel, giant bellflower, common violet, primrose, bluebell and pale wood violet. N of the wood, a wildflower meadow runs down to the River Weaver.

53.282313, -2.667597

 ### Brighton le Sands, Crosby
Walk among the 100 Anthony Gormley beach statues at low tide... then watch the sculptures vanish as the water comes in.

53.482582, -3.055066

Top TEN Formby Footprints, Raven Meols
Ephemeral prehistoric footprints from humans who walked these shores thousands of years ago. They are found sometimes in the silt along a 4.8km (3 miles) stretch of coast from Lifeboat Rd to Gypsy Wood (or Formby Point and the Ribble Estuary). Look roughly 50 to 100m (165 to 330ft) offshore from the dune edge. The prints are a snapshot of people and animals that walked across the mud before their imprints were baked by the sun and covered in hardened silt. These silt layers are occasionally eroded by 21st-century tides. The footprints survive for one day only, before the waters return 12 hours later and wipe them out... forever. Heartbreakingly wonderful, it's enough to bring a grown adult to tears.

53.548210, -3.106243

Walney

ENGLAND COAST PATH NORTH & EAST   329

THE BAY HORSE HOTEL & RESTAURANT, A 17th-century coaching inn where travellers would rest before making the journey by horse coach across the sands to Lancaster. Famous for being the birthplace of Stan Laurel, with many art festivals.

Canal Foot, Ulverston, LA12 9EL

www.thebayhorsehotel.co.uk

01229 583972

Formby, Sefton
Stunning. Pine trees, beach and swimming.

53.576166, -3.096401

Freshfield Dune Heath, Formby
Goldcrests and red squirrels flit around the birch and pine woodland.

53.576530, -3.075551

Ribble Estuary, Southport
Follow the path onto vast sands or kayak for wild camps.

53.678639, -3.001995

Lytham Windmill Museum, Lytham Green, E Beach, Lytham
Windmill built on the marshes before the area was drained and tourists arrived.

53.735649, -2.955570

Meldham Wood, Ashton with Stodday
Pine and broadleaf wood on sandy foreshore. FP between Glasson to S and Lancaster, 6.4km (4 miles) N.

54.009026, -2.831020

Lancaster Castle, Lancashire
A 12th-century castle overlooking a strategic ford.

54.04981, -2.80562

Freeman's Pools, Freeman's Wood, Aldcliffe
One of the UK's rarest trees stands here: a mature native black poplar.

54.046582, -2.832310

The Barrows, Heysham
The only sea cliffs in Lancashire. Woodland and open grassland over sand beach and rock pools.

54.044674, -2.9049503

Rock Cut Tomb, Heysham,
Two sets of tombs cut into the sandstone at St Peter's churchyard, thought to be more than 1,000 years old.

54.047070, -2.901659

Hunting Hill, Carnforth
Ancient settlement mound over the Keer Estuary where it feeds into Morecambe Bay. Several ancient tracks circle the hill. Good views over Warton Crag.

54.129161, -2.781476

Holmrook

THE DOWER HOUSE

 Country house for self-catering or B&B. On the site of an old packhorse inn overlooking the Duddon estuary, close to where the fells and salt marshes of the Duddon Estuary merge.

High Duddon, Duddon Bridge, Broughton-in-Furness, Cumbria, LA20 6ET

01229 716279

HARTLEY'S BEACH SHOP

 Wonderful sea views from outside tables. Good place to stop for food and drink after a clifftop walk.

Beach Rd, Saint Bees, CA27 0ES

www.facebook.com/hartleysbeachshop

01946 820175

Top TEN — Dog Holes, Millhead, Warton
Series of caves, chambers and passages in the limestone rock. Bolton Museum holds various finds recovered from the caves, including tools and bones.

54.150479, -2.792595

Jack Scout, Silverdale
Mixture of pine and broadleaf that falls down to the rocky foreshore and beach just N of Jenny Brown's Point.

54.157480, -2.830331

Top TEN — Humphrey Head, Nr Grange over Sands
Breathtaking woodland ramp where peregrines nest and bluebells flower.

54.158106, -2.932695

Beach Wood, Ulverston
Broadleaf woodland over Morecambe Bay's sandy W shore.

54.171873, -3.059390

Chapel Island, Leven Estuary, Morecambe Bay
A 7-acre wooded island, less than 1.6km (1 mile) from the shore.

54.173706, -3.041066

Top TEN — Sunbrick Stone Circle, Birkrigg Common
Double stone circle on an ancient common surrounded by FPs. 12 stones inside 20 more. Thought to date from the early Bronze Age, about 4,000 years ago.

54.156555, -3.085196

NATIONAL TRAILS

ENGLAND COAST PATH NORTH & EAST   331

BLACK SWAN INN
 Overlooking the harbour with sea views. Freshly cooked, locally sourced food.

2 Union St, Seahouses NE68 7RT

www.northcoastcollective.co.uk/black-swan-inn

01665 720227

THE JOLLY FISHERMAN INN
Fresh fish catches on the menu, including crab soup.

Haven Hill, Craster, Alnwick, NE66 3TR

www.thejollyfisherman craster.co.uk

01665 576461

Church of St Cuthbert, Aldingham
Peaceful graveyard sloping down to the beach.

54.1299714, -3.0980504

Foulney Island, Rampside
Island of pebbles formed by glaciers that 'rolled 'em round' during the last Ice Age. Terns nest on the island's shingle banks.

54.066398, -3.153592

Piel Castle, Barrow-in-Furness
Ruins of a 14th-century castle that guarded the harbour.

54.0626, -3.1733

Roanhead Beach, River Duddon, Askam-in-Furness
Sandy beach and dunes, with views up to the Lakeland mountains. Listen to the mating call of rare natterjack toads.

54.1714727, -3.2287749

Giants' Grave, Whicham
Two giant standing stones with sea views.

54.218343, -3.326297

Gutterby Spa, Whicham
Spa next to a freshwater spring on the beach.

54.247155, -3.379435

Berwick

THE ARCHES COUNTRY HOUSE

B&B accommodation within 800m (½ mile) of the coast path surrounded by farmland and a golf course.

Low Farm, Ings Ln, Brotton, TS12 2QX

www.thearcheshotel.co.uk

01287 555666

 Eskmeals Dunes, Nr Ravenglass
Otters around the mouth of the River Esk.

54.342258, -3.413584

 W Pier Lighthouse, Bransty, Whitehaven
A 19th-century lighthouse built into the Old Quay.

54.552739, -3.598490

 King Edward's Monument, Burgh by Sands
Monument to King Edward I, who died here with his army while waiting to cross the Solway estuary into Dumfries and Galloway.

54.938413, -3.053947

 Church of St Mary the Virgin, Rockcliffe
There's an ancient cross in the SE of the churchyard that may date back to the 10th century.

54.945098, -3.002363

 Scremerston, Ancroft
Plant and coral fossils in sandstone. Best where the rocky cliffs give way to pools and golden beaches before Cheswick Sands.

55.73883, -1.96464

 Bamburgh Castle, Bamburgh
The Vikings destroyed everything on this naze in AD 993. The Normans rebuilt the castle 70 years later. Open to the public, entrance charges apply. Much like Holy island, you really need at least two days to take it all in.

55.608, -1.709

 Annstead Dunes, between Beadnell and Seahouses
Exmoor ponies graze across 10m (33ft)-high dunes. There's a colony of common lizards on the site.

55.567658, -1.644778

 Long Nanny Bridge, Newton-by-the-Sea
Beautiful bridge over tidal creeks, one of which, called 'Long Nanny', twists N.

55.5374146, -1.641574

 Dunstanburgh Castle, Alnwick
Among the largest forts in England. The ruins and their rock defences span almost 3.2km (2 miles) of headland that have been occupied for thousands of years.

55.4911, -1.5932

Withernsea

HAVEN INN

Great-value rooms and food. Built in 1730 as a coaching inn for travellers using the nearby ferry. A dog-friendly hotel for long walks along the Humber.

Ferry Rd, Barrow-upon-Humber, DN19 7EX

www.thehaveninnltd.co.uk

01469 530247

Top TEN Sugar Sands /Howick/Whitefin Spring/Crow Wood

The oldest Stone Age settlement in England, dating to 7800 BC, was found here in 2002. More than 18,000 pieces of flint were recovered, as well as charred animal bone, hazelnut shells and red ochre.

55.442599, -1.592949

Alnmouth Wall Rock, Alnmouth

The cup-marked stone was found on top of the Alnmouth Wall. There's still debate about whether it is Stone Age art or created by nature.

55.392415, -1.609756

Warkworth Castle, Warkworth

A medieval castle in the loop of the River Coquet. Walks to the beach and inland.

55.3447, -1.6105

Cresswell Foreshore and Pond, Ellington and Linton

Five species of crab live in these rock pools. The 'pond' is a brackish lagoon created by a collapsed mine works, connected to the sea by Blakemoor Burn.

55.242988, -1.556457

Tynemouth Castle, Tynemouth
Three kings are buried in this moated castle, within the ruins of the Benedictine priory.

55.0175, -1.418889

Tynemouth Pier Lighthouse, N Tyneside
Huge stone pier extends 900m (½ mile) out to sea to protect the harbour. The walkway leads out to the lighthouse.

55.0145911, -1.4027328

Newcastle Castle Keep, Newcastle upon Tyne
William the Conqueror's eldest son built a castle here in 1080 to stop the Scots invading. It was rebuilt in stone by King Henry II around 1175.
www.newcastlecastle.co.uk

54.9688, -1.6105

Nose's Point, Dawdon
Caves and prehistoric beach at Nose's Point. Visit at low tide to make the best of exploring the caves. Lovely waterfall (54.821373, -1.322679) a few hundred metres S of the caves.

54.823251, -1.3230050

Brancaster

ENGLAND COAST PATH NORTH & EAST   335

Blackhall Rocks and Cross Gill Nature Reserve, Blackhall Colliery
The low-tide caves in the reef-limestone cliffs are the largest in Durham. Kelp forest over the rocky reef is home to cuttlefish, lobsters and sea slugs.

54.741059, -1.268388

Saltburn, Marske and New Marske
Wooded river valley to walk inland to Hazel Grove and Skelton Brook. Jurassic cliffs at Saltburn Scar for ammonites and other fossils.

54.586091, -0.967482

Street House Farm Burial, Easington
Bronze Age barrows and Neolithic finds have revealed human activity along this stretch of coastline dating back over 5,000 years.

54.566274, -0.862430

Staithes Harbour, Hinderwell
Cobbled streets and beaches for ammonites and other fossils.

54.55992, -0.78462

The Coomb, Stainton Dale
Seals, sloes and broadleaf trees along a cliff platform looking over the sea.

54.404615, -0.489340

Cornelian Bay, Savile's View, Osgodby
Swim the 'inner lake' channel protected offshore by the High Scar rocks.

54.258044, -0.371809

The Spittals, Old Town, Filey Brigg
Wall of red rock jutting out into the North Sea. Sensational views back to Filey Bay.

54.214914, -0.264042

Thornwick Bay Caves, Flamborough
Series of four sets of caves along a 800m (½ mile) stretch of sand coves.

54.131363, -0.113151

Flamborough Cliffs, E Riding of Yorkshire
One of the most important seabird colonies in Europe. Tens of thousands of breeding auks, gannets, gulls and puffins.

54.10431, -0.14204

Weybourne

Noah's Wood (Submarine Forest), Withernsea
Submerged forests were once thought to be remnants of the biblical flood.

53.732989, 0.035905

Spurn Head, River Humber, Easington
Harbour porpoises and minke whales swim here.

53.611436, 0.143460

Welwick Saltmarsh, E Riding of Yorkshire
Thousands of birds feed here, including hundreds of curve-billed curlews, on the edge of the salt marsh on the N bank of the River Humber. Look out for purple sea lavender and aster flowers in summer.

53.651293, 0.022913

S Ferriby Cliff, S Ferriby
Find ammonites and other fossils along a wooded shore.

53.686502, -0.493574

Killingholme Haven Pits, N Killingholme Haven
Flooded clay pits to watch spoonbills, avocets and egrets.

53.662614, -0.238389

Donna Nook National Nature Reserve, N Somercotes
Breeding colony of grey seals arrive in November and December, with more than 1,300 pups born annually.

53.475726, 0.141134

ENGLAND COAST PATH NORTH & EAST

Rimac Nature Reserve, Saltfleetby
Sea breezes and great views from the top of the dunes.

53.401741, 0.208088

Huttoft Beach, E Lindsey
Sandy secluded beach.
➤ Find the dead-end Ln to the beach, where Huttoft Bank Rd meets Sea Ln, LN13 9RR (53.282299, 0.305120). Parking by the beach.

53.282450, 0.310624

Gibraltar Point, Croft, E Lindsey
Little terns dive around in the shallows.

53.100442, 0.337090

Pilgrim Fathers Memorial, Fishtoft
Next to a creek known as 'The Haven'. Where the founding fathers are said to have set off on their voyage to the so-called 'New World', via mainland Europe.

52.941944, 0.023611

Clay Hole, Freiston Shore, Freiston, Boston
Possibly one of the most isolated places on the entire coast path – overlooking The Wash.

52.931791, 0.077459

Frampton Marsh, Boston
Hen harriers and merlins hunt over this part of The Wash.

52.916984, 0.012380

Moulton Marsh, The Moultons
Broadleaf woodland, scrub and lake beside the River Welland. Lagoons, creeks and salt marsh.

52.881514, -0.014059

W Nene Lighthouse, Sutton Bridge, S Holland
Built in the early 19th century. It's tall, fat and white.

52.8087404, 0.2110644

Lynn Museum, King's Lynn
Seahenge is here, the Bronze Age timber circle controversially removed from Holme beach. The 4,000-year-old structure was discovered after heavy tides removed some of the silt and mud that had covered it up.

52.753807, 0.399378

Wolferton Creek, Snettisham, King's Lynn and W Norfolk
Tide and fresh waters meet over the sands of Shepherd's Port.

52.869875, 0.443818

 Statue of Wolf, St Edmund's Chapel, Hunstanton
A carved wooden wolf sits near the ruins of the chapel. It marks the spot in legend where King Edmund first landed on these shores before he was killed by Viking invaders.

52.949125, 0.491539

 Holme-next-the-Sea, Flaxley
The original home of Seahenge I and II.

52.977704, 0.548412

 Blakeney Eye, Cley next the Sea
Stand over the (buried) remains of Blakeney Chapel that stood on this islet for 200 years.

52.966021, 1.037482

 RNLI Sheringham Lifeboat Station, Sheringham
Learn about the savage seas of this coast by exploring a working lifeboat station and meeting its volunteers.

52.933014, 1.301140

Trimingham

ENGLAND COAST PATH NORTH & EAST

THE CRAB HUT

Beside the harbour, freshly baked baguettes filled with seafood from the owners' boat, which fishes out of Brancaster Staithe. Simon Letzer also has a smokehouse where he smokes locally caught fish and prawns using traditional methods passed on from his father Paul Letzer.

Harbour Way, Brancaster, Staithe, King's Lynn PE31 8BW

www.explorewestnorfolk.co.uk/retail/the-crab-hut-31

07582 916652

 Overstrand Beach, Norfolk
Chalk full of fossils is exposed at low tide in winter.

52.91666, 1.34769

 Forest, Fritton and St. Olaves
Pine and broadleaf wood by the River Waveney.

52.552696, 1.624443

 Beach Rd, Hopton-on-Sea,
The ECP N path starts/ends 500m (⅓ mile) N of the Norfolk/Suffolk beach border. There's a good reason for that. The Peddars Way starts/ends here too, in Norfolk, at the bottom of Beach Rd, to the sound of waves and whining sea birds. What lies ahead and behind is a rare opportunity for connection to nature: foraging. Foraging is one of the best ways of connecting and interacting with nature and the outdoors, whether you are cooking a Norfolk crab on a fire or eating salted nettle tips on the move around The Wirral.

▶**Find** Potters Resorts, NR31 9BX (52.535362, 1.731512). Move 200m (655ft) N to Sea View Rise on the L (E). Follow the Rd for 90m (295ft), take the R turn into Beach Rd and follow the Rd down to the beach where it joins to point where the ECP meets the Peddars Way/Norfolk Coast Path.

52.536274, 1.737427

WILD THINGS TO DO BEFORE YOU DIE

SEE the rarest birds in England

LOOK for ephemeral prehistoric footprints

SING inside a double stone circle on an ancient common

STAND beside the home of Seahenge

CELEBRATE the Pilgrim Fathers

TOUCH the only sea cliffs in Lancashire

WATCH peregrines nest on a woodland tidal ramp

EXPLORE the oldest Stone Age settlement in England

LISTEN to the most important seabird colonies in Europe

 Top TEN

 Benacre Broad, More than 10 species of dragonfly flit around.
52.473339, 1.686884

 Dunwich Forest, Wild ponies graze over more than 7.8km² (3 miles²) of pine and broadleaf woodland.
52.289950, 1.627029

 Cudmore Grove, Prehistoric beach renowned for mammoths.
51.791777, 0.996831

 The Broomway, A prehistoric path, officially dubbed the most dangerous Rd in England.
51.548196, 0.840260

 Ghost Wood, Find a ghost wood on the London Thames: fossil oak stumps at low tide – remnants of the great forests that lined the Thames valley about 11,000 years ago.
51.699657, 0.757269

 Milton Locks and Eastley Lake, Kayak a salt lake trapped inside Langston Harbour.
50.795027, -1.038573

 Farlington Marshes, Watch avocets feed over this salt marsh harbour.
50.829365, -1.034584

 Beaulieu River W, One of the most isolated and inaccessible pieces of coastline on the English shore. Kayak or boat only.

 Elmley Marshes, Cloud-like murmurations in the winter skies at dusk as thousands of birds arrive to roost here.
51.370585, 0.774305

 Wainlode Cliff, Wooded cliff face that towers over the Severn. Keep eye out for cliff falls as good fossils can be found.

ENGLAND COAST PATH SOUTH

BEST FOR: CANOE ADVENTURES

Canoes, camping, cooking

START: SUFFOLK   FINISH: GLOUCESTER

If the S coast is canoe and kayak camp heaven, then Essex is its mecca. The chalk streams of the River Stort mark the boundary between Essex and Hertfordshire.

This is where mud creeks and the Thames basin begins. Chalk streams are by their very nature shallow runs that rarely run dry. Mud creeks are the opposite. They are fast, tidal and switched on and off by the moon twice a day. This makes canoe camping on creeks the obvious and inevitable life hack of tidal travel. Because when the tide goes out, there's nothing left to do but sit, cook, eat... and sleep until it comes back.

Outside of Essex, the best waters for kayaks and canoes are the free-flowing rivers of S and N Devon, to the tidal inlets of Kent, Sussex and Suffolk.

Kayaks, canoes, paddleboards and packrafts open up every possibility to camp and explore. Tidal navigation — apart from some exceptions that are unworthy of mention here — is a right enshrined in English law.

BASIC SAFETY
- Check tide times
- Do not kayak alone
- Always carry warm clothing and spare sets
- Always let other people know where you are going
- Carry a radio or, at the very least, a well-charged phone with spare batteries

The S coast is the best place for wild camping. Once you are prepared for occasional mishaps and weather changes, the two most important justifications for wild camping around England's coast are enshrined in English law: tidal fishing and tidal navigation.

Around the tidal coast, time is of no consequence. So if we choose to fish for cod or mackerel on a beach for two weeks or two months, that's a reasonable thing to do... in law, it's a 24-hours-a-day right. There is no right to sleep, but it is a legitimate pursuit to sleep in a bivvy on the foreshore (below the high-tide mark) while waiting for the tide, and the fish, to return.

There is a right in law that allows you to wait on the foreshore with your boat for the tide to return in six or seven hours' time before navigating off to your next destination. The function of sleeping forms a legitimate part of that travel on the foreshore, below the high-tide mark. And spending the night is the best way to get intimate with nature.

Walton Backwaters

Benacre Broad

THE WHITE HART INN

 A 16th-century pub with views across the Blyth estuary. Four dog-friendly en-suite rooms, twin or doubles. Traditional ales from Adnams and home-cooked dishes.

London Rd, Blythburgh, Halesworth, Suffolk, IP19 9LQ

www.blythburgh-whitehart.co.uk

01502 478217

HARBOUR LIGHTS RESTAURANT

 Worth the visit for the drive and harbour views alone.

Titchmarsh Marina, Coles Ln, Walton on the Naze, CO14 8SL

https:// harbourlightswalton.co.uk

Beach Rd, Hopton-on-Sea

ECP S path starts/ends 500m (⅓ mile) N of the Norfolk/Suffolk beach border. The Peddars Way starts/ends here too, in Norfolk. What lies ahead and behind are some of the most isolated coastal areas that trails just don't reach. These are often accessible from a sea kayak launch or even a small packraft, often by using the tide.

➤**Find** Potters Resorts, NR31 9BX (52.535023, 1.7318558). Move 200m (665ft) N to Sea View Rise on the L (E). Follow the Rd for 90m (295ft) and take the R turn into Beach Road and follow the Rd down to the beach where it joins to point where the ECP meets the Peddars Way/Norfolk Coast Path.

52.536274, 1.737427

Benacre Broad, Covehithe *(Top TEN)*

More than 10 species of dragonfly flit around this tidal lagoon surrounded by gorse, woodland, bogs, flowers and birdlife. Access is from the beach only. Fast tides and isolated.

52.387846, 1.719188

Dunwich Forest, Westleton *(Top TEN)*

Wild Dartmoor ponies graze over more than 8km² (3 miles²) of pine and broadleaf woodland.

52.289950, 1.627029

Trimley Marshes, Trimley St Mary

The lagoon and islands attract migrating waders such as common sandpipers, curlews sandpipers and greenshanks. Avocets and ringed plovers nest here in spring.

51.972092, 1.281768

ENGLAND COAST PATH SOUTH

THE ROSE AND CROWN, WIVENHOE

 Tables and chairs beside the River Colne. Wonderful at sunset.

The Quay, Wivenhoe, Colchester, Essex, CO7 9BX

www.greeneking.co.uk/pubs/essex/rose-and-crown

01206 826371

THE OTHONA COMMUNITY

Sleepover in yurts or communal rooms. Prices include all food and are wonderful value. The birdsong at dawn is deafeningly sensational. Othona began as an experiment in Christian community back in 1946, but welcomes everyone.

E End Rd, Bradwell-on-Sea, Essex, CM0 7PN

www.othonaessex.org.uk

01621 776564

 ### Skipper's Island, Walton Backwaters
Flooded causeway onto magical island of freshwater pools and sea lavender.

51.872247, 1.220585

 ### Jaywick Sands, Clacton-on-Sea
The best beach in Essex is only a few minutes' walk from Clacton, but several 90m (295ft) offshore on a low tide.

51.774921, 1.125784

 ### Ray Island Nature Reserve, Mersea
Remote island backdrop to Sabine Baring-Gould's 1880 novel *Mehalah*. Fresh water, woodland and shelter, with direct access to the mainland via the Strood.

51.794460, 0.903233

 ### Top TEN Cudmore Grove, Mersea, Colchester
Prehistoric beach overlooking the Colne and Blackwater estuaries. Renowned for mammoths – a giant tusk was discovered here in 2018.

51.791777, 0.996831

 ### Shingle Head Point, Tollesbury Wick
Sandy and isolated headland at the end of grassy islands and shallow salt marshes. Perfect place for swims and wallowing.

51.757333, 0.881138

Chapel of St Peter-on-the-Wall, Bradwell-on-Sea
The 7th-century chapel where pagan Britons were converted to Christianity. Swim after waking at dawn to the rising tide.

51.735278, 0.94

Hyebridge Basin

THE CROOKED BILLET

 Sit outside on the cobbled streets by Leigh Creek sipping ale and eating Leigh cockles. A wonderful place all year, but best in high summer when the streets are packed.

51 High St, Leigh-on-Sea, Essex, SS9 2EP

www.nicholsonspubs.co.uk/restaurants/eastofengland/

The Broomway, Great Wakering
Top TEN

A prehistoric path, officially dubbed the most dangerous Rd in England because it floods twice a day under seawater. It still has 'road' status and links Foulness Island to the mainland.

51.548196, 0.840260

The Ray, River Thames, Leigh on Sea

Sandbanks and tidal creek exposed once a day when the tide goes out. Get there by walking 800m (½ mile) along an old 'cockle path'.

51.536231, 0.628579

Ghost Wood, River Thames, Rainham
Top TEN

Fossil oak stumps at low tide – remnants of the great forests that lined the Thames Valley before the glaciers last cut them down about 11,000 years ago.

51.488015, 0.219001

Dartford Marshes, Dartford

A green lung between the Dartford Crossing and London. Walk the bank where the River Darent meets the Thames.

51.474575, 0.230137

Baty's Marsh, Rochester

Watch graceful cormorants skilfully dive for fish beside the marina on Wickham Reach, River Medway, close to the Medway M2 bridge crossing.

51.375752, 0.483839

St Margaret of Antioch Church, Halstow

Beautiful 8th-century Saxon church next to a small creek and harbour on the River Medway. Church contains a fresco of the crucifixion of St Andrew.

51.375361, 0.671173

Pegwell

Dymchurch

SPORTSMAN

 Seafood on the harbour from local fishing boats. Remarkable sunsets on the English Channel. Fish from the local boats are caught daily and sold in the restaurant and fish market. Stunning. Located on the old coastal Rd between Whitstable and Faversham. Fruit and veg from a small kitchen garden. Try the oysters.

Faversham Rd, Seasalter, Whitstable CT5 4BP

www.thesportsmanseasalter.co.uk

01227 273370

THE VIKING SHIP CAFE

 Views across the cliffs and Pegwell Bay, with a field for kids to play in. There's also a Viking ship monument.

Sandwich Rd, Cliffsend, Ramsgate CT12 5JB

www.facebook.com/TheVikingShipCafe

01843 577577

 ### Elmley Marshes, Minster-on-Sea, Swale
Top TEN
Cloud-like murmurations in the winter skies at dusk as thousands of birds arrive to roost here.

51.370585, 0.774305

 ### Botany Bay, Broadstairs
White cliffs and steps down to a sandy beach, secret caves and uniquely beautiful turquoise/green waters.

51.3893, 1.4352

 ### Shell Ness, Pegwell Bay
Stunning dune pasture peppered with butterflies, birds and the sound of nightingales in spring.

51.312259, 1.370008

 ### St Margaret's Bay, St Margaret's at Cliffe
Sweeping sand and shingle bay at St Margaret's for swimming. Find fossils around the beach, chalk cliffs or inside some of the boulder-sized stones.

51.156847, 1.392964

 ### Dover Castle, Dover
England's most important harbour for thousands of years.

51.129524, 1.323919

 ### Samphire Hoe, Aycliffe
Towering chalk cliffs over waterside meadows. Good for butterflies that feed on hundreds of species of wildflower.

51.10480, 1.27553

 ### Dungeness, Lade
Pebble beach defined as a navigational beacon for migrating birds.

50.931641, 0.944549

 ### Rye Harbour, Rother
Tranquil path on the banks of the River Rother. Leads out to Rye Bay and the beaches.

50.936840, 0.762592

Camber Sands

WINCHELSEA BEACH CAFE

 Perfect after a long walk. No sea views, but right next to the seawall and a lovely beach. Sheltered outdoor seating.

Pett Level Rd, Winchelsea, E Sussex, TN36 4ND

www.winchelseabeachcafe.com

01797 227918

 ### Winchelsea Beach, Icklesham
Magical shingle beach that exposes sand and clay at low tide. Take a 1.6km (1 mile) beach stroll W to the equally enchanting Royal Military Canal Path.

50.906209, 0.720104

 ### Covehurst Wood, Clive Vale
Rocky nudist beach that is usually deserted.

50.862971, 0.627667

 ### Bexhill and Cooden, Hastings
Dinosaur footprints can sometimes be found on the beach at Bexhill. Best visited after a storm and high tides.

50.84360, 0.50536

 ### Cuckmere River, Seaford
Kayakers, walkers, cyclists and anglers meet at this natural mecca of fresh water and tides.

50.759595, 0.151838

 ### Castle Hill, Newhaven
Clifftop views over Seaford, from the W shore of Newhaven Harbour. Best in spring when the place is awash with yellow buttercups, butterflies and birdsong.

50.781554, 0.049765

 ### Shoreham Fort and dunes, Kingston Buci
Formidable fort at the entrance to Shoreham Harbour and the River Adur.

50.826576, -0.251378

ENGLAND COAST PATH SOUTH   347

THE BRIDGE INN

Panoramic views of the River Adur. Simple food made from local ingredients, including beef or fish from the pub's own companies.

87 High Street, Shoreham-by-Sea, BN43 5DE

www.bridgeshoreham.co.uk

01273 452477

THE CRAB & LOBSTER
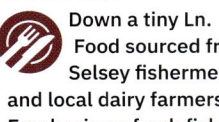
Down a tiny Ln. Food sourced from Selsey fishermen and local dairy farmers. Emphasis on fresh fish, crab and lobster. Also traditional English and Mediterranean dishes. Rooms with harbour views.

Mill Ln, Sidlesham, W Sussex, PO20 7NB

www.crab-lobster.co.uk

01243 641233

THE SHIP INN

At the heart of the beautiful sailing village of Itchenor. Popular with walkers and cyclists – 180m (590ft) from the harbour. Self-catering accommodation in a 3-bed cottage or 2-bedroom apartment.

The St, Itchenor, Chichester, W Sussex, PO20 7AH

www.theshipinnitchenor.co.uk

01243 512284

 ## Littlehampton Fort, Arun
Fort ruin that in its 19th-century pomp was the cutting edge of military innovation. Still impressive on the dunes of the River Arun.

50.800930, -0.544005

 ## E Head Spit, W Wittering
Vast stretch of isolated beach and dunes to explore. Walk the spit head at low tide to appreciate the peaceful beauty of the sandy expanse.

50.781833, -0.916127

 ## W Thorney Church and Hard, Chichester
Waterside church beside a hard into the Thorney Channel.
Church Rd, Thorney Island PO10 8DS

50.816624, -0.908384

 ## Nore Barn Woods, Emsworth
Woodland beach with harbour views. Good for kayak landing point.

50.841259, -0.955400

 ## Quay and BW, Langstone
Treacherous tidal BW best seen at low tide. One of the original tracks onto Hayling Island before the Langstone Rd bridge was built.

50.835569, -0.974528

 ## Farlington Marshes, Solent Way
Watch avocets feed over this salt marsh harbour fed by the Broom Channel. Short-eared owls hunt around the most southerly parts of the marsh before dusk.

50.829365, -1.034584

 ## Milton Locks and Eastley Lake, Milton
Kayak a salt lake trapped inside Langston Harbour.

50.795027, -1.038573

 ## Titchfield Haven, River Meon, Stubbington
Stunning septarian nodules are occasionally found along this cliff shore W of the tiny harbour.

50.819042, -1.248995

Hook Ln, Fleetend
Sand and shingle hook shaped by nature over more than 1,000 years at the Solent funnel. Watch the terns. Walk in the water.

50.845138, -1.307702

Allwoods Copse, Fawley, Calshot
Wood meets tidal beach on the edge of the New Forest.

50.794835, -1.335668

Rye Harbour

THE SHIP INN

Enjoy fresh, locally- caught fish and cask ales in this old mill overlooking Langstone Harbour.

Langstone Rd, Langstone, Havant, Hampshire, PO9 1RD

www.shiplangstone.co.uk

02392 471719

THE JOLLY ROGER

Indoor and outdoor seating on the waterfront overlooking Portsmouth Harbour.

156 Priory Rd, Gosport, PO12 4LQ

www.jollyrogergosport.co.uk

02392 004925

Top TEN Beaulieu River W, Beaulieu
One of the most isolated and inaccessible pieces of coastline on the English shore. Kayak or boat only.

50.776920, -1.397561

Taddiford Gap Beach, New Milton
Find crocodile, shark and mammal fossils.

50.729664, -1.631588

Barton Wood, Whippingham
Wooded shore on Osborne Bay, facing Hampshire and Portsmouth. Walk S towards boat launch at Barton Hard, which is next to a small beach.

50.750501, -1.246977

Whitecliff Bay, Bembridge
Where geology gets groovy. Colourful mix of chalk, shingles, clays and sand against wooded cliffs. And a swim.

50.67234, -1.09496

Fort Albert, Norton
Outstanding Cliff End naze within touching distance of mainland Hampshire across the Solent.

50.700266, -1.534496

ENGLAND COAST PATH SOUTH 349

PREMIER INN
A budget hotel on the edge of the River Medina. Better prices if booking in advance.

Seaclose, Fairlee Rd, Newport, Isle of Wight, PO30 2DN

www.premierinn.com
0871 527 8556

Bouldnor Forest, Yarmouth
Red squirrels and goldcrests in a pine forest.

50.708483, -1.481609

Lytchett Bay DWT/ARC Nature Reserve, Upton
Where heather merges into marshland around a bird-rich bay.

50.732112, -2.031120

Brownsea Island, Poole Harbour
Spoonbills, avocets, wildfowl and flocks of waders on a spectacular pine-ringed lagoon. Breeding common terns and sandwich terns in summer. Red squirrels, sika deer and kingfishers. Island admission and ferry fare applies to non-National Trust members; members pay the ferry fare only. Harbourside café for lunch, cake and ice cream.
➤ **Find** regular ferries onto the island from Poole Quay.

50.689844, -1.961725

Berrow Beach, Berrow
Unique tide and sands. Banks are hard enough for horses and bikes, but they're constantly shifting as the Bristol Channel has a tidal range of 15m (50ft), second only to the Bay of Fundy, in Canada.

51.263646, -3.020065

St Mary's Church, Burnham-on-Sea
Church separated from the beach and dunes by a links golf course but linked by a BW.

51.266710, -3.013932

Brean Beach, Brean
Km of open beach at low tide. Park right on the sand or hard ground.

51.322402, -3.012081

Newhaven

THE BARGEMAN'S REST

 Seabass fillets served with garlic butter and prawns where the River Medina meets the Lukely Brook. Wander around the converted warehouses of an old quay. Quay Arts Centre is next door.

Little London Quay, Newport, Isle of Wight, PO30 5BS

www.bargemansrest.com

01983 525828

BEACH HOUSE

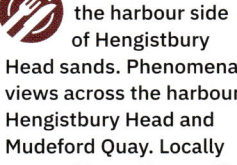 Restaurant on the harbour side of Hengistbury Head sands. Phenomenal views across the harbour, Hengistbury Head and Mudeford Quay. Locally sourced ingredients. If in season, try the scallops in garlic or fish fillets with asparagus.

The Spit, Mudeford, BH6 4EN

www.beachhousecafe.co.uk

01202 423474 or 07517 620464

Seafarers Memorial Stone, Portishead
Ship-watch at high tide from Portishead Point.

51.494170, -2.7715480

Leigh Woods, Stoke Bishop
Wooded shores of Avon Gorge. Walk with the shore on your L shoulder into Bristol Harbour.

51.465115, -2.636350

Littleton Brick Pits, Littleton-upon-Severn
Migrating birds feed along this chain of estuary reed beds, 3.2km (2 miles) E of the Severn Rd Bridge.

51.617860, -2.593933

St Arilda's Church, Oldbury-on-Severn
Sacred mound with beautiful sunset views from the church.

51.624636, -2.567232

Hock Cliff, Arlingham
Tree-lined clifftops of Long and Smith's woods. Fossils in the limestone and shale.

51.77845, -2.39236

Awen Stone, Arlingham
Stone carving linked to St Mary's Church, Arlingham.

51.786927, -2.414607

Mawnan

ENGLAND COAST PATH SOUTH   351

THE CLIFF HOUSE

Clifftop dining with panoramic views of the Solent. Try the Cliff House fish cakes. Six en-suite rooms named after ports and places with a maritime heritage linked to the English coast – Dover, Wight, Portland, Plymouth, Biscay and Thames.

Marine Dr W, Barton on Sea, New Milton, Hampshire, BH25 7QL

www.thecliffhouse.co.uk

01425 619333

Alney Island, Oxleaze
This flood plain has escaped development because of its high water table.

51.863231, -2.260473

Wainlode Cliff, Norton
Top TEN
Wooded cliff face that towers over the Severn. Keep an eye out for cliff falls as good fossils can be found.

51.93002, -2.22592

Odda's Chapel, Deerhurst
The ECP S starts/ends at Odda's Chapel. A triad of value: chapel, next to St Mary's Church, and only a 200-yard walk from the river and the Severn Way. This start/end is not currently official. In a sense, it's something of a path extension, pushing the boundaries. The very thing that makes it so magical. What lies ahead and behind are some of the best waterways in England to explore by kayak, canoe or paddleboard. Watercraft opens up every possibility to camp and explore via tidal navigation – one of the most important rights enshrined in English law.

▶ **Find** Odda's Chapel, GL19 4BX, right next to a little car park. The path to the river is right opposite the chapel.

51.966918, -2.192055

WILD THINGS TO DO BEFORE YOU DIE

WALK the most dangerous road in England... where you'll never see a car

KAYAK a salt lake trapped inside a harbour

FEEL a ghost wood on the London Thames

LISTEN to bird murmurations in winter skies

FIND fossils after cliff collapses beside the River Severn

SWIM a tidal creek at the end of an old 'cockle path'

SMELL the scent of where wood meets tidal beach

WATCH ten species of dragonfly over a tidal 'broad'

EXPLORE a prehistoric beach renowned for mammoth remains

TOUCH the water in England's most important harbour

CONWAY
Bloomsbury Publishing Plc
50 Bedford Square, London, WC1B 3DP, UK
Bloomsbury Publishing Ireland Limited,
29 Earlsfort Terrace, Dublin 2, D02 AY28, Ireland

BLOOMSBURY, CONWAY and the Conway logo are trademarks of Bloomsbury Publishing Plc

First published in Great Britain 2025

Copyright © Stephen Neale, 2025

Stephen Neale has asserted his right under the Copyright, Designs and Patents Act, 1988,
to be identified as Author of this work

This book is a guide for when you spend time outdoors. Undertaking any activity outdoors carries with it some risks that cannot be entirely eliminated. For example, you might get lost on a route or caught in bad weather. Before you spend time outdoors, we therefore advise that you always take the necessary precautions, such as checking weather forecasts and ensuring that you have all the equipment you need. Any walking routes that are described in this book should not be relied upon as a sole means of navigation, so we recommend that you refer to an Ordnance Survey map or authoritative equivalent.

This book may also reference businesses and venues. Whilst every effort is made by the author and the publisher to ensure the accuracy of the business and venue information contained in our books before they go to print, changes to such information can occur during the production and lifetime of a publication. Therefore, we also advise that you check with businesses or venues for the latest information before setting out.

All internet addresses given in this book were correct at the time of going to press. Bloomsbury Publishing Plc does not have any control over, or responsibility for, any third-party websites referred to or in this book. The author and the publisher regret any inconvenience caused if some facts have changed or sites have ceased to exist, but can accept no responsibility for any such changes.

All rights reserved. No part of this publication may be: i) reproduced or transmitted in any form, electronic or mechanical, including photocopying, recording or by means of any information storage or retrieval system without prior permission in writing from the publishers; or ii) used or reproduced in any way for the training, development or operation of artificial intelligence (AI) technologies, including generative AI technologies. The rights holders expressly reserve this publication from the text and data mining exception as per Article 4(3) of the Digital Single Market Directive (EU) 2019/790

A catalogue record for this book is available from the British Library

Library of Congress Cataloguing-in-Publication data has been applied for

ISBN: PB: 978-1-8448-6673-1; ePub: 978-1-8448-6675-5; ePDF: 978-1-8448-6674-8

2 4 6 8 10 9 7 5 3 1

Typeset in IBM Plex Sans by Nick Avery Design
Printed and bound in India by Replika Press Pvt. Ltd.

To find out more about our authors and books visit www.bloomsbury.com and sign up for our newsletters
For product safety related questions contact productsafety@bloomsbury.com